To Mum and Dad.

Contents

1 Summary

1.1 Goals of this Work

In the scope of this work a control architecture for the vehicle of the SUAVE project (see chapter 3) is to be designed. The architecture has to include all necessary features in order to perform missions in the scope of the SUAVE project.

The navigation, map building and memory management structures have to be defined in detail. Their tasks and the algorithms to perform these tasks have to be chosen, as well as the interfaces between the modules and the data structures.

The "local" parts of the memory manager and the navigation module and the map building algorithms have to be implemented in "C", evaluated and improved using extensive simulations of relevant AMV mission types. The system is considered a research platform to investigate Control Architectures, Navigation and Map Building algorithms, as well as sensor system architectures.

1.2 Approach

This thesis partly bases on prior work done at the department. The SUAVE vehicle has been designed and built, the control hardware mounted on the vehicle, and the motion controller implemented on the on-board control chip. The ultrasonic sensors have been set up and software access is given to trigger the sensors and to collect the sensor data. Quadtree manipulation, serial communication, and real-time software packages have been developed and were used in this work. Another source of experience were first implementations of potential fields navigation.

In this work one PC which is linked to the sensors was used to implement the Map Building algorithms. A second PC holds the framework of the control architecture, and the planning, navigation and memory management modules. This is linked to the motion controller of the vehicle.

Based on literature on existing control architectures for autonomous mobile vehicles (AMVs), on navigation techniques, and on map building using range sensors the modules of the control architecture were designed. Then data structures for the maps and the description of the vehicles path on four levels of abstraction and the interfaces between all the modules were defined. A communication system that allows open communication between the single modules was developed.

IN the second part the navigation module and the algorithms for map building and memory management were designed in detail. The local navigation and the local map were implemented in C, as well as the map building algorithms. The code was debugged and improved and used for simulations in order to evaluate the performance of the modules. The simulation sequence covers 14 different missions in environments that are likely to be encountered by an AMV in its mission, and that require different skills, e.g. a doorway, a corridor, a corner, single or multiple obstacles, etc.

1.3 Results

The Local Navigation Module (LNM) consisting of a deliberative path planning module, PILOT, and a potential field based reactive navigation module, the MOTOR-SCHEMA-EXECUTOR, is able to create smooth paths to the goal. If the potential field module cannot find a solution due to local minima, local replanning creates an alternative path when possible.

The structure used for the local map is efficient in terms of memory requirements and processing speed, thus provides sufficient accuracy in order to model obstacles. Moving obstacles are reflected in the map as well as static obstacles.

The ultrasonic sensor model transforms the raw sensor data into a data form useful for the map building algorithm where noise is filtered using a Kalman Filter.

The LNM and the Memory Manager are par of the CA^{2}MOV-control architecture. The module definition and the module communication is effective and very flexible.

All software is implemented in "C".

2 Autonomous Mobile Vehicles (AMVs)

Autonomous Mobile Vehicles (AMVs) have been of considerable interest in the research community for the last few decades. The first serious efforts in building a complete AMV was the development of "Shakey" at the Stanford Research Institute in the early sixties [4, 6].

AMVs might replace human labour in for human beings inconvenient, dangerous or impossible tasks.

In order to fulfil its mission an AMV must combine at least three skills: Mobility, Perception of its environment, and some form of Intelligence. Mobility is realised by a mechanical vehicle with wheels, tracks or similar devices and one or many motors or engines. Perception, more accurately measuring certain properties of the environment, is realized by the sensor system. Intelligence constitutes the link between perception and action and is implemented in the control structure of the AMV.

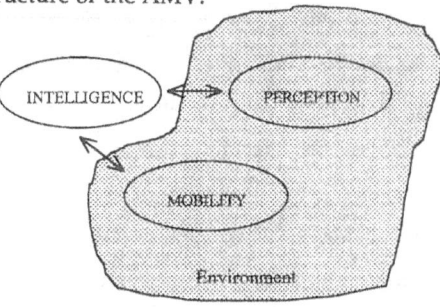

Figure 1: Three Skills of an AMV

Examples of the use of AMVs are in manufacturing for transport of tools or materials, in health-care for transportation of meals or medicine (HELPMATE [3]), in security to patrol a certain area, in building construction or exploration in space (Jet Propulsion Laboratory's Planetary Rover Navigation Testbed "Robby" [5]) or sub-sea.

In the beginning of the history of the development of AMVs most machines were designed for applications in manufacturing. More sophisticated control algorithms and sensor systems enable AMVs today to be used successfully in outdoor applications such as agriculture, mining, etc. where the environment can not be prepared as much for the vehicle.

The operating environment of an AMV can be characterised in four categories:

- A priori information: unknown/ known
- Time behaviour: Static/ dynamic
- Type: indoor/ outdoor
- Surrounding element: ground/ air/ see/ sub-sea/ space

3 "SUAVE" Project

SUAVE is an acronym for "Sydney University Autonomous Vehicle Experiment" and summarises the research on AMVs at The Department of Mechanical and Mechatronic Engineering. It is used in parallel for the experimental mobile platform built at the department.

3.1 Project Goals

The goals of the SUAVE project are to develop an AMV system that is able to operate in any environment on a solid ground with a reasonable flat surface.

Based on the current state of research the optimal combination of navigation techniques are selected, adapted and combined in a control architecture in order to create a navigation system that is able to cope with static and moving obstacles in large and small two-dimensional environments. Previous implementation of navigation architectures are mostly limited to static obstacles, or small environments, or both. Furthermore a human operator should be able to specify general characteristics such as safety level against collision, preference for unknown or known areas, and explorative behaviour.

New map structures based on the well-known Quadtree structure are developed and implemented to extend the use of Quadtrees from vision data processing to AMV navigation. Currently used map building techniques are adapted to the new map structure and extended by new models of prediction to cope with unexpected sensor measurements in order to obtain maximal noise filtering and reactivity of the map building process.

New models for ultrasonic sensors are developed and used to build the map based on previous work in this area. Later multiple sensors are used and their data fused in order to enhance the data provided by the sensor system for map building.

In a final state of the project when the AMV is prepared for specific tasks additional external devices such as a cleaning brush should be controlled by the vehicle control architecture

3.2 Vehicle Design

The mobile platform used for experiments related to this research was built at the department and uses a design suggestion of Killough and Pin [1]. This design enables the platform to perform omnidirectional non-holonomic motion, i.e. translation and rotation are independent from each other. It is a deduction from the "generalised wheel" which is described in [1]. A circular plate that carries the control hardware is mounted on a construction of three pairs of wheels. Each wheel pair is driven by a DC motor. Each motor is equipped with a shaft encoder to measure the wheel position and velocity. 24 Ultrasonic sensors are fixed to a second plate on the top of the vehicle.

$$\omega_1 = \frac{V}{2R}\left(\sin\theta - \sqrt{3}\cos\theta\right) + \frac{\Psi L_1}{R} \quad (2.1)$$

$$\omega_2 = -\frac{V}{R}\sin\theta + \frac{\Psi L_2}{R} \qquad\qquad (2.2)$$

$$\omega_3 = \frac{V}{2R}\left(\sin\theta - \sqrt{3}\cos\theta\right) + \frac{\Psi L_3}{R} \quad (2.3)$$

Figure 2: Wheel Design

The diameter of the platform is 500 mm, the height including the sensor module is approximately 400 mm. The weight is approximately 11 kg. For a full description of the vehicle the reader is referred to [2].

Figure 3: SUAVE Wheel assembly and Control Hardware

3.3 Motion Controller

The motion controller is implemented in an Intel 80C196K microprocessor which is equipped with two serial interfaces. A half-size 486DX IBM-compatible microcomputer with flash ROM-disc is going to run major parts of the control structure presented in this work, and is currently being mounted on the platform.

The motion controller is implemented as a position controller using global coordinates and one PID-velocity controller per wheel. It monitors the current position of the vehicle and angular velocities of each of the wheels with a frequency of 50 Hz using the shaft encoder information.

The input is a position setpoint in absolute world coordinates (X,Y,ψ). While the vehicle is travelling position setpoints are provided continuously to guide it on the desired path where the velocity does not change necessarily at a position setpoint. When a certain area around the current position Setpoint is reached a request for a new Setpoint is issued on the serial port. A diamond shape is chosen due to faster computation compared to a circular shape. It is absolutely necessary that this request is satisfied quickly enough to ensure that the next Setpoint is available before the current one is reached to create a smooth sequence of position Setpoints.

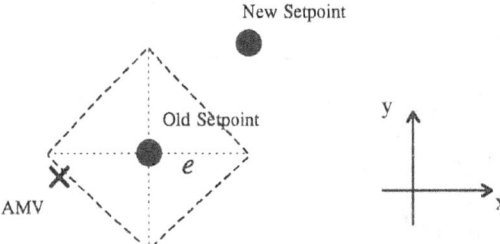

Figure 4: Request of New Position Setpoint

The diamond shaped area around the new setpoint is described using its diagonal e. The condition for the request of a new position setpoint is therefore

$$\left| X_R - X_{SP} \right| + \left| Y_R - Y_{SP} \right| <= e \qquad [1.]$$

where (X_R, Y_R) is the AMV's position and (X_{SP}, Y_{SP}) is the position of the current setpoint.

The time from issuing the request for a new setpoint until the new position Setpoint is used must satisfy the condition

$$T_R <= \frac{e}{\sqrt{2}V_R} \qquad [2.]$$

with v_R being the maximum velocity of the AMV to ensure a smooth path.

3.4 Dead Reckoning

Dead-reckoning is the easiest and most widely used method to keep track of an AMV's position. Assuming a known start position integration of the drive shaft encoder information can be used to estimate the current position. Due to slippage between the wheels and the ground surface and other inaccuracies, however, random errors accumulate and increase the total error unbounded with the distance travelled. Dead-reckoning can therefore be used successfully to solve the localisation problem of an AMV only for short trajectories.

The dead-reckoning accuracy of this vehicle has been determined experimentally to be smaller than 0.6% for straight line trajectories, and smaller than 1% for a squared trajectory [2]. This error is expected to be significantly larger for complex trajectories defined by a sequence of single position setpoints with small distances.

4 Control Architecture

An AMV's control architecture realises the "intelligence" skill (see chapter 2) and links the "intelligence" with the two other skills: mobility, i.e. the motor drives, and perception, i.e. the sensor system.

Many different types of architectures have been developed and used in AMV applications and research. The requirements of an AMV architecture and some of the basic architectures are introduced briefly in the following chapters.

4.1 Requirements for an AMV Control Architecture

Certain performance properties of an AMV control architecture can be identified:

- Reactivity: time to react to relevant changes in the environment
- Robustness: ability of the system to handle unexpected events, imperfections, and failures
- Reliability: ability to operate without unrecoverable failure for a considerable period of time

In addition some design characteristics are of certain interest:

- Modularity: The architecture should be divided into smaller modules each performing a well defined task, each module should be replaceable with a different approach or implementation to per form this task
- Expandability: different application may require additional modules to be added to the system, this should be possible without major changes in other modules or undesired interaction between the modules
- Adaptability: The operator should have the possibility to specify certain parameters to influence the system to adapt its behaviour to a change in operating conditions.

4.2 Review of Control Architectures

4.2.1 SMPA-Architecture

The "Sense-Model-Plan-Act" (SMPA) control architecture is a minimal architecture to connect the three basic skills of an AMV (see chapter 2). It is suitable for one-processor hardware architectures and features only Local Navigation.

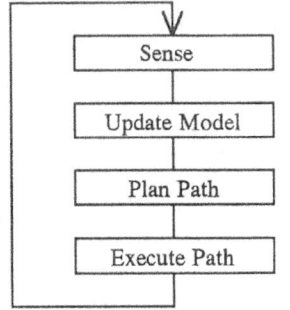

Figure 5: SMPA-Control-Architecture

The sensor system is used to collect data about the current environment (perception), the model (map) is updated, the path for this cycle is planned (intelligence), and finally this path is executed (mobility) [38]. The SMPA-approach is equivalent to "Process based control" described in [36].

4.2.2 Blackboard Architecture

In a Blackboard Architecture several agents or modules that are each responsible for a specific task, e.g. sensing, path planning, motion control, run in parallel and use a Blackboard as communication medium [37].

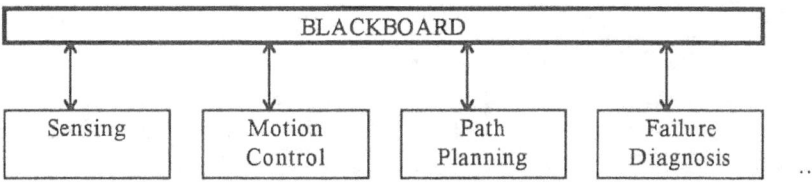

Figure 6: Blackboard Control Architecture

This architecture is due to its parallel nature limited to multi-tasking or multi-processor systems. Basis of successful implementation is the definition of an efficient communication format, since all interactions between the modules are limited by the types available messages from and to the Blackboard. Another important factor is the level of decomposition of tasks for the single modules which determines the intensity of communication.

4.2.3 Hierarchical Architecture

Hierarchical architectures are based on the decomposition of the control problem into progressive levels of abstraction [37, 39, 40]. The different modules use environment models of decreasing abstraction with lower levels in the hierarchy.

Environment Model   **Navigation Module**   **Vehicle**

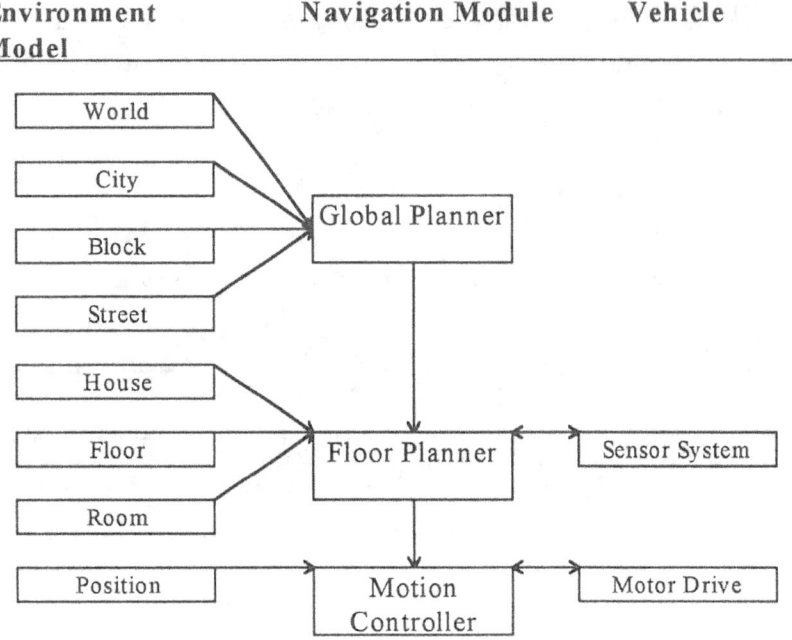

Figure 7: Hierarchical Control Architecture (example)

4.2.4 Subsumption Architecture

In the Subsumption Architecture behavioural modules are defined as layers of decreasing priority [36]. Each layer represents a single behaviour, and higher levels can override (subsume) lower levels.

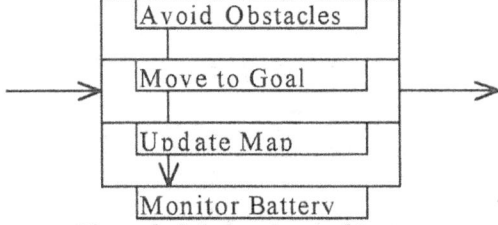

Figure 8: Subsumption Architecture

This type of architecture is used to implement behaviour based navigation consisting of many behaviours with different priorities.

4.2.5 Hybrid Architecture

Hybrid Architectures are any combination of elements of the architecture types described above. They seek to combine the strengths of Blackboard, Hierarchical, and/ or Subsumption Architecture [42] and are of higher complexity and individuality. A general structure can therefore not be given.

4.3 Design of the CA²MOV Control Architecture

"CA²MOV" is short for "Control Architecture for Autonomous Mobile Vehicles". This architecture is part of the SUAVE project and is the basis for future developments, improvements and expansions.

4.3.1 Specifications

The CA²MOV architecture has of course to meet the requirements of the SUAVE project as outlined in chapter 3.1. However, it should not be limited to the vehicle used for experiments during this research (see chapter 3.2).

The architecture bases on the following assumptions regarding the environment: Large areas of operation should be considered, e.g. a city, a university campus. The environment consists of a planar surface, i.e. paths are limited to two dimensions. It is structured or unstructured and it is populated with for the vehicle untraversable areas, in the following summarised as obstacles, that may be fixed or moving.

The vehicle is considered to be omnidirectional, i.e. two Cartesian coordinates plus the heading angle describe its position and changes in the heading angle are decoupled from changes in the position of the centre of the vehicle. Autonomy in terms of battery life and other hardware requirements is assumed for a considerable time. The motion controller is using the same input as SUAVE's motion controller (see chapter 3.3). Additional devices such as cleaning brushes, welding equipment etc. might be attached to the platform.

4.3.2 Module Definitions

The architecture is divided into six modules which each represent a basic task and support functions. These six modules are PLANNER, NAVIGATION, MEMORY, EXTERNAL DEVICE MANAGER, MAP BUILDING, LOCALISATION. The modules interface with a human operator who specifies the AMV's mission and receives certain information, the vehicle and the sensor system which interacts with the environment.

The PLANNER interfaces with the operator and executes a mission of the AMV by calling the appropriate modules and providing the necessary data.

The Navigation's task is to generate the input to the AMV's motion controller in order to guide it to the specified target position with the desired path characteristics.

A model of the environment and the AMV's current position estimation is stored in the MEMORY. The MEMORY also features a number of access function to this model.

MAP BUILDING builds and updates the environment model and triggers the sensors.

LOCALISATION keeps track of the AMV's position in the environment as accurately as possible.

The EXTERNAL DEVICE MANAGER invokes hardware devices for other tasks than navigation or sensing, e.g. a cleaning brush, welding equipment, etc..

SUPPORT FUNCTIONS are functions available to all modules and are mainly used for the software implementation, e.g. calculating the distance between two points.

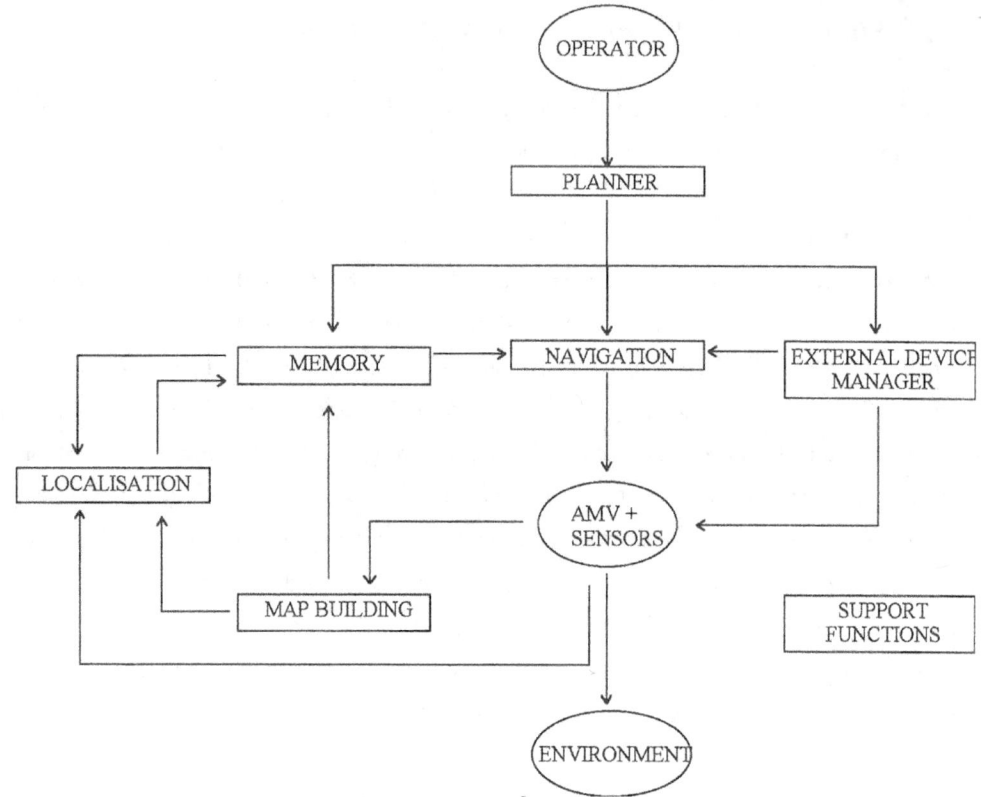

Figure 9: Overview CA²MOV Architecture

The interfaces between these modules are summarised in the following table:

From	To	Data
OPERATOR	PLANNER	• Mission specification • A priori map
PLANNER	OPERATOR	• Mission status
PLANNER	NAVIGATION	• Motion command
PLANNER	MEMORY	• A priori map • Map update specifications
PLANNER	EXTERNAL DEVICE MANAGER	• Activate/ Deactivate device • Operating data
NAVIGATION	AMV	• Position Setpoints
MEMORY	MAP BUILDING	• Current map
MAP BUILDING	MEMORY	• Updated map
LOCALISATION	MEMORY	• Updated AMV position
MEMORY	LOCALISATION	• Current AMV position
EXTERNAL DEVICE MANAGER	NAVIGATION	• Motion command

MAP BUILDING	AMV	• Sensor trigger
AMV	MAP BUILDING	• Raw sensor data
ENVIRONMENT	AMV	• Interaction with wheels
		• Interaction with sensor beam

The CA²MOV architecture features hierarchical and subsumption characteristics in the NAVIGATION, and blackboard characteristics in the MAP BUILDING and EXTERNAL DEVICE MANAGER and is therefore of a hybrid type.

4.3.3 Hardware Configuration

In addition to the C196 motion controller of the vehicle used two PC486 are currently used. One carries out the Planning and Navigation task and Memory, the other the sensor managing and map building task.

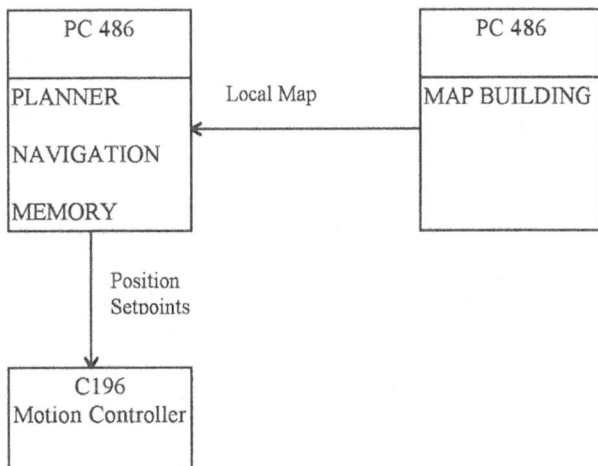

Figure 10: Hardware Configuration

4.3.4 Module Communication

The modules communicate using two structures: Boards and Lists. Boards hold a predefined set of parameters of a fixed length. The parameters in a Board are public message that can be read by any module. Lists consist of a variable number of sets of parameters each of which consists of the same number and types of parameters. They are used to store data, and they are public to be read and written. The lists are implemented as linked circular lists with pointers to the head and the tail.

In the current implementation the following Lists and Boards exist:

List of ...

COMMANDS	No - Command-Type - No. of Parameters
SUBPATHS	No - X_{from} - Y_{from} - X_{to} - Y_{to} - ψ_{to} - v
SETPOINTS	X_{from} - Y_{from} - X_{to} - Y_{to} - ψ_{to} - v

Board of ...

COMMAND	Command-Type
GOTO	X_{to} - Y_{to} - ψ_{to} - v
WAIT	t
SUBPATH	X_{from} - Y_{from} - X_{to} - Y_{to} - ψ_{to} - v
ELASTIC BAND	X_{from} - Y_{from} - X_{to} - Y_{to} - ψ_{to} - v
Status PLANNER	Status-Type
Status NAVIGATOR	Status-Type
Status PILOT	Status-Type
Status MSE	Status-Type

The available Status-Types are

- Idle
- Executing
- Terminated Successfully
- Local Failure
- Global Failure

Local Failure indicates a failure in a module which leaves the option of recovery on a higher level. Global Failure excludes the possibility of a failure recovery and leads to an unsuccessful termination of the mission.

As the architecture is completed in its implementation the necessary lists and boards are defined as desired or extended, respectively.

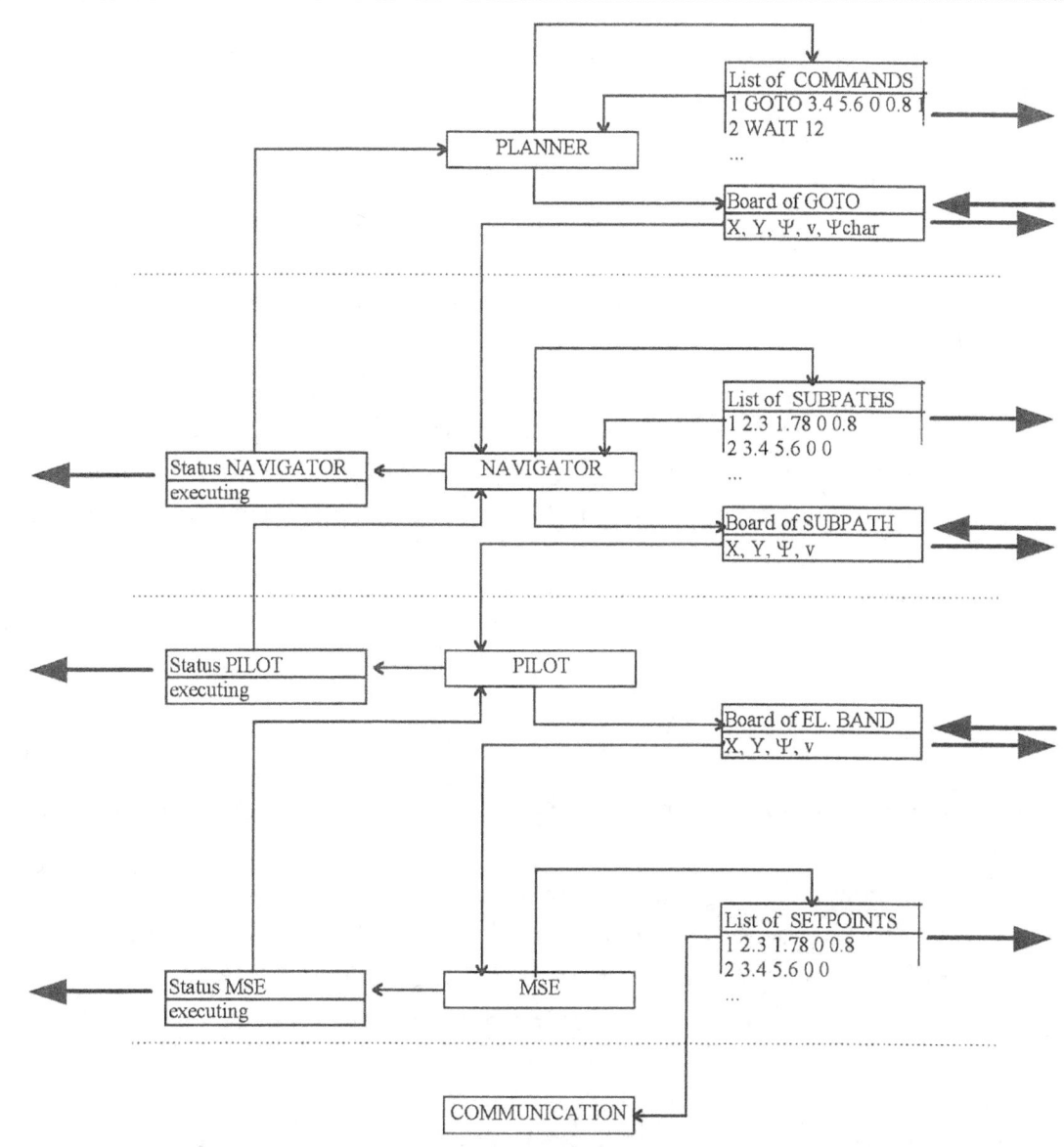

Figure 253: Communication in the Navigation Module

This open communication and data transfer system allows any module to monitor the activities of all other modules. All modules can be invoked by any other module by providing the necessary data in the appropriate board(s) and calling their main routine. An interesting application of this capability is the ability of the Local Navigation module to be driven by an external task instead of the Global Navigation module. For this an external task has to create a Subpath that describes the desired movement of the AMV, write it to the Board of Subpath and call the PILOT.

4.3.5 Mission Types and Path Characteristics

The types of missions that are supported by this architecture are

- Goto a certain point in the operating space using certain path characteristics
- Wait for a specified time at the current position
- Explore a specified area, i.e. move such that the map of the entire area can be updated
- Turn an external hardware device on or off
- Cover a certain area with the application of a certain external tool, e.g. clean a part of the floor
- Patrol a certain area
- Dock at a workstation

These missions can be decomposed into a number of basic mission types: to cover a certain area with a tool is a sequence of Goto the specified area, Turn the tool on, followed by a series of Goto commands that cover the entire area. To Patrol an area is a series of Goto commands that build a closed path, e.g. a square. These basic missions are

- GOTO
- EXPLORE
- WAIT
- TURN EXTERNAL DEVICE ON/ OFF

A Goto mission consists of a target point and a number of path characteristics. The path characteristics to be considered are

- The orientation (heading angle) of the vehicle as it moves
- Conservative/ adventurous/ shortest path
- Security against collision with obstacles
- Patience when waiting for moving obstacles to clear a blocked path

4.3.6 PLANNER

4.3.6.1 Mission Description and Execution

A number of mission planning systems for AMVs have been developed. Borenstein et al.'s "Tour Plan Generator" [43] concentrates on navigation functions and features routing optimisation techniques. Pearson et al. [44] describe a knowledge based mission planner that integrates navigation functions. The planning system developed in this work does not perform any other task than to specify the mission as a list of single commands and to execute this list (see Figure 11).

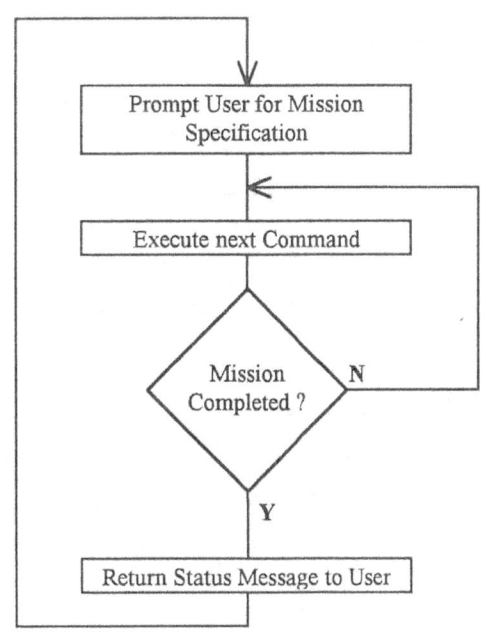

Figure 11: PLANNER Flow Diagram

Each command results in a call to the Navigation or External Device Management module as shown in the flow diagram in Figure 12.

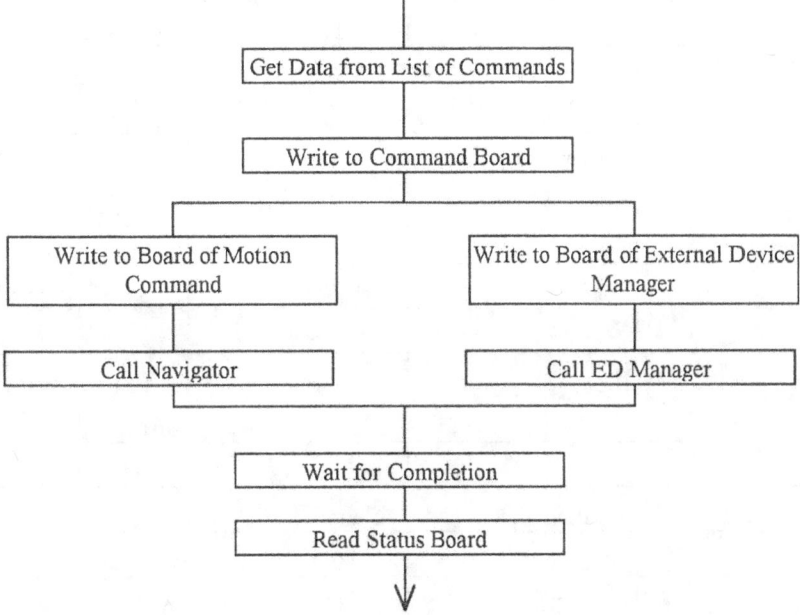

Figure 12: PLANNER - Execution of a command

4.3.6.2 Mission Commands

The commands that are used to specify the AMV's mission are summarised in the following table:

Mission Command	Parameter Name	Range	Remark
GOTO			
	X	Global Map	Global Coordinate of Target Point
	Y	Global Map	Global Coordinate of Target Point
	Ψ	0-360°	Heading Angle
	v	0 - 100 %	Velocity to be travelled at
	ORIENTATION	HOLD	Heading Angle is kept constant to global north
		AHEAD	Heading angle is kept constant towards current moving direction
	PATH	CONSERVATIVE	Known areas of environment are preferred
		ADVENTURE	Unknown areas of map are preferred
		SHORT	Shortest path is preferred
	SECURITY	0 - 100 %	Security level with respect to collisions
	PATIENCE	0 - 100 %	Patience of the Local Navigation module towards other moving obstacles
EXPLORE	X1	Global Map	Top left of exploration area
	Y1		
	X2		Bottom right of exploration area
	Y2		
	ORIENTATION	Arbitrary	Auto-set
	SECURITY	100 %	Auto-set
	PATIENCE	100 %	Auto-set
	T	0-infinity	in seconds [s]
WAIT	N	0,1,2,3,...	Non-Navigation Task Number
TASK		ON, OFF	

An example for a complete mission command is

> GOTO 12,25,25,80
>
> ORIENTATION HOLD
>
> PATH ADVENTURE
>
> SECURITY 70
>
> PATIENCE 50

where the vehicle travels from the current position to the position (12,25) with 80% of its maximum velocity, and a heading angle of 25° towards the direction of movement. The path is preferably in areas that are unknown in the map and the security and patience levels are 70% or 50%, respectively.

5 Memory System, Navigation and Map Building

5.1 Memory System

5.1.1 Introduction

The memory system holds the model of the environment of the AMV; this model is called "map". Properties of the environment that have to be included for navigation purposes are areas that are traversable (free space) and areas that are not traversable (obstacles) for the AMV. The definition of "traversable" is dependent on the vehicle design and may include or exclude rough surface, water, sand, etc.. Changes in the environment should be incorporated in the map as accurately and as quickly as possible. The update rate and accuracy of the map limit reactivity and accuracy of the navigation module, respectively.

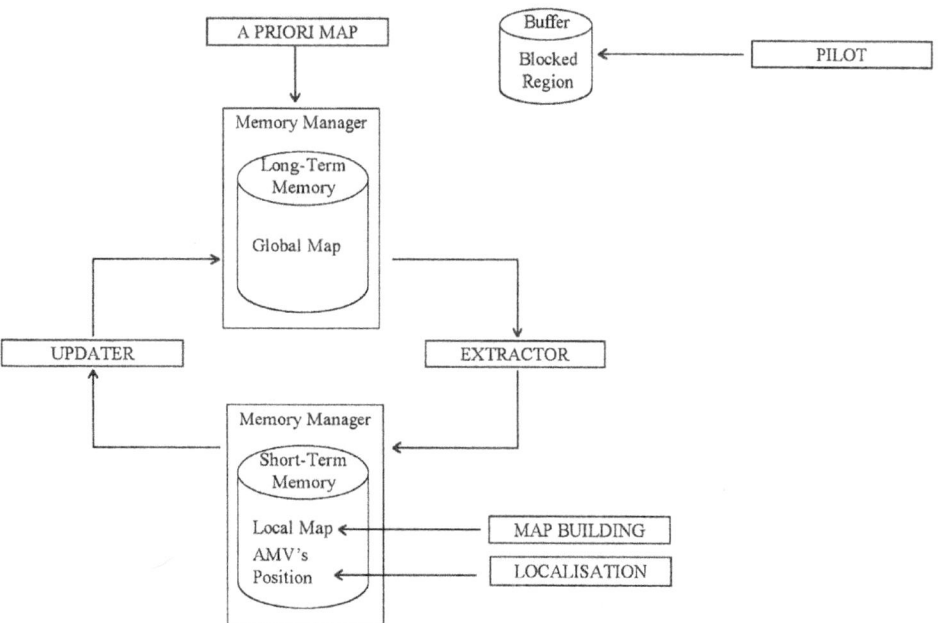

Figure 13: Memory System

As described above navigation techniques can be divided into Local and Global Navigation techniques. The requirements for the models are different for local and Local Navigation techniques, therefore a twofold model is introduced: a "Local Map" and a "Global Map".

The Global Map is stored in the Long Term Memory (LTM), the Local Map in the Short Term Memory (STM). The STM also holds the AMV's actual position estimation. The LTM is stored in a harddrive, the STM in a

RAM. Additional memory space is reserved for a "Blocked Region" which is used for Global Re-planning (see 4.4.2.2.2.1.2.).

5.1.2 Global Map

The Global Map covers the entire area of operation of the AMV. It is used for Global Navigation techniques, i.e. Pre-planning of a global path, and contains only static data of high reliability (e.g. walls, trees, etc.). Parts of it might be a priori data that is provided by the operator prior to the AMV's mission. The size of the Global Map is only limited by the available storage space.

The AMV's position in the Global Map is specified using the Cartesian coordinates (X_A, Y_A) and the orientation angle Ψ_A measured clockwise between the global north defined in positive Y-direction and the vehicle's north from 0 to 2π. Negative X and Y values are used if necessary.

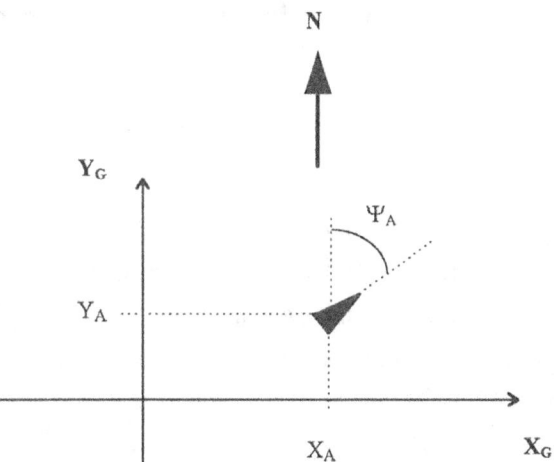

Figure 14: Global Map and AMV Coordinates

5.1.3 Local Map

The Local Map covers a squared area of the Global Map and holds static and dynamic data of arbitrary reliability, e.g. people, moving cars, etc. It is used by Local Navigation techniques. Map building is done only for the Local Map (see chapter 5.3.2). The size of the Local Map depends on the range of the available sensors to be able to incorporate all sensor data.

As the AMV moves the Local Map is switched to a new position whenever the PILOT calculates a new "Elastic Band" (see chapter 5.2.3.3.1.1).

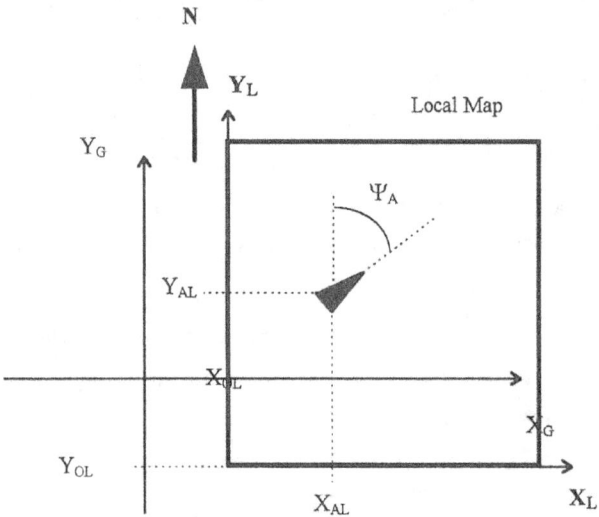

Figure 15: Local Map and AMV Coordinates

The position of the AMV in the Local Map is described using the Cartesian coordinates (X_{AL}, Y_{AL}) and the orientation Ψ_A. Since the North of the Local Map and the Global Map are both pointing in the same direction the orientation angle is equivalent in both coordinate systems.

The necessary resolution of the Local Map is determined using a well-known benchmark situation for AMVs: passing through a door.

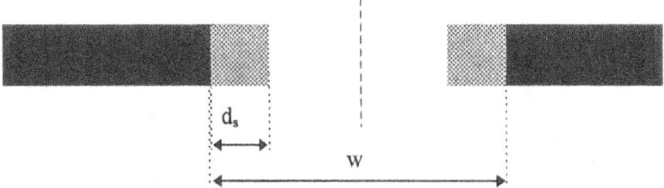

Figure 16: Pass through Door Problem

The resolution necessary to be able to pass through a door expressed as the minimum length reflected in the map (the maximum sidelength of a cell in a grid based map) is determined to

$$s_{\min} = \frac{w - d_{AMV} - d_s}{2}$$

[3.]

where w is the width of the smallest door that has to be passed, d_{AMV} the diameter of the (assumed to be circular) AMV and d_s the security distance the AMV has to keep to each obstacle.

5.1.4 Map Structure

5.1.4.1 Review of Common Map Structures

The environment is represented by a collection of entities. Each entity describes a certain area of the environment, and the minimum area described by one entity is the maximum resolution of the map. Each entity has a number of properties assigned that describe the area represented by this entity.

Entity n
Area represented
Property 1
Property 2
Property 3
...

Entity n+1
Area represented
Property 1
Property 2
Property 3
...

...

Figure 16b: General Map Structure

The type of entity (= decomposition) chosen determines fundamental properties of the map system, such as

- Access speed
- Flexibility
- Memory requirement
- Available algorithms
- Ability to represent desired properties of the environment

Two major types of map structures can be distinguished: feature based maps, e.g. in [45] and grid based decompositions of space, e.g. using hexagons [27] or squares [46].

Feature based maps basically consist of a list of features (objects) present in the environment. Each feature has its position and size and properties to describe the area covered by this feature assigned. Feature based maps require feature recognition or extraction from sensor data which increases computational cost. The features in the map are usually chosen from a list of available features which limits the ability to model the environment accurately. Some feature based map systems are able to learn new features and extend the set of available features.

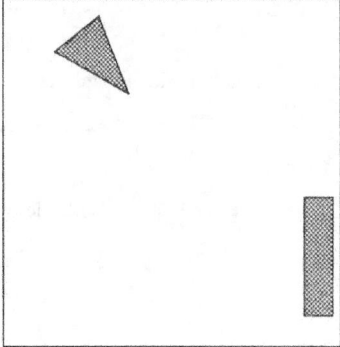

Figure 17: Example Environment with two Obstacles

Advantages of feature based maps are fast access due to a comparable small number of entries in the list and high accuracy of the model if all occurring objects are available in the set of features. One major drawback is the problem of detecting overlapping or touching features.

Feature Classification	Position	Size
TRIANGLE	X,Y,Ψ	l_1,l_2,l_3
RECTANGLE	X,Y,Ψ	l_1,l_2

Feature Map:
Number of Entries: 2
Total number of information bytes: 13

Figure 18: Feature Based Map

Maps based on regular decompositions of space use equally shaped cells, e.g. squares, polygons, etc., that each cover a certain area. Each cell is then assigned the properties describing this area. The advantages of this technique is fast access to the properties of a point in the environment. Major drawback is the necessity to process all cells if the entire map is to be processed.

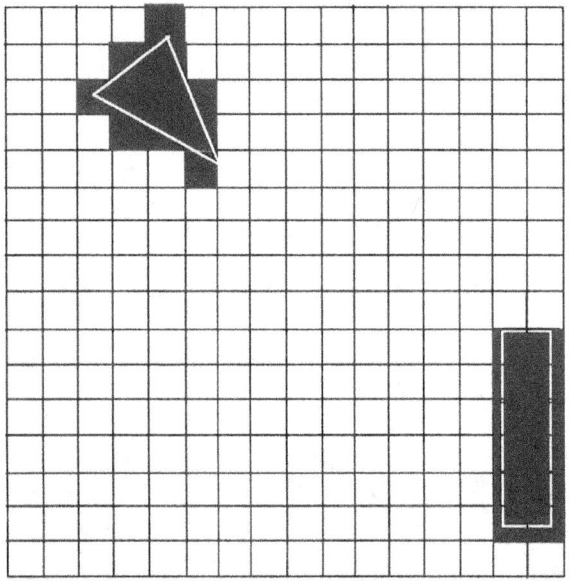

Regular Squared Grid:
Total number of grid elements: 256
Number of occupied grid elements: 23

Figure 19: Regular Squared Grid Map

Samet [47] introduced a Quadtree decomposition which combines some of the advantages of feature and regular grid based maps. A Quadtree Data Structure (QDS) uses a grid of flexible resolution to represent space. Each node of the quadtree represents a squared area. Adjacent areas of space with the same environment properties may so be described using a smaller number of cells compared with the regular shaped grid decomposition.

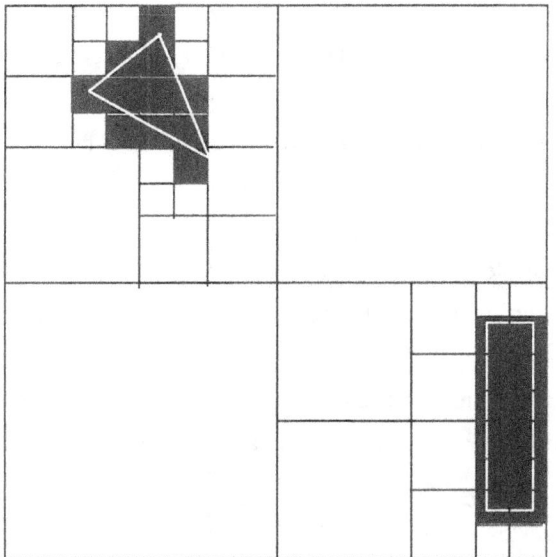

Quadtree Representation:
Total number of Nodes: 52
Number of occupied Nodes: 14

Figure 20: Quadtree based Map

The QDS representing the example environment from Figure 17 is shown in Figure 20. The data structure is shown in Figure 21, white nodes indicate empty space, black nodes occupied space, grey nodes do not contain information of the environment and are only needed to link the tree.

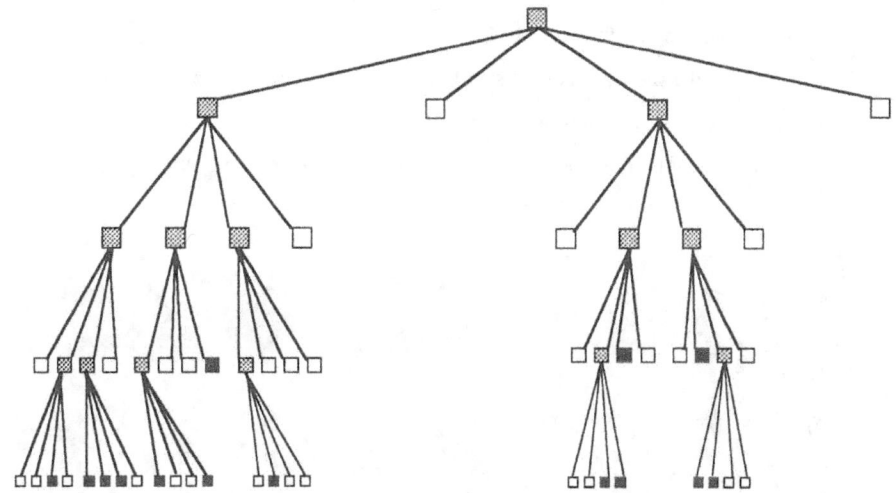

Figure 21: QDS of Example Environment

Comparing the QDS with a feature and a regular grid based map it is apparent that the number of entities in the map is the lowest for feature based maps, and the largest for regular grid based maps; memory requirements will be accordingly.

Discussing processing speed two basic types of map operations are considered: access time to one entity and the time to perform an action to a certain area of the map, whereas the latter is dependent on the size of the area of one entity. The access speed is dependent on the total number of entities and the type of access and order that is maintained (pointer or array). The feature based map is expected to provide the fastest access speed, the QDS the slowest due to some overhead in tree operations. Considering operations that have to be performed on an area of the map, or the entire map, the QDS is expected to be quicker compared to the regular grid due to the smaller number of entities that has to be processed.

Samet [48] points out that the number of nodes in a QDS is proportional to the perimeter of obstacles contained in an environment map. Increasing the resolution leads to a linear growth in the number of nodes in a QDS, whereas doubling of the resolution leads to a quadrupling of the cells of a regular grid. Therefore a QDS is preferable for high resolution maps.

Zelinsky [22] carried out extensive comparisons in terms of processing speed and memory requirements of the QDS and regular grid maps using some navigation algorithms. He favours QDS for high resolution maps and less cluttered environments.

Flajolet et al. [49] describe an investigation of the costs of various types of searches in quadtrees.

5.1.4.2 Quadtree Data Structure (QDS) for Local and Global Map

In the CA²MOV architecture a QDS is used for the Global Map because of its memory efficiency and for the Local Map mainly because its lower computational cost for high resolution. The Global Map covers a large area with low resolution, the Local Map a small area with high resolution. Additionally, using the same data structure simplifies the exchange of data between the Local and the Global Map.

The QDS of the Local Map is described using

- s_{LM}, the sidelength of the Local Map, in [m]
- $s_N = s_{min}$, the sidelength of the smallest nodes on the lowest level of the QDS, in [m]
- m_{max}, the number of levels of the tree
- n_{max}, the maximum number of nodes on the lowest level of the QDS

which are related as follows

$$m_{max} = \frac{s_{LM}}{s_N} \qquad\qquad [4.]$$

$$n_{max} = 2^{2 m_{max}} \qquad\qquad [5.]$$

$$s_N = \frac{s_{LM}}{\sqrt{n_{max}}} \qquad\qquad [6.]$$

The nodes of the QDS are used to store properties of the area covered by each node. Since the maps are used for navigation purposes it is necessary to describe an area as traversable, "empty", or untraversable, "occupied", for the AMV. Widely used is a simple marking of the cells as empty or occupied. In order to consider uncertainties in the way the map is built it is desirable to store a measure of confidence in the information whether the node is empty or occupied. This uncertainty can result from sensor uncertainty, uncertainties in the map building algorithm or in the AMV's position. Therefore the probability P that a node is occupied is defined as one property that is stored in each node. *P* ranges from *-1*, empty with very high certainty, to *+1*, occupied with very high certainty. *P=0* indicates an unknown state of the node.

Comparing a moving with a static obstacle the static obstacle's probability will be constant, apart from noise in the measurements, the moving obstacle's probability will increase at the position it has just reached and decrease at nodes it has just left. It seems useful to keep track of the change of P, and therefore the dynamics value *D* is introduced. *D* is defined as the derivative of *P* to the time and ranges from *-1*, high negative change of *P*, to *0*, static node, to *+1*, high positive change of *P*.

$$D = c * \frac{dP}{dt} = c * \frac{\Delta P}{\Delta t}$$ [7.]

In equation 7 *c* is a scaling constant.

To accurately determine *D* changes in *P*, that occur when the map is being updated, have to be time stamped. To avoid this, *D* can alternatively be defined as

$$D = \frac{\Delta P}{2}$$ [8.]

where *ΔP* is the change of *P* between two consecutive sensor measurements which introduces some inaccuracy since not all nodes in the map are covered by each cycle of map updating. Sensing frequency and the nature of environment actually encountered by the AMV decide whether this approximation is feasible.

In the Global Map *D* is per definitionem always = *0*.

The structure of a node in the Local or Global Map is summarised in Figure 22.

Position		Size		
P		D		
Pointer to Parent Node	Pointer to Child 1	Pointer to Child 2	Pointer to Child 3	Pointer to Child 4

Figure 22: QDS Node Structure

The *P-D* plane represents the state space of one node which is divided in four states: EMPTY, FULL, TIP, and TAIL. EMPTY node are static and traversable for the AMV, FULL nodes are static and not traversable, TIP nodes are nodes with increasing *P*, and TAIL nodes are nodes with decreasing *P*. The fifth state is UNKNOWN which means that neither a priori data nor data from map building is available. To account for changes in *P* due to noise a threshold D_{th} is defined to clarify the difference between static and dynamic nodes.

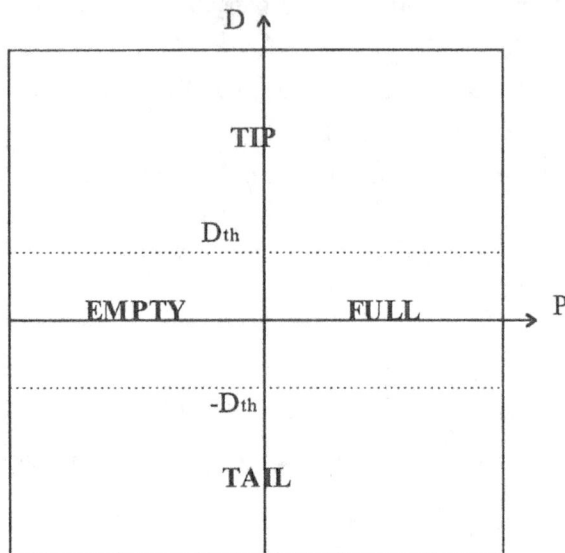

Figure 23: Node State Space Plane

Using these five states a state transition diagram can be constructed as in Figure 24.

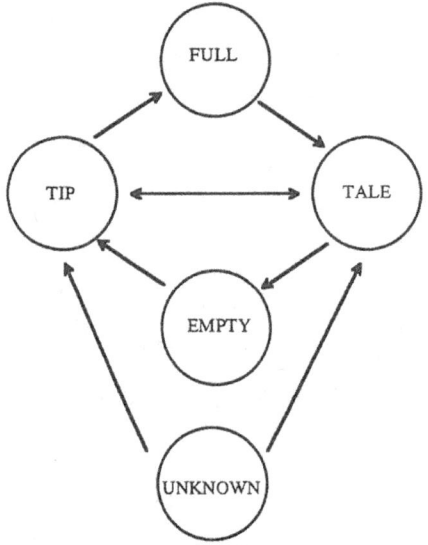

Figure 24: Node State Transition Diagram

The transition from EMPTY to FULL is shown for a simulation in the node state space plane in Figure 25 in a simulation. Each square represents the position of the state vector in the state space plane after one map updating cycle.

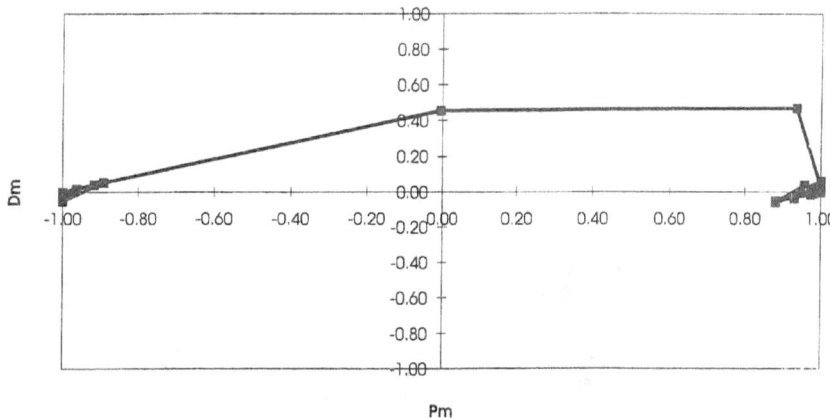

Figure 25: Transition EMPTY - FULL in State Space Plane

5.1.5 Short Term Memory Manager (STMM)

The Short-Term-Memory-Manager (STMM) is the access module to the Local Map and the AMV's position. It uses various algorithms for the QDS in order to perform the necessary procedures.

The STMM is a collection of public functions that will be expanded as necessary as the architecture is expanded. For an overview of all available functions at the current state of implementation see Appendix A.

5.1.6 Long Term Memory Manager (LTMM)

The Long-Term-Memory-Manager (LTMM) is the equivalent to the STMM regarding the Global Map. If the same form of QDS is used for the Local Map and the Global Map as proposed, many functions of the STMM and the LTMM are similar and can therefore be easily adapted.

5.1.7 UPDATER

As the AMV moves through the environment the Local Map's position in the Global Map is switched accordingly whenever the PILOT calculates a new Elastic Band (see chapter 5.2.3.3.1.1) to a new position to include the new Elastic Band in the Local Map. "Switching" the Local Map has to be done in three steps:

- Update the Global Map
- Adjust Local Map parameters, e.g. its position in the Global Map
- Extract information about area covered by the Local Map from the Global Map

The second step is performed by the STMM.

Updating the Global Map is task of the UPDATER-Module. It searches the Local Map for entries which are of the nature of the Global Map, i.e. static data of high reliability. The according areas in the node state space plane are marked black in Figure 26. Nodes with these properties are simply copied to the Global Map. More sophisticated rules for updating the Global Map can be formulated after experimentation with large environments has been carried out.

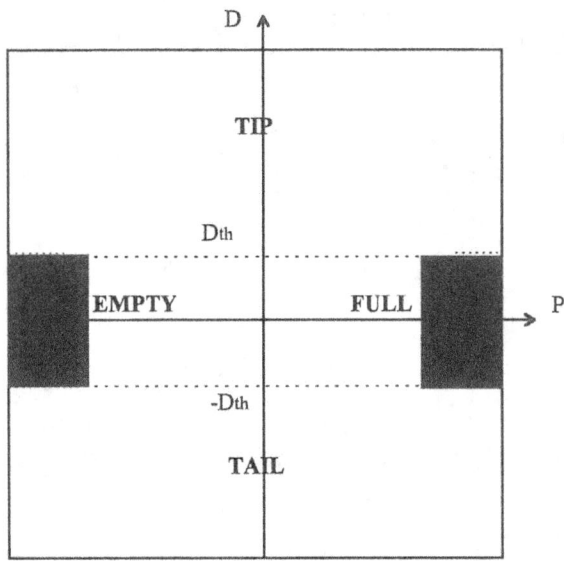

Figure 26: Nodes Used for Updating

The criteria for selecting node candidates for updating may be altered by the PLANNER for exploration missions where the task is to build the Global Map and nodes with less reliable data should be incorporated to build the Global Map, too.

5.1.8 EXTRACTOR

The Extractor is responsible for step three (see previous chapter) of switching the Local Map. When the new position of the Local Map has been determined in step two the data of the area represented by the Local Map is simply copied from the Global Map into the Local Map for areas that were not covered by the old position of the Local Map. Overlapping areas should retain their values.

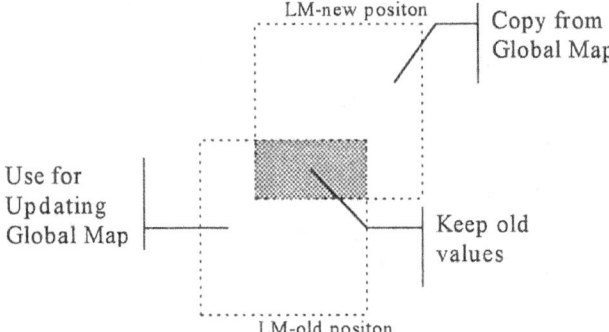

Figure 27: Switching the Local Map

5.2 Navigation

5.2.1 Global and Local Navigation

Navigation can generally be divided into Global and Local Navigation. Global Navigation considers the entire area of operation of the vehicle. It is of low reactivity towards changes in the environment and usually plans a path of the AMV in advance to its execution. It can therefore only consider static elements of the environment. Global Navigation usually uses some sort of optimisation technique considering the whole path from start to goal point, e.g. the shortest or quickest path.

Local Navigation is of higher reactivity towards changes in the environment, and can therefore cope with dynamic elements in an environment, e.g. moving obstacles. It determines an AMV's path on-line and can not insure optimality of the path as a whole. Usually Local Navigation is restricted to the range of the AMV's sensor system. AMVs operating only in a small environment, e.g. office, laboratory, may be sufficiently equipped with Local Navigation. Global Navigation is generally necessary if the vehicle is supposed to operate in a fairly large environment, e.g. a town, lake, hospital, factory, etc.

Some navigation techniques are more useful for Global Navigation, some for Local Navigation, and a few are suitable for both.

5.2.2 Introduction to Navigation Techniques

Navigation can be defined as "The science of getting ships, aircraft, or spacecraft from place to place; esp.: the method of determining position, course, and distance travelled" [7]. This traditional definition is modified with respect to AMVs as "the task of guiding a mobile vehicle from a start position to another desired position along a path with certain characteristics".

Navigation in this sense requires the localisation problem to be solved. The navigation task assumes the position of the vehicle to be known at all times with sufficient accuracy.

The two main desired path characteristics all navigation techniques have in common is

- Reach of the goal position
- Collision avoidance

Common optimisation goals are

- Minimise total path length
- Minimise travel time
- Minimise fuel/ electricity use
- Minimise curvature
- Maximise safety (distance to obstacles)

5.2.2.1 Vertex Graph Path Planning

Vertex Graph path planning bases on a map that models all obstacles in the environment geometrically. Prior to the path planning the obstacles are expanded by the radius of the AMV (assuming circular shape of the platform) plus a security distance, the AMV is then considered a point. All possible collision free paths are constructed by connecting the vertices of the expanded obstacles that are of free line of sight. These paths are then searched for an optimal path using the desired optimisation criteria using a standard search algorithm, e.g. "breadth first" or "A*" [8, 9, 10]. An example is given in Figure 28: The path from the start position (circle) to the goal position (cross) is determined considering two obstacles. All possible paths are shown in fine black lines, the solution path in a thick grey line.

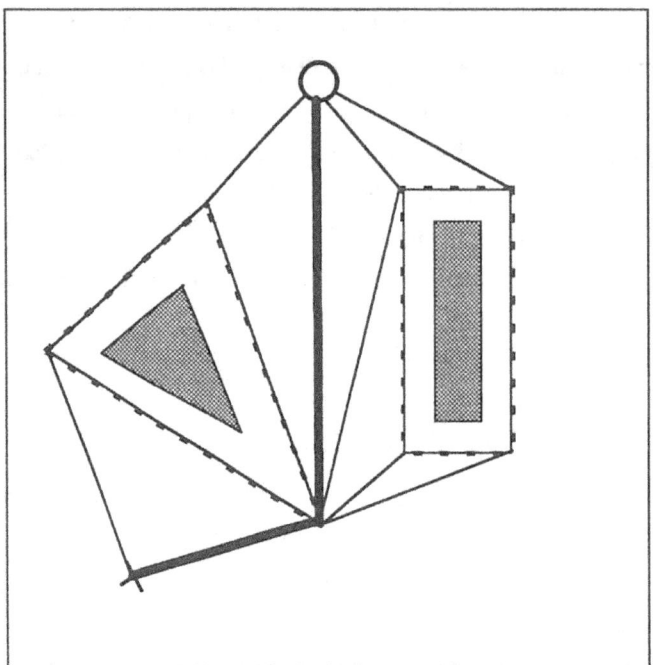

Figure 28: Vertex Graph Navigation

A drawback of Vertex Graph Navigation is its limitation to optimisation criteria that are related to properties of the straight lines between the vertices, e.g. the shortest path. It has no mechanism to deal with unknown regions of the environment. Used for reactive (local) navigation the entire path from the current location to the goal has to be re-planned continuously, which would waste computing resources. Vertex Graph path planning is therefore more suitable for Global Navigation.

In-depth information on Vertex Graph path planning can be found in [11, 12, 13, 14, 15].

5.2.2.2 Free Space Path Planning

Free space navigation considers free space rather than obstacles to determine the path for an AMV. Free space is modelled as convex polygons [16, 17], generalised cones [18] or a combination called "mixed space" [19] after the obstacles have been expanded in the same fashion as described in the previous chapter.

All these methods have in common that a set of possible paths is constructed linking the centres of passable free space corridors. This set is searched for an optimal solution using search algorithms as in the Vertex Graph method (see 3.1.5.).

An example using the same environment as in the previous chapter is given in Figure 29: all possible paths are shown in broken lines.

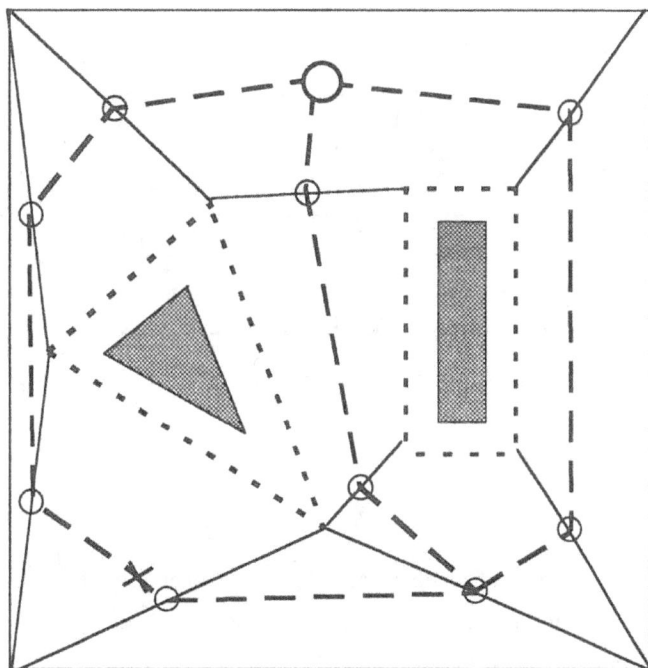

Figure 29: Free Space Navigation

The main drawback of this method is often referred to as the "too far problem", which means the solution path tends to be too conservative, the AMV is keeping a distance from obstacles that might be larger than the specified security distance. Free space navigation is therefore limited to find the safest path. This is fatal in large environments populated with only a few obstacles where the solution path might be much longer than necessary. Furthermore free space navigation suffers the same limitations with respect to reactive navigation as Vertex Graph navigation.

5.2.2.3 Grid Based Navigation

This navigation technique uses a grid map or needs to superimpose a grid on the existing map. Each grid cell is marked as free or occupied. The obstacles are again expanded by the AMV's diameter plus a security distance. Each grid point can now be "four or eight connected" to its neighbour points, depending on the inclusion or exclusion of diagonal neighbours. The set of possible paths is now searched for an optimal path using one of the standard search algorithms (see 3.1.2) [20, 21].

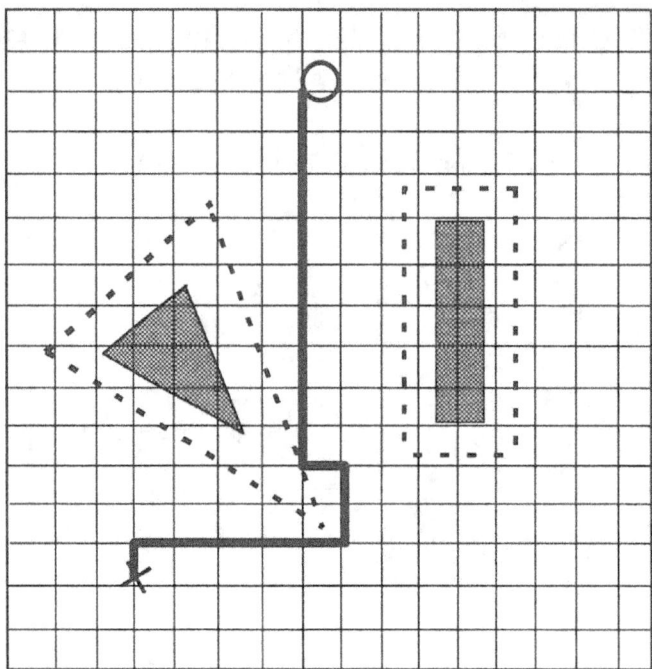

Figure 30: Four Connected Grid Navigation

Obviously the resolution of the path is dependent on the resolution of the grid. On order to obtain a path that is not too conservative a relatively small grid size is necessary. This however leads to a very large set of possible paths and a need for powerful computing resources. Another drawback is the extra effort to build the grid if not already present in form of a grid based map.

5.2.2.4 Distance Transforms

First presented by Byrne [20] Distance Transforms are a novel approach of path planning offering some significant advantages. A grid is superimposed on the environment map and each cell is assigned a value that represents the distance from this cell to the cell in which the goal is. These distance values are calculated from the goal (=0) "flowing" around obstacles whose cells are assigned the value "∞" until all cells are calculated. The solution path is then found as a sequence of cells going downhill in distance values from the start cell to the goal cell. If there is no downhill path from a cell than it can be concluded that there is no solution path, i.e. the goal is unreachable. If there are two neighbour cells with the same value, the two paths are equivalent.

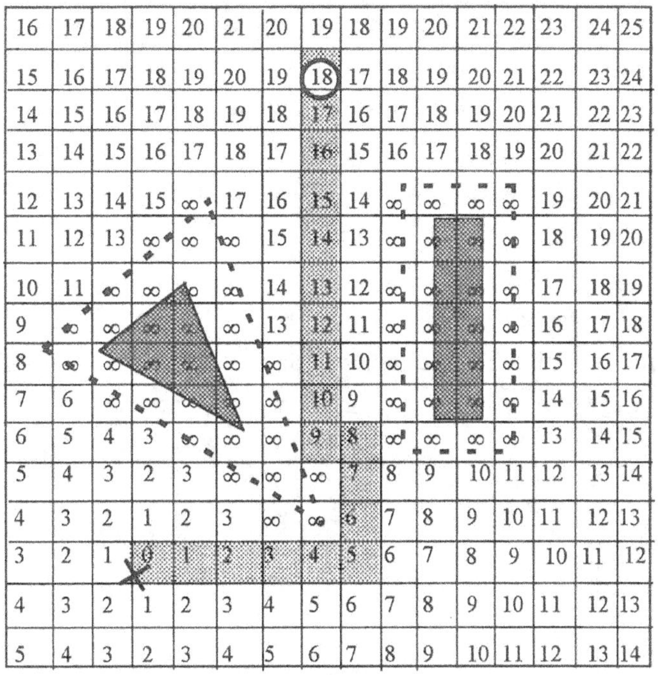

16	17	18	19	20	21	20	19	18	19	20	21	22	23	24	25
15	16	17	18	19	20	19	⑱	17	18	19	20	21	22	23	24
14	15	16	17	18	19	18	17	16	17	18	19	20	21	22	23
13	14	15	16	17	18	17	16	15	16	17	18	19	20	21	22
12	13	14	15	∞	17	16	15	14	∞	∞	∞	∞	19	20	21
11	12	13	∞	∞	∞	15	14	13	∞	∞	∞	∞	18	19	20
10	11	∞	∞	∞	14	13	12	∞	∞	∞	∞	17	18	19
9	∞	∞	∞	∞	13	12	11	∞	∞	∞	16	17	18
8	∞	∞	∞	∞	∞	11	10	∞	∞	∞	15	16	17
7	6	∞	∞	∞	∞	10	9	∞	∞	∞	14	15	16
6	5	4	3	∞	∞	∞	9	8	∞	∞	∞	∞	13	14	15
5	4	3	2	3	∞	∞	∞	7	8	9	10	11	12	13	14
4	3	2	1	2	3	∞	∞	6	7	8	9	10	11	12	13
3	2	1	0	1	2	3	4	5	6	7	8	9	10	11	12
4	3	2	1	2	3	4	5	6	7	8	9	10	11	12	13
5	4	3	2	3	4	5	6	7	8	9	10	11	12	13	14

Figure 31: Distance Transform Navigation

The main drawback of distance transforms is the large computing overhead for building the grid, if not already present, and calculating the distance transform values.

However it offers some major advantages: So is the optimal path known from every grid cell in the map, such that multiple robot systems are supported. Also multiple goals of same priority are easily considered, in this case the AMV selects automatically the goal that can be reached with minimum cost.

Very important is that the distance transform values are not limited to reflect the Euclidean distance to the goal. It is straightforward to implement all kinds of cost functions, such that the distance transform values reflect directly the cost of the path from each cell to the goal. This way path characteristics such as "conservative", "adventurous", etc. can be realised [22]. Zelinsky [23] presents an exploration algorithm which exhibits a "visit all" path using distance transforms.

Distance transform methods are furthermore very flexible in their implementation. They can be very accurate when considering not only perpendicular neighbours, but also diagonal neighbours with the distance calculated from the centre of the cells (see Figure 32)

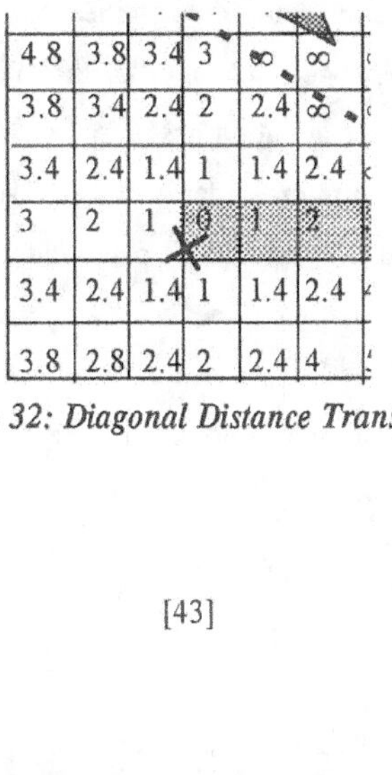

4.8	3.8	3.4	3	∞	∞
3.8	3.4	2.4	2	2.4	∞
3.4	2.4	1.4	1	1.4	2.4
3	2	1	0	1	2
3.4	2.4	1.4	1	1.4	2.4
3.8	2.8	2.4	2	2.4	4

Figure 32: Diagonal Distance Transform

Of considerable importance, especially with large cell size, is the transition from the solution cell sequence to the actual solution path. This is a purely geometric step and can be done in many ways. The easiest method is to connect the centres of the cells. This introduces some conservativeness and can be replaced with more sophisticated methods.

Distance transform techniques are not suitable for reactive navigation due to their large computational overhead. However they are a flexible and efficient method for off-line Pre-planning of an AMV's path (Global Navigation).

5.2.2.5 Potential Field Navigation

Potential field navigation techniques make use of artificial forces: Repulsive forces at impassable areas, obstacles, rivers, etc., keep the vehicle away, an attractive force at the goal point moves it towards the goal [23, 24, 25, 26, 27].

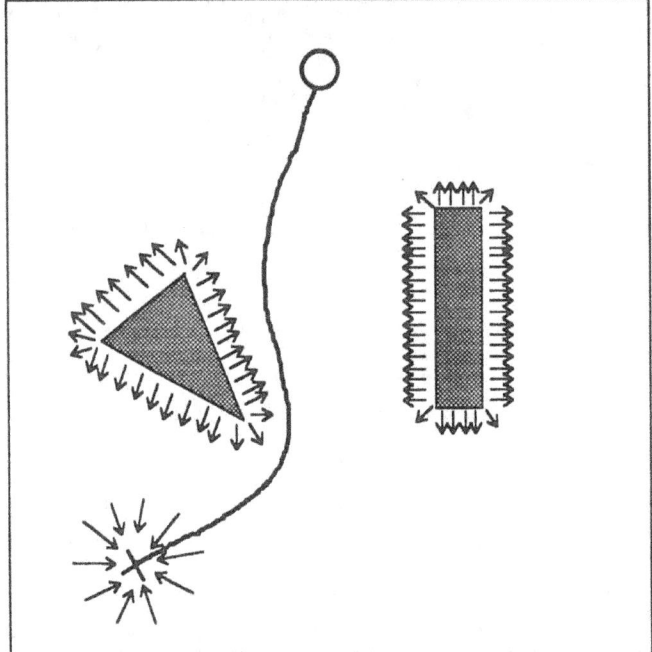

Figure 33: Potential Field Navigation

The potential fields have to be tuned such that the AMV can never be dragged inside an obstacle and keeps a specified security distance, but moves towards the goal from all points in the environment. This is limited by the existence of local minima. There the resultant force on the AMV disappears and a solution path can not be found. Local minima exist e.g. on the opposite goal side of obstacles. The local minima problem has not been solved up to date completely, though considerable attention has been given to it: Arkin [24] suggests a random movement of the AMV hoping to escape a local minimum, Adams et al [23] suggests to relocate the goal temporarily when stuck in a local minimum. Hou at al [27] assume the path around a local minimum turns into an infinite loop and avoid this problem by marking areas that have been visited already as impassable.

All these methods do not avoid the existence of local minima and are not always successful in their solutions. Another drawback is that no optimisation techniques can be applied.

Potential field navigation is very suitable for Local Navigation since the environment has only to be known in the vicinity of the vehicle and only a short piece of the path is calculated with each evaluation of the force fields. On-line path generation can be implemented easily and effectively.

5.2.2.6 Heuristic Navigation

Heuristic navigation does not use an environment model (map) but can use sensor information directly. The AMV's behaviour consists of simple rules [28, 29], e.g. minimising the current distance to the goal, minimise the deviation angle form the current moving direction to the straight line to the goal, etc.

Heuristic navigation is very limited in the situations it can solve but might be a cost effective fast alternative for some simple applications.

5.2.2.7 Behaviour Based Navigation

Behaviour Based Navigation for mobile vehicles was introduced by Brooks [30] and is based on breaking up the navigation task into basic behaviours, e.g. "avoid obstacles", "follow wall", "stay on path", etc. The combination of these "micro-behaviours" result in the desired "macro-behaviour" of the AMV. This approach results in solution paths that may be hard to foresee, but present an opportunity for reactive navigation independent from geometric path modelling models.

Arkin [24, 31, 32] defined these behaviours as "Motor-schemas". Motor-schemas origin in psychology and neurology and describe the interaction between perception and action of living beings.

Motor-schemas are usually implemented using artificial potential fields. Each Motor-schema is implemented using a separate field or field property, e.g. "Move-towards-Goal" is reflected by an attractive force of the goal. Combining all Motor-schemas or behaviours is usually done by simply adding all forces at the AMV's position vectorially. One advantage of Motor-schemas is that they can be activated or de-activate separately as desired. E.g. when travelling over a bridge a "stay-on-path" behaviour is essential, but it may be de-activated when travelling in a large area of free space in order to give the vehicle more flexibility in its path. Alternatively the schemas might be given different priorities in case of opposing objectives.

5.2.2.8 Navigation Techniques for Moving Obstacles

Most navigation techniques above assume a static environment, some reactive navigation techniques can cope with moving obstacles in a "quasi-static" fashion. Re-planning of the path or calculating of the next step in the path and updating of the environment model is done fast enough to be able to include (slowly) moving obstacles in the path planning. However the velocity of elements in the environment is not included in the model.

A number of path planners extend the two- or three-dimensional space by the dimension time and are able to consider the velocity of obstacles[34, 35]. Fujimura et al. [33] model obstacles as polygons and assign a velocity vector. Space and time are represented in a three-dimensional model and the path is determined using an optimisation technique. All navigation techniques considering moving obstacles suffer from the assumption that the obstacles continue to move at constant velocity, acceleration, and/ or direction.

5.2.3 CA²MOV Navigation Module

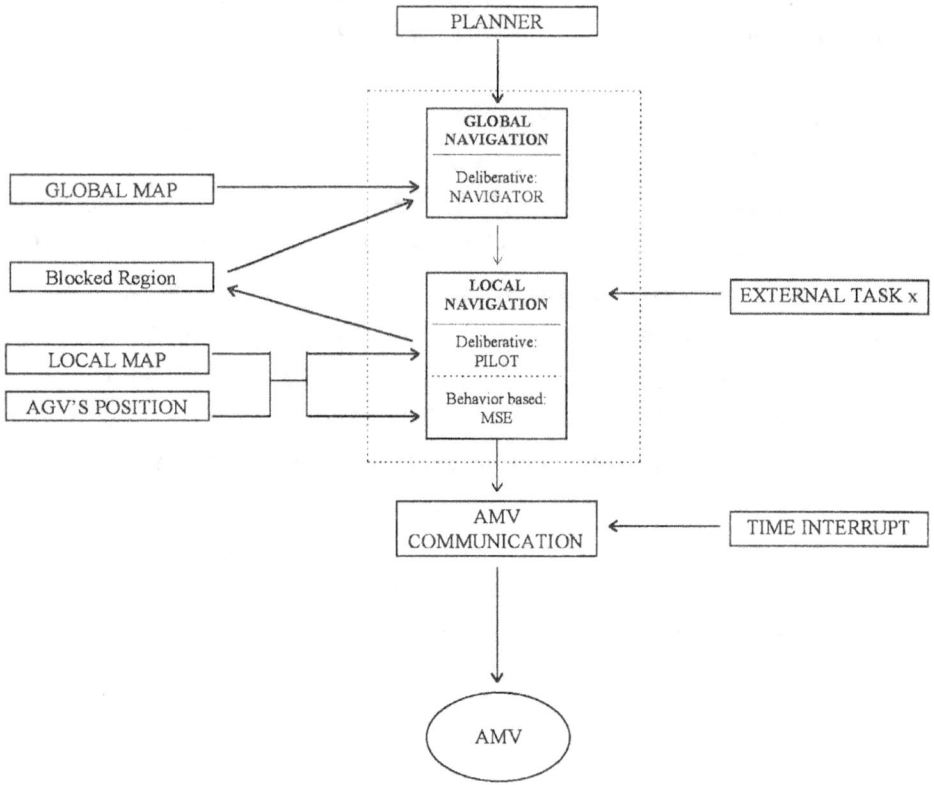

Figure 34: Navigation Module - Overview

The Navigation task is implemented using three modules: NAVIGATOR, PILOT, AND MOTOR-SCHEMA-EXECUTOR (MSE). In Figure 34 the hybrid nature of the Navigation module is apparent: Navigator, Pilot, and MSE are building a hierarchy, the MSE is a behaviour based subsumption module.

The Navigation module receives a motion command, GOTO or EXPLORE, (see chapter 4.3.6.2) and the appropriate path parameters. The task of the Navigation module is to calculate position setpoints that are stored in a list, the list of setpoints (see chapter 4.3.4) and are used by the motion controller of SUAVE (see chapter 3.3) to guide the vehicle. The list of position setpoints is a first-in-first-out (FIFO) list that acts as buffer.

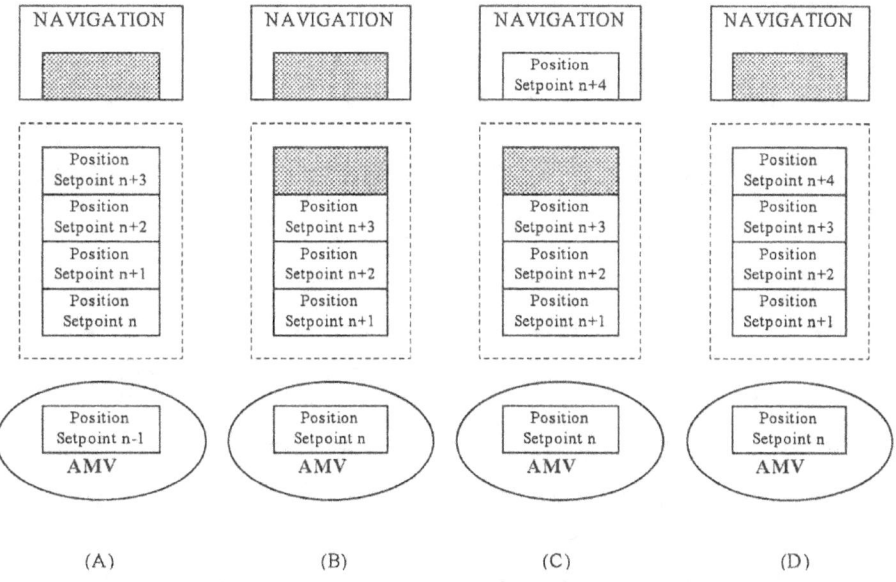

Figure 35: List of Position Setpoints

Figure 35 shows how the list of position setpoints links the AMV's motion controller with the Navigation module. In (A) the AMV is using setpoint (n-1) as input to its motion controller, the Navigation module is running idle and the list is full (assuming a list size of four setpoints). In Figure (B) the AMV has reached setpoint (n-1) and requested setpoint (n), the list size has shrunk to three setpoints. (C) shows how setpoint (n-4) is calculated in the Navigation module. In (D) the list is filled up again and the cycle starts over.

The buffer function is necessary since in some cases new setpoints might be requested by SUAVE more frequently than the Navigation module can calculate new setpoints. The list must never run empty, this would lead to a sudden emergency stop of the vehicle and a failed mission. The minimum number of setpoints in the list is determined to

$$N_{min} = N_{worst_{max}} * \left(T_{calc_{max}} - T_{R_{min}} \right) \qquad [9.]$$

with $N_{worst\ max}$ being the maximum number of consecutive setpoints under the worst condition, i.e. the calculation of the new setpoint takes the maximum time, $T_{calc\ max}$ and the time between the request of two setpoints is minimal $T_{R\ min}$:

$$T_{R_{min}} = \frac{d_{sp_{min}}}{V_{R_{max}}} \qquad [10.]$$

where $d_{sp,min}$ is the minimal distance between two consecutive setpoints and $v_{R,max}$ is the maximum velocity of the AMV.

5.2.3.1 Path Description

The path of the AMV that is determined by the three Navigation modules, NAVIGATOR, PILOT, and MSE, is described geometrically on four levels of increasing accuracy and decreasing levels of abstraction.

Level 1	PLANNER	--->	Endpoint of Motion Command
Level 2	NAVIGATOR	--->	Subpath
Level 3	PILOT	--->	Elastic Band
Level 4	MSE	--->	Position Setpoint

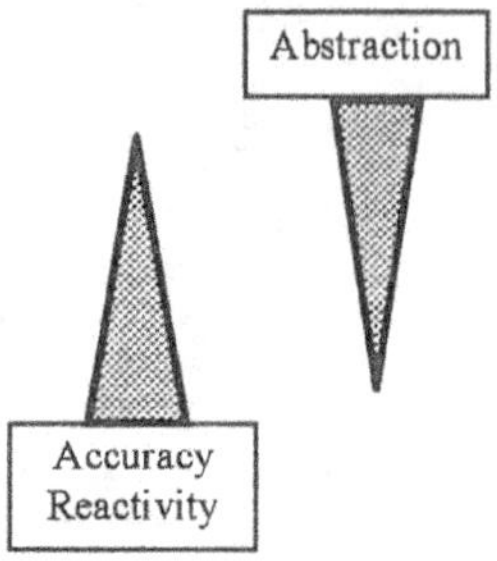

Abstraction

Accuracy
Reactivity

Figure 36: Four Levels of Path Description

The path description should be as accurate and detailed as necessary in order to allow the appropriate module to carry out its task, and as abstract as possible in order to minimise processing cost.

The description levels in detail are:

The endpoint of a motion command (GOTO or EXPLORE) is specified by the user or determined by the PLANNER in the case of a mission that is decomposed into several single motion commands (see chapter 4.3) in the form of the three global coordinates (X, Y, Ψ).

A Subpath is a straight line segment specified by its endpoints. One motion command is subdivided into a collection of Subpaths that form a complete collision free path from the start to the end point. The subpaths are determined by the NAVIGATOR and consider all obstacles in the Global Map.

Elastic Bands are created by the PILOT by breaking the current Subpath up into shorter pieces that fit into the Local Map. The PILOT might also relocate the endpoint of an Elastic Band away from the original Subpath in case an obstacle in the Local Map is too close to the Subpath, this function is called "Local Pre-planning" and is described in detail in chapter 5.2.3.3.1.1. Elastic Bands are defined by start and endpoint in global coordinates, too.

The MSE uses the Elastic Bands to calculate position setpoints according to the actual estimated position of the AMV and the current state of the Local Map: reactive navigation.

The Subpaths are pre-planned, i.e. before the AMV starts moving, the Elastic Bands are calculated as needed, i.e. when the MSE requests the next one. The Position Setpoints are calculated on-line as requested by the AMV motion controller and consist of the global coordinates and the magnitude of the velocity (X, Y, ψ, v).

Using an environment populated with three types of obstacles in Figure 37 an example path is shown on the description levels 1, 2, and 3 in Figure 38, and on level 4 in Figure 39.

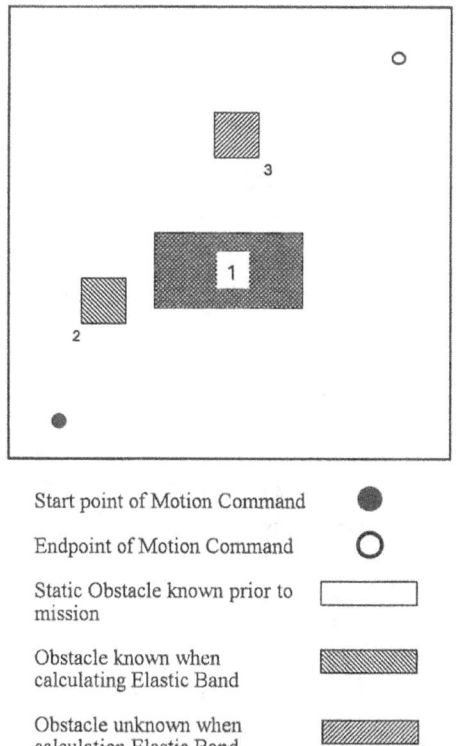

Start point of Motion Command   ●

Endpoint of Motion Command   ○

Static Obstacle known prior to mission

Obstacle known when calculating Elastic Band

Obstacle unknown when calculation Elastic Band

Figure 37: **Example Environment Populated with three Obstacles**

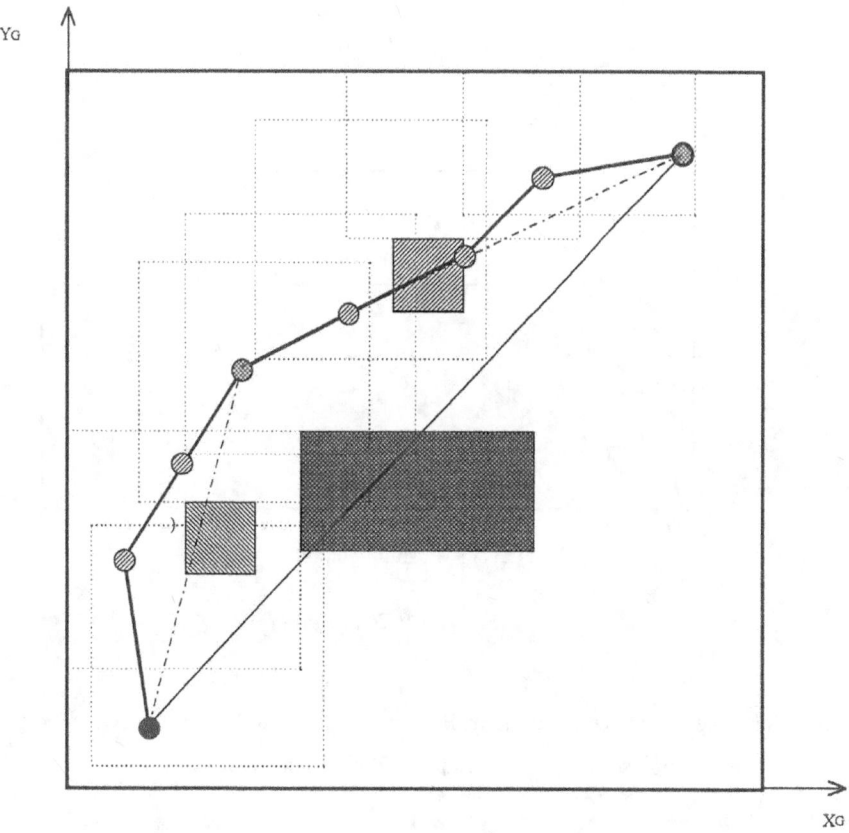

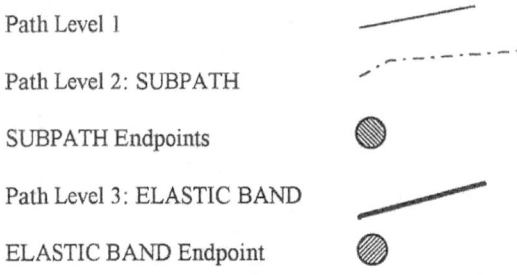

Path Level 1

Path Level 2: SUBPATH

SUBPATH Endpoints

Path Level 3: ELASTIC BAND

ELASTIC BAND Endpoint

Figure 38: Path Levels one, two, and three

The Global Map and the Local Map (dotted square) at its different positions when calculating the Elastic Bands are shown.

Note that the Subpaths do only consider the big obstacle since this is the only one included in the Global Map. Important is furthermore that the position setpoints do not necessarily reach the endpoints of the Elastic Bands. This is due to the way the Elastic Bands are implemented which is described in chapter 5.2.3.3.2.10. Only the endpoint of the motion command must be reached exactly by the AMV and is therefore always a position setpoint.

The first Elastic Band has been located away from the Subpath due to the obstacle 2: Local Pre-planning.

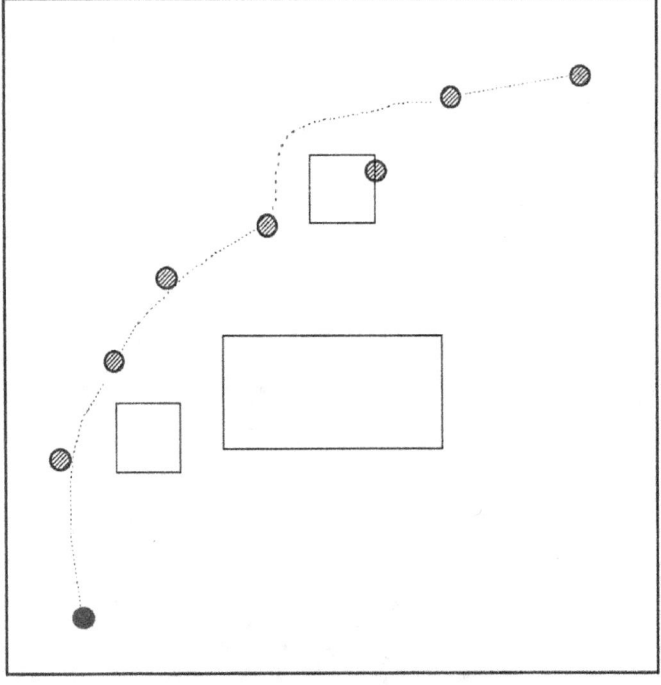

Path Level 4: Position Setpoints

Figure 39: Path Level four

Obstacle 3 could not be considered when Elastic Band 5 was determined and is therefore used only by the MSE when calculating the position setpoints, that "bend" the Elastic Band at these positions.

Module	Element used	Element Created	Map Used	Obstacles in Map
Planner	User input	Motion command, end-point	-	-
Navigator	Motion Command	Subpath 1, and 2	Global Map	Obstacle 1
Pilot	Subpath 1	Elastic Band 1	Local Map	Obstacle 1 and 2
MSE	Elastic Band 1	Position Setpoints	Local Map	Obstacle 1 and 2
Pilot	Subpath 1	Elastic Band 2	Local Map	Obstacle 2
MSE	Elastic Band 2	Position Setpoints	Local Map	Obstacle 2
Pilot	Subpath 1	Elastic Band 3	Local Map	Obstacle 1
MSE	Elastic Band 3	Position Setpoints	Local Map	Obstacle 1
Pilot	Subpath 2	Elastic Band 4	Local Map	Obstacle 1
MSE	Elastic Band 4	Position Setpoints	Local Map	Obstacle 1
Pilot	Subpath 2	Elastic Band 5	Local Map	-
MSE	Elastic Band 5	Position Setpoints	Local Map	Obstacle 3
Pilot	Subpath 2	Elastic Band 6	Local Map	-
MSE	Elastic Band 6	Position Setpoints	Local Map	-
Pilot	Subpath 2, Motion Command	Elastic Band 7	Local Map	-
MSE	Elastic Band 7	Position Setpoints	Local Map	-

Figure 40: Steps in Mission Example

5.2.3.2 Global Navigation

The basic nature of Global Navigation has been described in chapter 5.2.1. In the CA^{2}MOV architecture Global Navigation is carried out as pre-planning of a set of Subpaths. This will be implemented in one module, the (global) NAVIGATOR.

The NAVIGATOR has not been implemented yet, such that no simulation or experimental results are presented. The initial ideas outlined in this chapter have to be verified and improved in a real-time implementation in the future.

5.2.3.2.1 NAVIGATOR

5.2.3.2.1.1 Global Pre-planning

With the set of commands defined in chapter 4.3.6.2, the NAVIGATOR is called by the PLANNER as result of the two motion commands GOTO and EXPLORE. They have two profound different goals: move to a specified position with certain path characteristics and explore a certain area, such that two separate are necessary. Additionally since the Global Map is stored in a QDS these algorithms should be able to use this data structure efficiently. Zelinsky [21a] provides an efficient algorithm to perform distance transform algorithms (see chapter 5.2.2.4) in conjunction of a QDS. He also provides an adjusted distance transform algorithm that ensures "visit all" behaviour for a specified region [22]. Taking furthermore the advantages of the distance transform for Global Navigation techniques into account makes this the technique of choice for the NAVIGATOR. The disadvantage of distance transforms, a certain inaccuracy and conservativeness of the solution path is irrelevant on this high level of path generation, since the Subpaths are adjusted twice prior to the execution of the AMV.

It is possible to use this distance transform algorithm to implement the desired path characteristics (see chapter 4.3.6) of a GOTO command as well as to use the probability of occupancy of a node as stored in the map to influence the solution path. The distance transformation values are then rather general "avoidance values" C, i.e. the tendency to avoid a particular node in path generation, than the pure distance values to the goal. The other influences on C are summarised in C_d:

$$C = f\left(distance\ to\ goal, C_d\right) \qquad\qquad [11.]$$

The parameter PATH-SHORTEST will result in the following dependency of the avoidance values on the probability P:

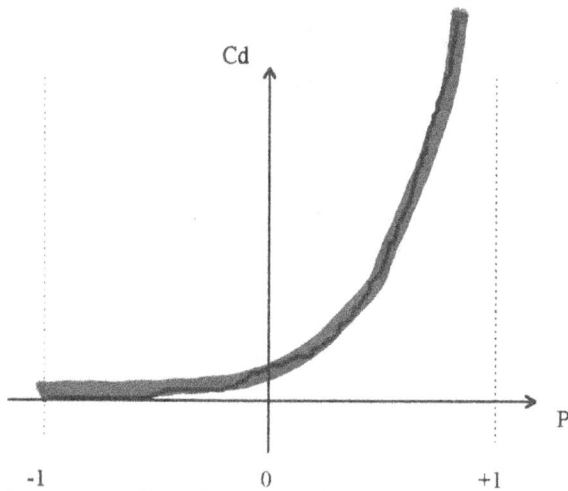

Figure 41: Avoidance Values for PATH-SHORTEST (conceptual)

The only criteria is the collision avoidance of occupied nodes.

Figure 42 shows how this dependency differs for the PATH-ADVENTUROUS characteristic. Obviously nodes in the vicinity of (P=0), i.e. unknown, are preferred in the path generation compared to nodes that are empty.

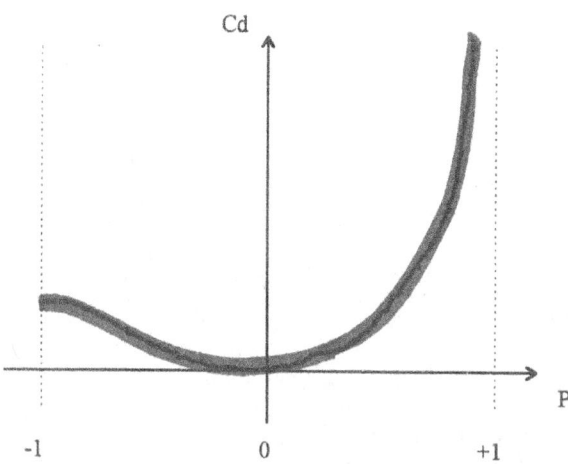

Figure 42: Avoidance values for PATH-ADVENTUROUS (conceptual)

In the case of PATH-CONSERVATIVE the path should avoid unknown/ undetermined areas.

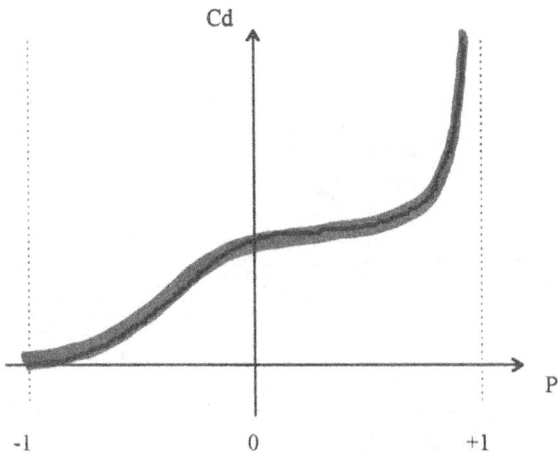

Figure 43: Avoidance Values for PATH-CONSERVATIVE (conceptual)

The effect of the SECURITY parameter is most easily implemented by a shift of the $C_c(P)$ functions as explained in an example for the PATH-SHORTEST characteristic in Figure 44.

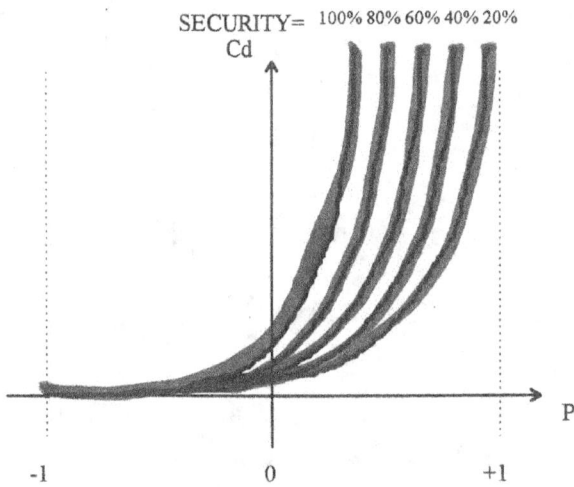

Figure 44: Effect of SECURITY Parameter (conceptual)

The way the NAVIGATOR combines Global Pre- and Re-planning and the call of the Local Navigation is summarised in the flow-diagram of Figure 45.

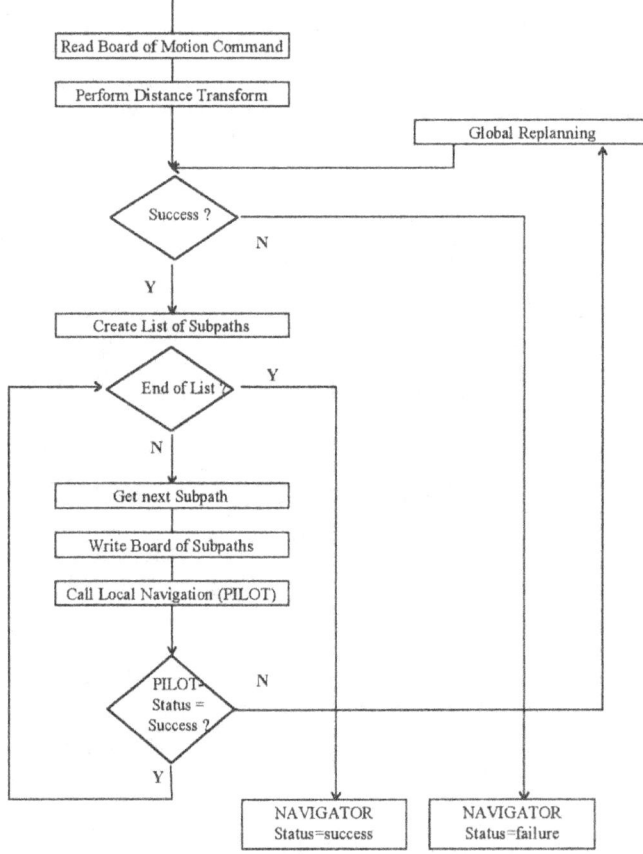

Figure 45: Flow Diagram NAVIGATOR

Performing the distance transform involves the following steps:

- Enlarge obstacles by the AMV radius plus a security distance
- Apply the regular distance transform, or the explore-algorithm [22] for an EXPLORE command
- Determine node solution sequence by going down-hill the avoidance values from start point to goal point
- Determine List of Subpaths

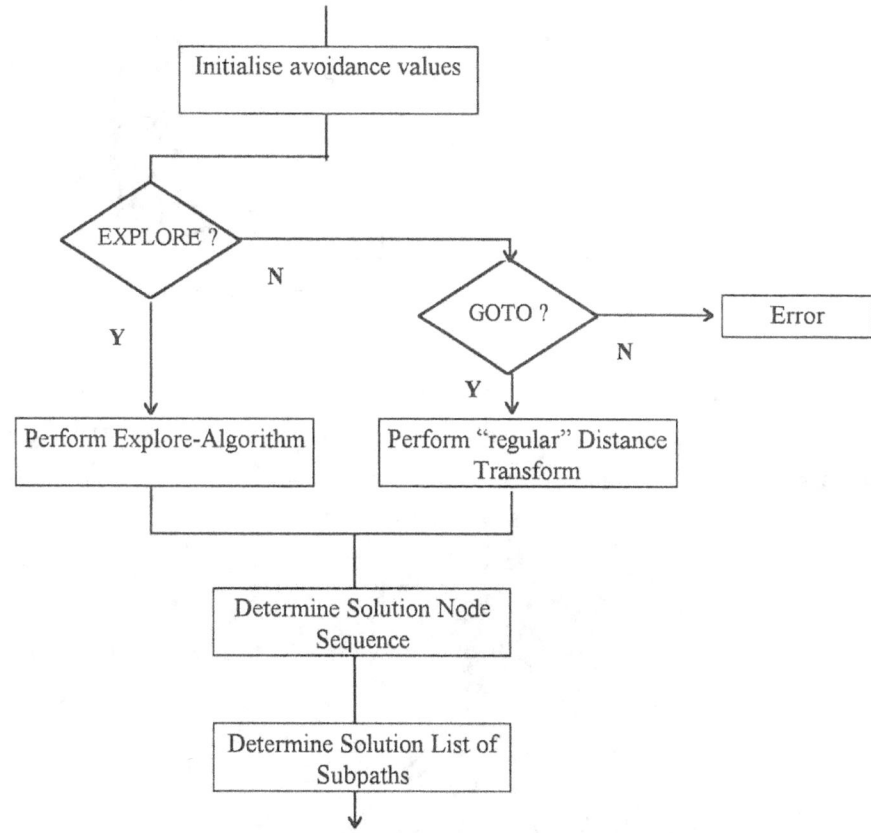

Figure 46: Perform Distance Transform

The step from the solution node sequence to the list of Subpaths is important for a successful implementation. The easiest method is to simply connect the centres of the solution nodes. However, this may lead to unnecessary curvature and conservativeness in the path, especially in the case of adjacent nodes of different size. It seems better to consider the corners of each node as possible endpoints of a Subpath and to choose the shortest of all possible connections. This is computationally more expensive but is still feasible since the Subpaths are determined off-line.

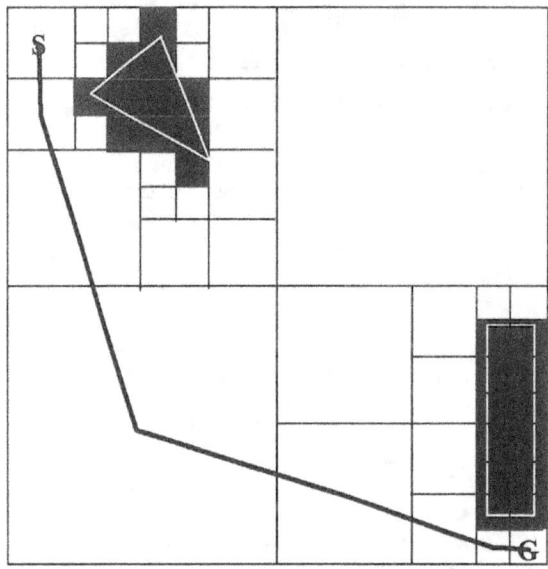

Figure 47: Solution Subpaths for Centre Solution

Figure 47 shows the drawbacks of the centre solution when using the two obstacle environment of chapter 5.1.4.1 and a SHORTEST path characteristic (for simplicity the obstacles are here not enlarged by the security distance). The path is obviously too conservative.

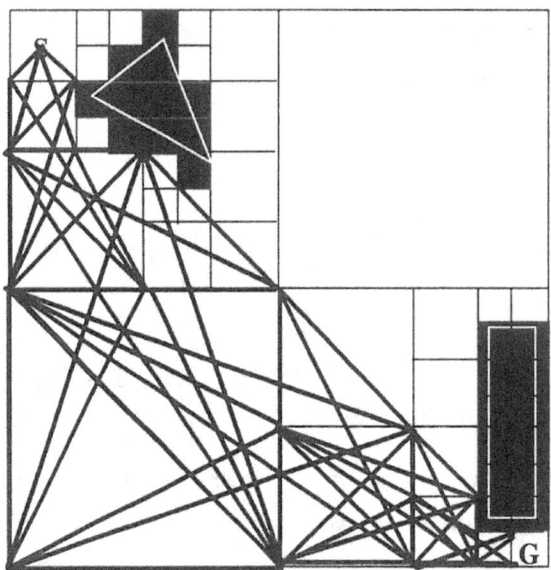

Figure 48: Set of Possible Subpaths for Corner Solution

Figure 48 shows all possible solution paths using the corner solution. This set of solution paths is searched for the shortest solution subsequently for each pair of neighbour nodes.

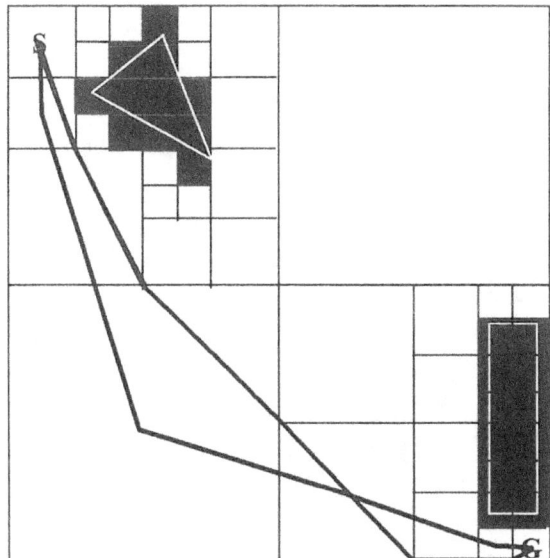

Figure 49: Solution Subpaths for Corner and Centre Solution

In Figure 49 the solution Subpath for the corner solution is shown and compared to the solution path for the centre solution. The latter is approximately 7% longer than the firsts in this example, but the corner solution is still approximately 8.5% longer than the shortest possible path. The corner solution method is only one suggestion to optimise the step from the solution node sequence to the solution Subpaths. Other more sophisticated methods may be derived and implemented.

5.2.3.2.1.2 Global Re-planning

Global Re-planning is invoked when the Local Navigation module fails to reach its goal, i.e. the endpoint of the current Subpath. In this case the status of the PILOT is set to "local failure".

Global Re-planning is similar to the Global Pre-planning with the additional consideration of a "Blocked Region". The Blocked Region is part of the Memory (see chapter 5.1.1). It is defined by the PILOT before returning to the NAVIGATOR for Global Re-planning and describes the area in the global map that caused the Local Navigation to fail, e.g. a door that is closed. The Blocked Region must be excluded from Re-planning which means the appropriate avoidance values are set to infinity by an additional step in the distance transform.

The use of the extra buffer for the Blocked Region decouples updating the Global Map and excluding a certain area from the set of solution Subpaths. Obstacles that are not eligible for the Global Map but do cause the Local Navigation to fail, e.g. a group of people blocking a door for a certain time, can so be treated.

5.2.3.3 Local Navigation

As mentioned earlier the Local Navigation uses only the Local Map, and through this concentration to the vicinity of the AMV processing cost is reduced and reactivity increased.

5.2.3.3.1 PILOT

The PILOT is called by the NAVIGATOR and uses a Subpath as input. It determines an Elastic Band, performs Local Pre-planning, and calls the MSE. In case the MSE fails, the PILOT tries to determine alternative Elastic Bands in Local Re-planning. This is summarised in the flow diagram in Figure 50.

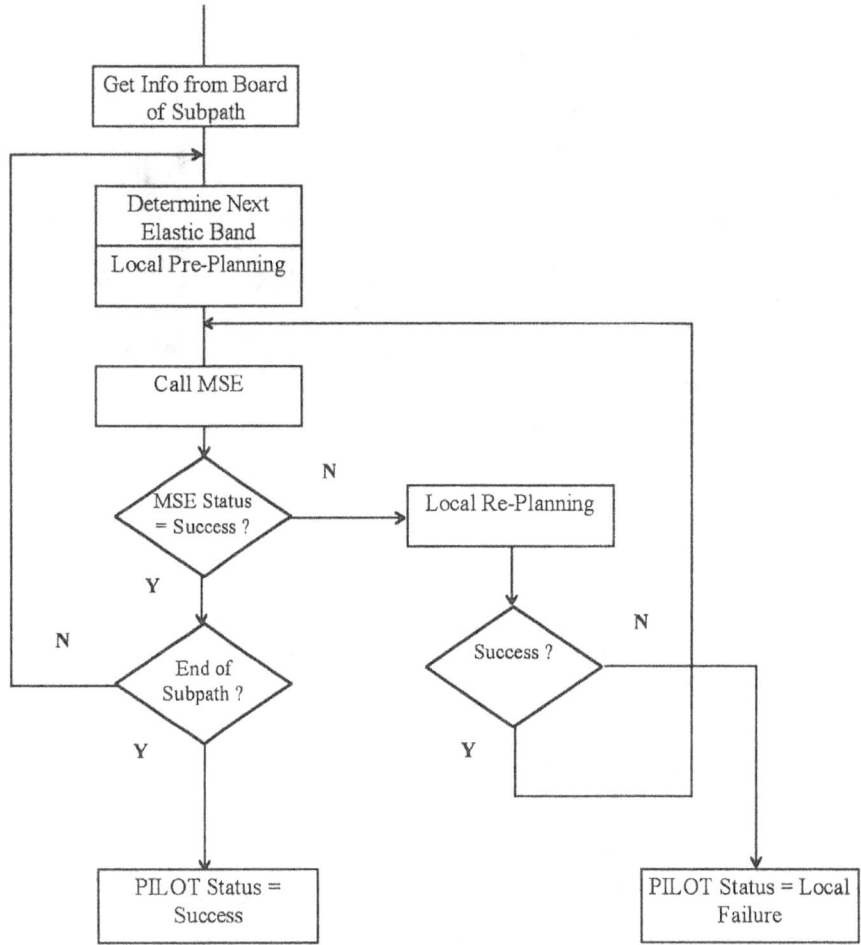

Figure 50: Flow Diagram PILOT

5.2.3.3.1.1 Local Pre-planning

The task of Local Pre-planning is to break down the current Subpath into Elastic Bands one-by-one. The Length of Elastic Bands is limited by the size of the Local Map, their startpoint is the current position of the AMV if it is stationary, or the last setpoint in the list of setpoints as this is the expected position of the AMV at the time when the Elastic Band is used for calculating the next position setpoint.

Is the Elastic Band endpoint too close to an obstacle in the Local Map the PILOT tries to relocate the endpoint in a safe area.

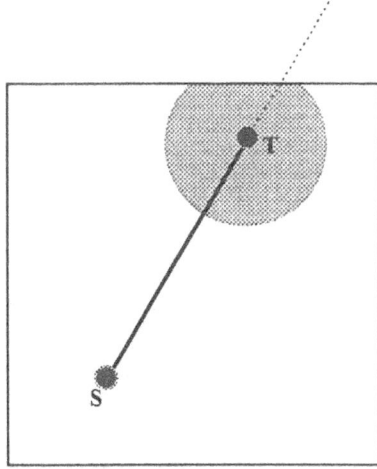

Figure 51: Subpath --> Elastic Band in Empty Local Map

Figure 51 shows how the Elastic Band (thick grey line) is determined from the Subpath (broken line) in an empty Local Map. The grey circle indicates the security zone that is checked for obstacles.

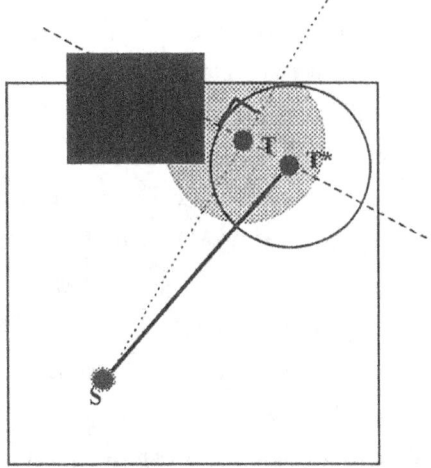

Figure 52: Local Pre-planning

In Figure 52 an obstacle (dark) violates the security zone and the PILOT tries to relocate the target point of the Elastic Band. In the current implementation the PILOT tries to find new target points along a straight line perpendicular to the Subpath, dashed line in the figure. If two solutions T* exist the shorter Elastic Band is selected. More sophisticated algorithms for Local Pre-planning might have to be developed when the importance of this step is clarified in future experiments using different environment types.

In a simulation an environment with two obstacle is used. Figure 53 shows two different paths, with and without local Pre-planning. The latter makes it possible to maintain a specified security distance to the obstacle by relocating the endpoints of the Elastic Bands.

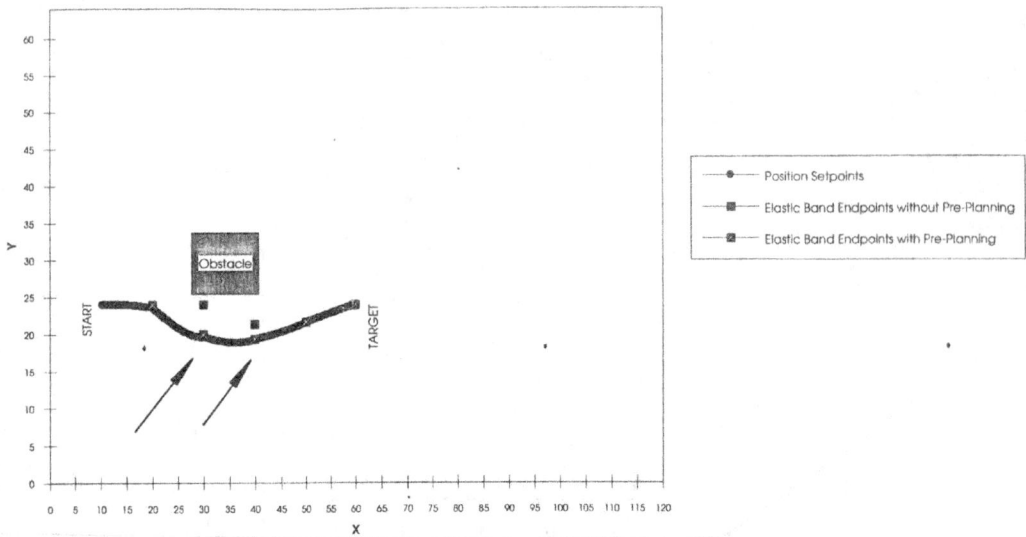

Figure 53: Local Pre-planning in Simulation

5.2.3.3.1.1.1 Local Re-planning

If the MSE fails to follow an Elastic Band the task of Local Re-planning is to find a sequence of new Elastic Bands from the AMV's current position to the endpoint of the current Elastic Band. This additional way is described using additional Elastic Bands. The algorithm chosen for this task is the Distance Transform using QDSs as described in [22a] as "corner-sweep-algorithm". The avoidance values are calculated by subsequent "sweeps" from the upper left-hand corner to the lower right-hand corner and vice-versa until no change in the avoidance values is made. Its efficient use of the QDS of the Local Map makes it the quickest and therefore preferred method.

The avoidance values are determined according to the shortest path characteristic (see chapter 5.2.3.2.1.1). The limited accuracy of the Distance Transform is enhanced by an expansion of the QDS to lower levels, i.e. all bigger nodes are split recursively to a specified node size of the children nodes. This expansion is reversed after the Re-planning by compression of the tree. The procedures of splitting and compressing the tree is adopted from [59]. The solution node sequence is determined considering only perpendicular neighbour nodes (dark grey in Figure 54) for reasons of processing speed and going down-hill the avoidance values. The maintenance of a minimum distance from obstacles is currently implemented by considering only nodes of a minimum sidelength of twice the security distance. This may result in unnecessary conservativeness and should preferably be replaced by an expansion of all obstacles by the AMV's radius plus the security distance prior to the distance transform.

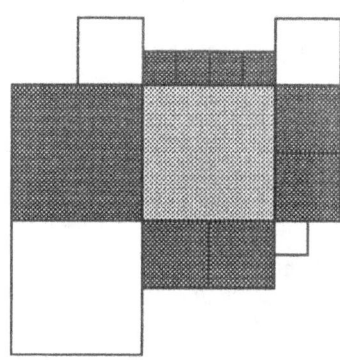

Figure 54: Neighbour Nodes Considered for Local Re-planning

The solution Elastic Bands are determined from the solution node sequence by connecting the node centres and fusing subsequent Elastic Bands that are in a straight line to a single one. Then the MSE is called using these new Elastic Bands until the original Elastic Band is completely processed. Local Re-planning can be called recursively up to a specified depth

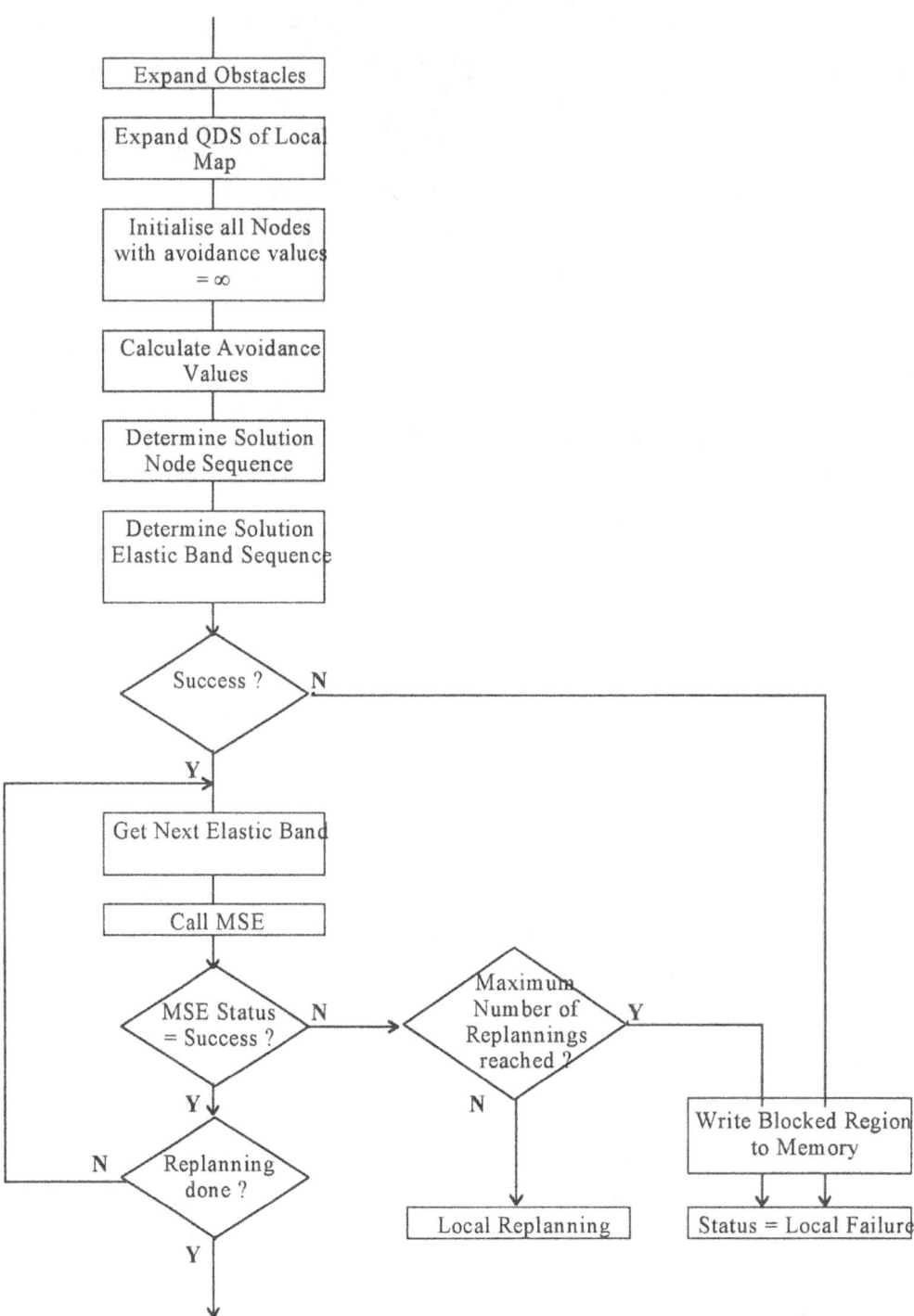

Figure 55: Flow Diagram Local Re-planning

In the following simulation the environment is populated with a U-shaped obstacle in which the AMV gets
trapped. The circles indicate the start and target points of Elastic Bands. White dots show position setpoints for

the AMV. In Figure 56 the AMV is stuck in the 4th Elastic Band. In Figure 57 the solution node sequence from the distance transform is marked in light grey.

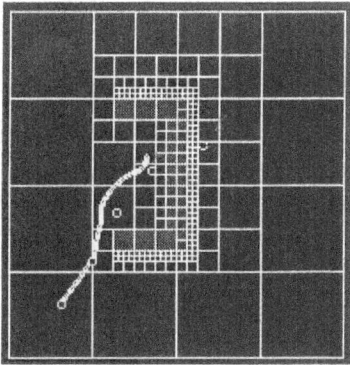

Figure 56: AMV is Stuck in Local Minimum

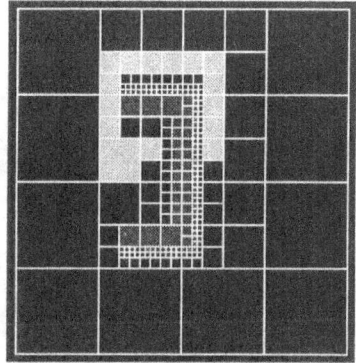

Figure 57: Solution Node Sequence from Local Re-planning

In Figure 58 the solution sequence of Elastic Bands is displayed as white circles. The AMV is travelling around the obstacle.

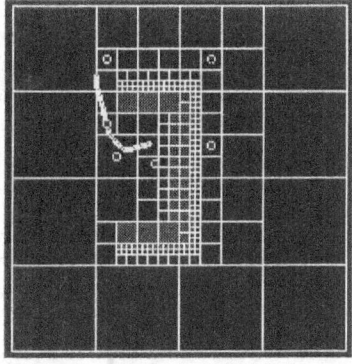

Figure 58: AMV on Re-planned Path

Figure 59 finally shows the completion of the motion command after the replanning was successful.

[63]

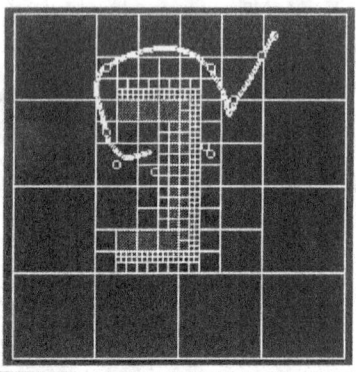

Figure 59: Completion of Motion Command after successful Local Re-planning

The Distance Transform needs 6 "sweeps" to complete the calculation of the avoidance values in this example. For simplicity the obstacle was not expanded and the resolution of the distance transform was not enhanced by expansion of the QDS in this example. Figures 60 to 65 show the avoidance values for each of the six „sweeps".

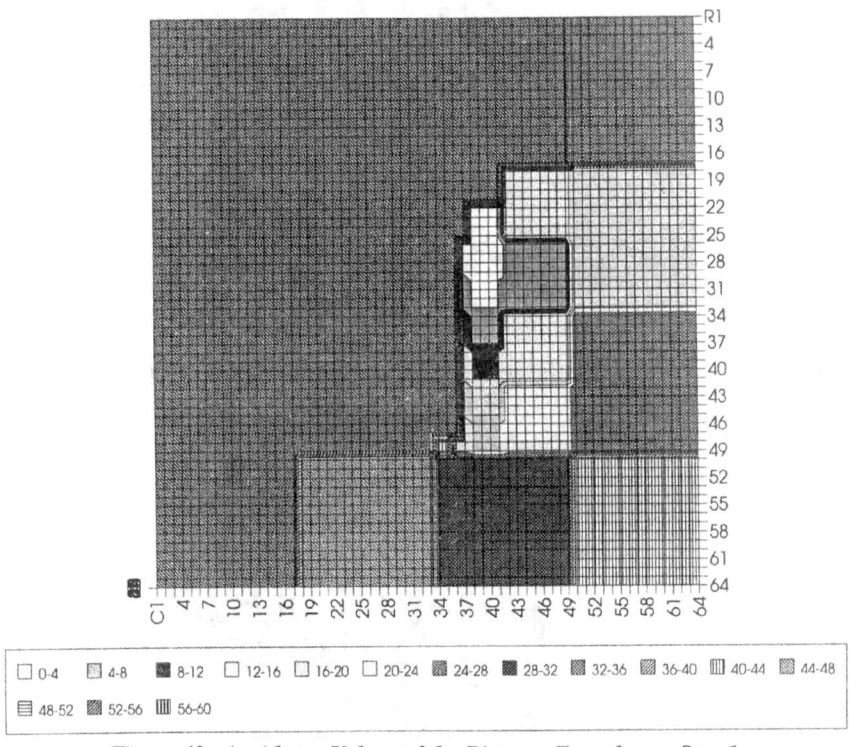

Figure 60: Avoidance Values of the Distance Transform - Step 1

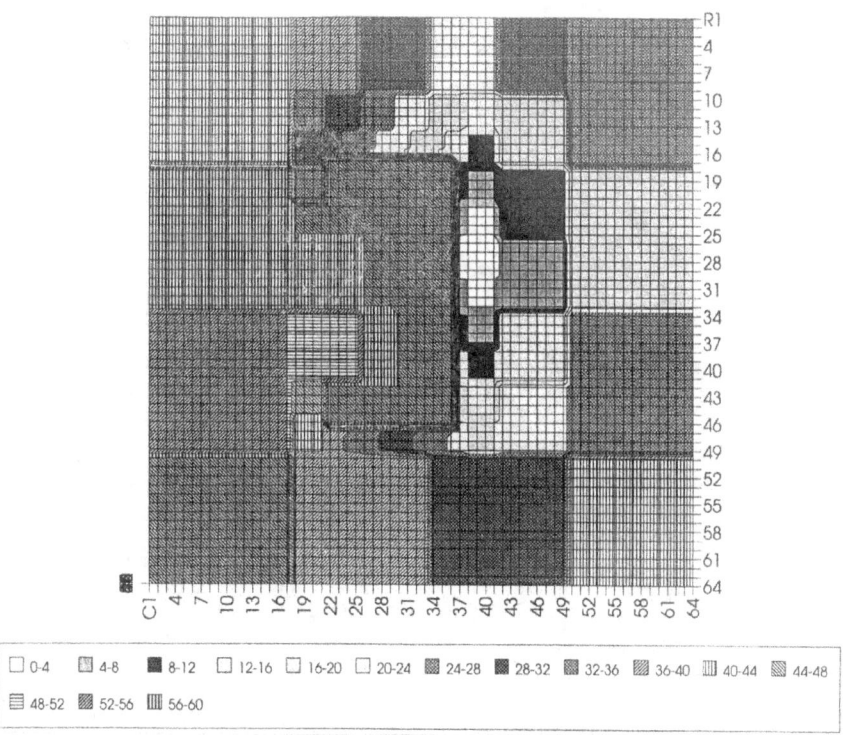

Figure 61: Avoidance Values of the Distance Transform - Step 2

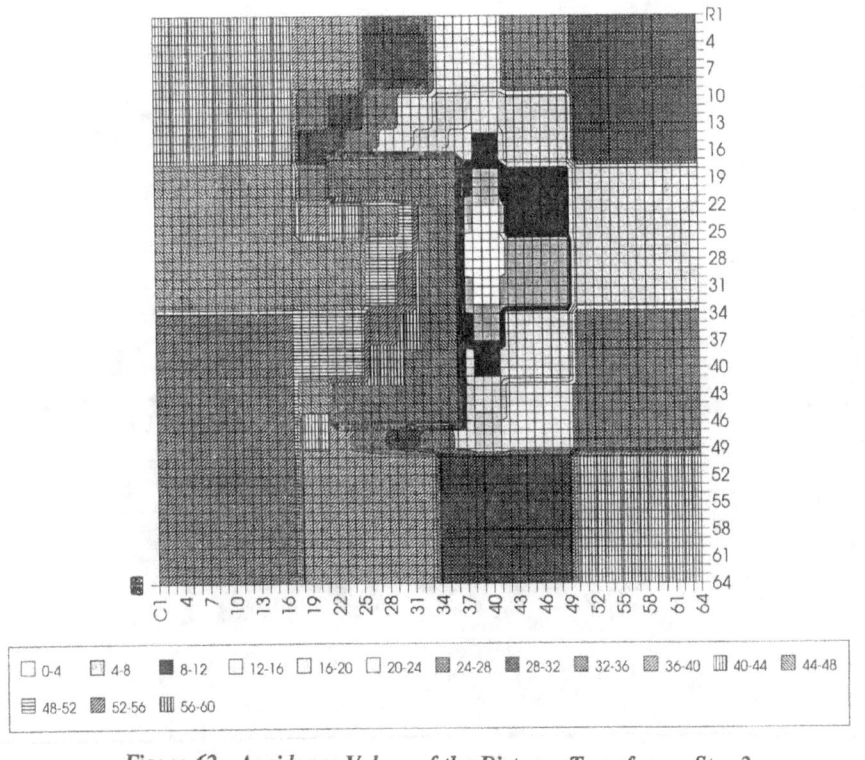

Figure 62: Avoidance Values of the Distance Transform - Step 3

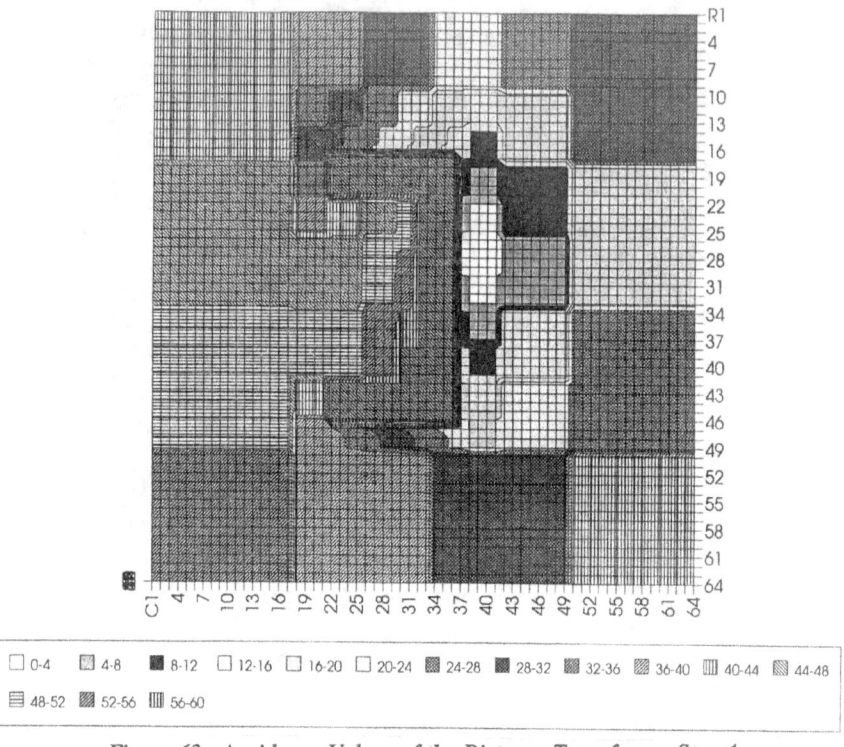

Figure 63: Avoidance Values of the Distance Transform - Step 4

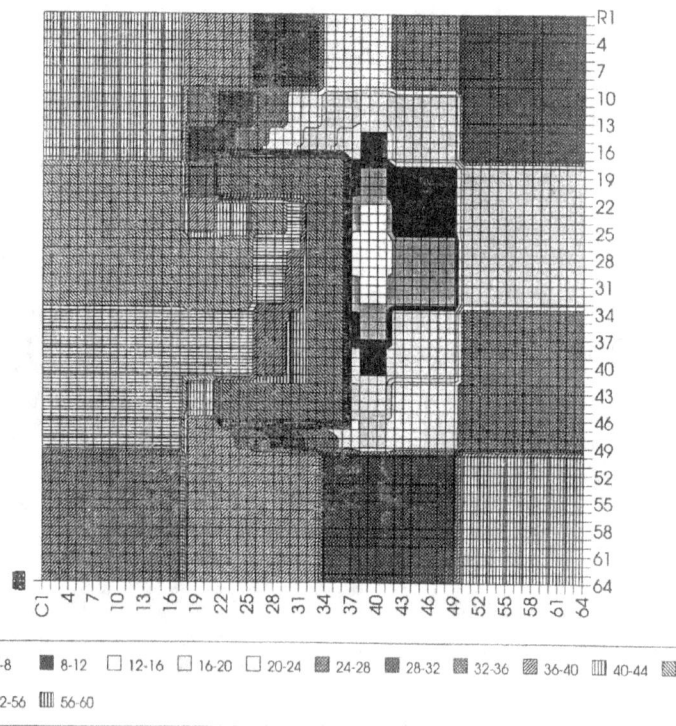

Figure 64: Avoidance Values of the Distance Transform - Step 5

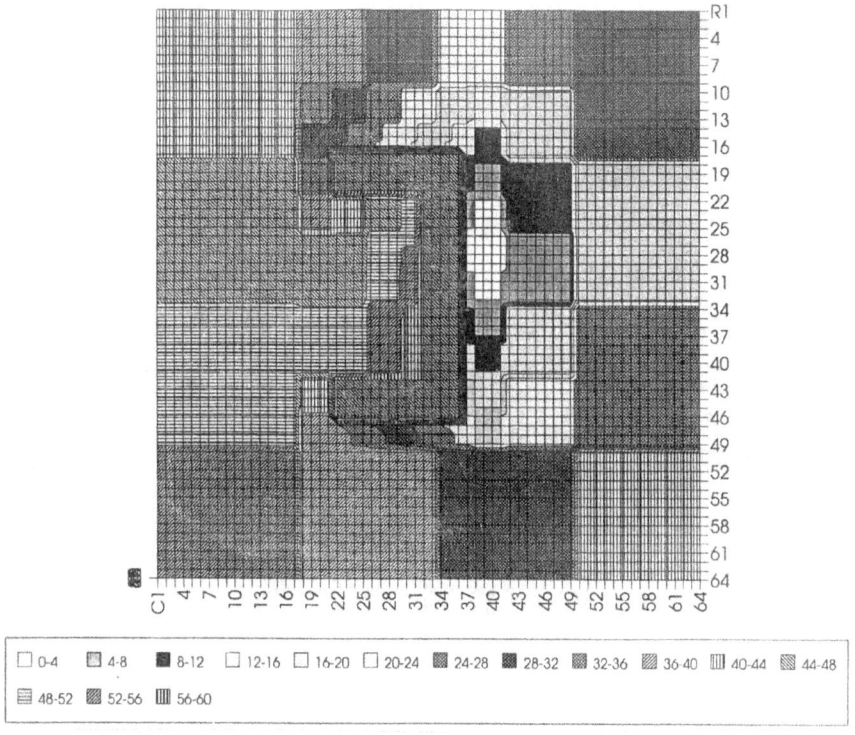

Figure 65: Avoidance Values of the Distance Transform - Step 6

5.2.3.3.2 MOTOR-SCHEMA EXECUTOR (MSE)

5.2.3.3.2.1 *Introduction*

The MSE is the reactive part of the Local Navigation and uses Motor-schemas. Motor-schemas, first introduced by Arkin [24] have their origin in psychology and neurology. They describe the interaction between perception and action, e.g. a frog recognises a fly and activates the muscles of its tongue.

The Motor-schemas to be considered in the MSE are

- Go-to-goal
- Avoid-static-obstacles
- Avoid-moving-obstacles
- Stay-on-path

These Motor-schemas are implemented using potential fields. The basic idea of potential fields navigation is to determine an AMV's path along a decreasing potential which is artificially created from a number of force fields. Each Motor-Schema results in the creation of a particular force field. This is very important in order to have the opportunity to turn individual schemas on or off, or to implement different priorities for the different schemas. The AMV is assumed to exhibit only translatory motion in two dimensions according to SUAVE's kinematics (see chapter 3.2).

5.2.3.3.2.2 Artificial Potential Fields

The creation of the artificial potential fields and experiments regarding their implementation bases partially on [50]. Latombe [51] describes the mathematical basis for navigation with potential fields.

Generally the virtual force $F(q)$ acting on the AMV (located at q) is found from an artificial potential field U by

$$F(q) = -\nabla U(q) \qquad\qquad [12.]$$

Latombe introduces an attractive field at the target point and repulsive force fields around obstacles and determines the resultant force at the AMV's position by adding these two forces vectorially.

Ikegami et al. [52] present a "distance value model" in which the repulsive force field around obstacles increases with decreasing distance of the AMV to the obstacle, and the attractive force field is of constant magnitude in the entire environment distance dependent field modelling.

5.2.3.3.2.3 Got-to-goal Motor-schema

This is implemented adopting Ikegami et al.'s proposal (see chapter 5.2.3.3.2.2) of an attractive force of constant magnitude at the goal. The attractive potential field becomes

$$U_{att} = u_0 \qquad\qquad [13.]$$

and the attractive force is

$$\bar{F}_{att} = -\nabla U_{att} \qquad\qquad [14.]$$
$$= -u_0 \left[\frac{d\bar{a}}{dx}, \frac{d\bar{a}}{dy} \right]$$

where $\bar{a}$ is a unit vector pointing from the AMV's position towards the goal and u_o is a constant.

5.2.3.3.2.4 Avoid-static-obstacles Motor-schema

Considering the Local Map in a QDS it is not possible to identify and separate single obstacles without major efforts. Therefore each node that is not empty ($P=-1$) is considered one single obstacle.

Following Ikegami et al.'s proposal a distance dependant repulsive force for each obstacle is created. Usually the repulsive potential fields decrease with the square of the distance, however, in simulations good results could be achieved with potential fields of third order. This could be more appropriate in highly cluttered and densely populated environments where the AMV has to navigate close to obstacles most of the time.

The potential function for this schema is

$$U_{rep} = u_1 * \frac{1}{\Phi^2} \qquad\qquad [15.]$$

or

$$U_{rep} = u_1 * \frac{1}{\Phi^3} \qquad\qquad [16.]$$

respectively, where Φ is the distance from the AMV to the border of the static obstacle, i.e. an occupied node, and u_1 is a constant.

The repulsive force results to

$$\overline{F}_{rep} = -\nabla U_{att}$$

$$= -u_1 * \frac{1}{\Phi^2} \left[\frac{\partial \overline{b}}{\partial x}, \frac{\partial \overline{b}}{\partial y} \right]$$

[17.]

where $\overline{b}$ is a unit vector from the AMV's position to the obstacle, i.e. the occupied node.
For each obstacle one repulsive force is created.

5.2.3.3.2.4.1 Shape of the Repulsive Force Field

The shape of the repulsive force field was implied to be circular in the previous chapter. This has a great influence on the resulting path. Apart from the circular shape two other models are considered in this work: a squared field with quarter circles at the edges and a combination in which the direction of the force is circular but the magnitude is determined by a square, see Figures 66 to 69.

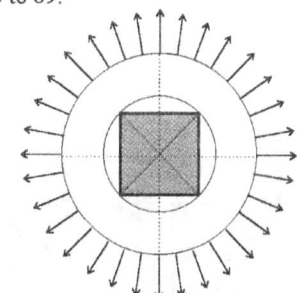

Figure 66: Circular Field Model (I)

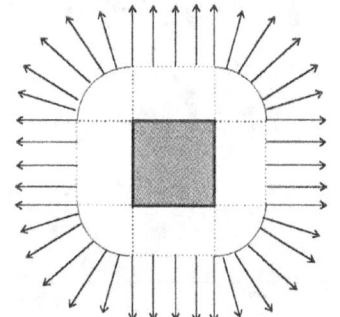

Figure 67: Squared Field Model (II)

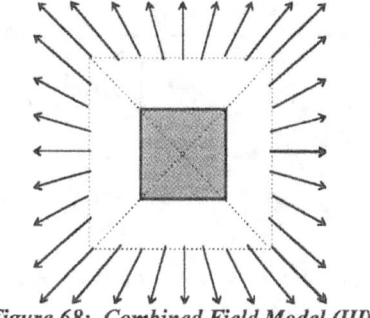

Figure 68: Combined Field Model (III)

In simulations Model (I) has lead to an oscillating path when the AMV is moving along a wall, because the force component perpendicular to the straight path parallel to the wall is not. Figure 69 shows a wall consisting of four nodes, their separate force fields and a path.

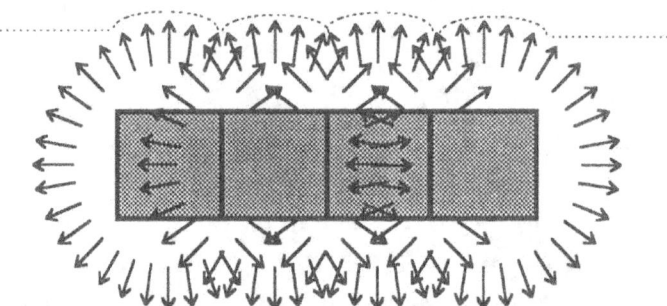

Figure 69: Oscillating Path when Moving along a Wall

Figure 70 is a simulation path where the AMV moves from the start point in the lower left-hand corner to the goal point in the upper right-hand corner through a corridor. The oscillations are apparent. The Repulsive Force in x and y-direction and the resultant force are displayed in Figures 71 and 72.

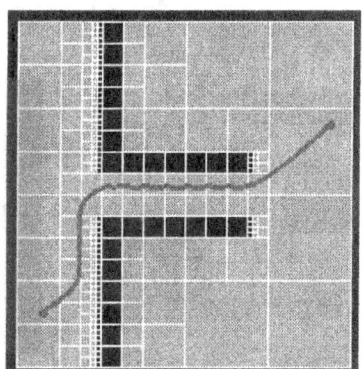

Figure 70: Oscillating Path, Model (I)

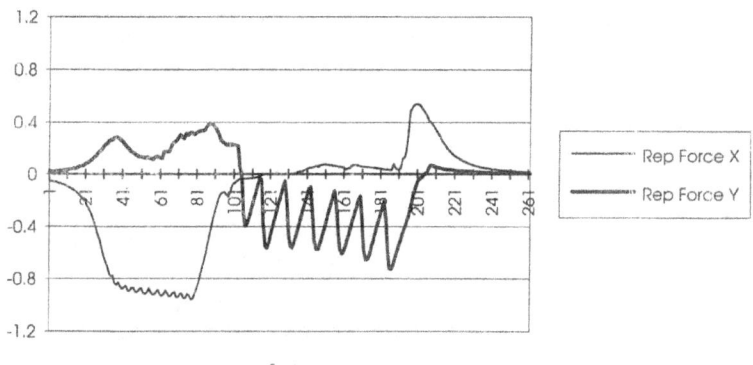

Figure 71: Repulsive Force in Simulation, Model (I)

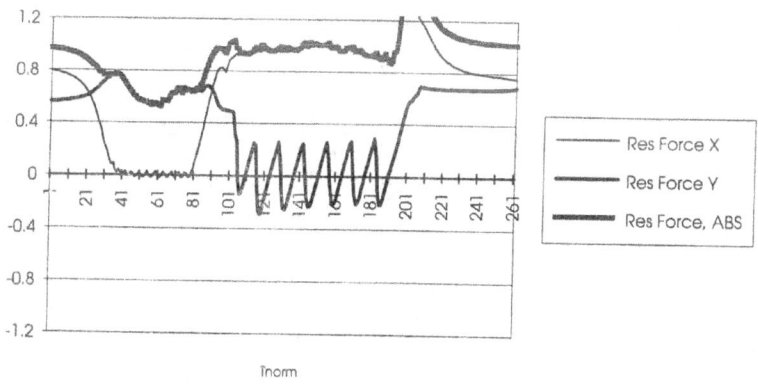

Figure 72: Resultant Force in Simulation, Model (I)

Model (II) overcomes this problem by accurately modelling the shape of the squared node. The path resulting from this Model and the forces are given in Figures 73 to 76.

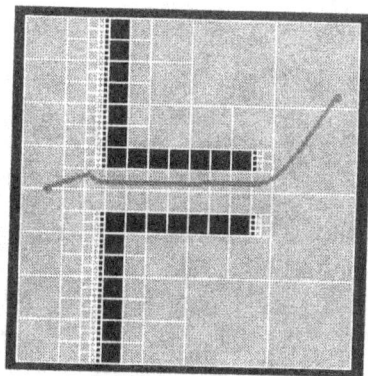

Figure 73: Simulation Path, Model (II)

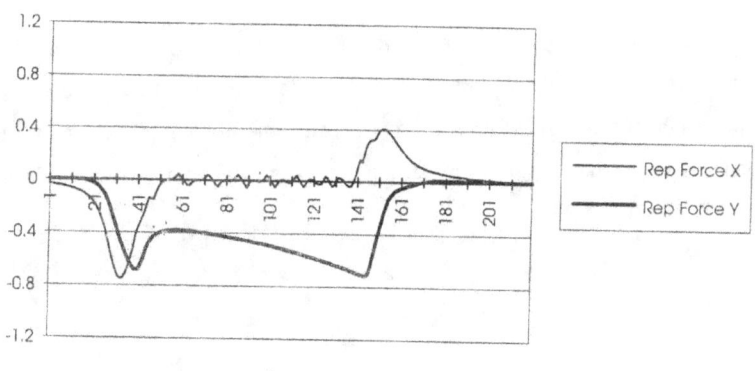

Figure 74: Repulsive Force in Simulation, Model (II)

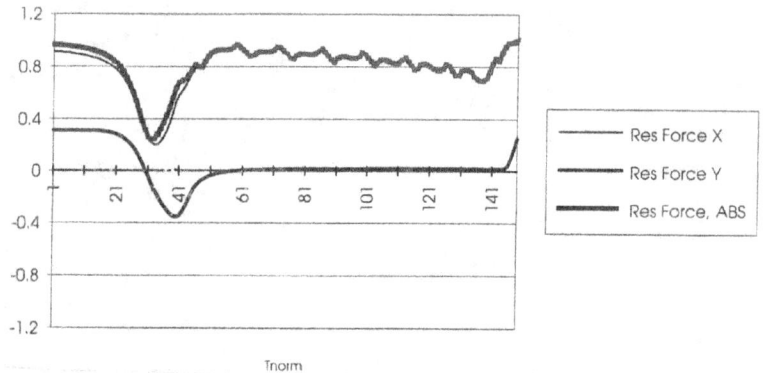

Figure 75: Resultant Force in Simulation, Model (II)

A drawback encountered with model (II) is the higher density of local minima since the forces along a side of the node all have the same direction. A local minimum is always present when the goal point is in the projection of the side of the node opposite to the AMV, see Figure 76.

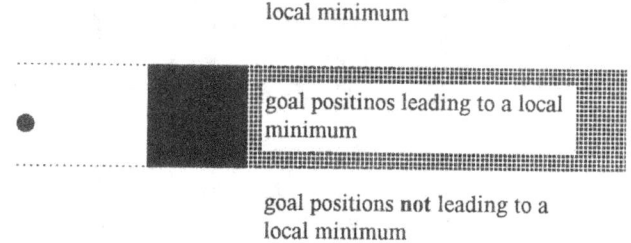

Figure 76: Local Minima behind Obstacle with Model (II)

The circular model (I) tends to push the AMV around the node since there is a force component parallel to the node surface.

Model (III) seeks to combine the advantages of model (I) and (II). The force component perpendicular to the node surface is constant, and there is a force component parallel to the surface unless the AMV's position is exactly at the projection of the centre of the surface. Using this model the AMV is expected to be pushed around a node whenever the goal point is off the projection of the centre of the node centre. This is verified in a simulation in Figure 77.

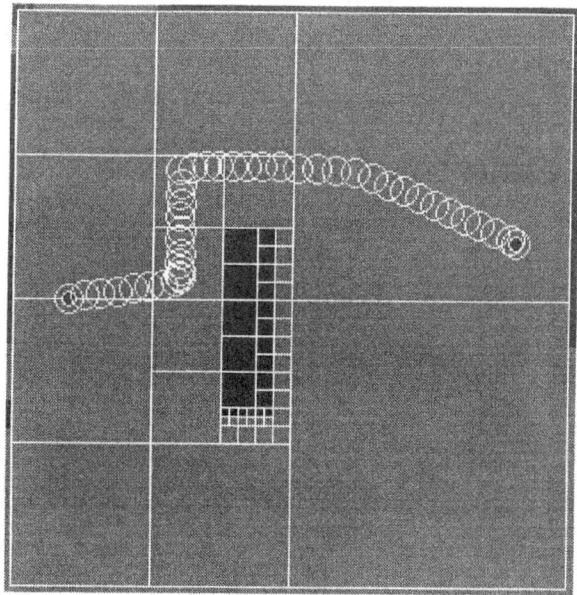

Figure 77: Moving Successfully around a Wall, Model (III)

The repulsive force components in x and y direction are given in Figure 78.

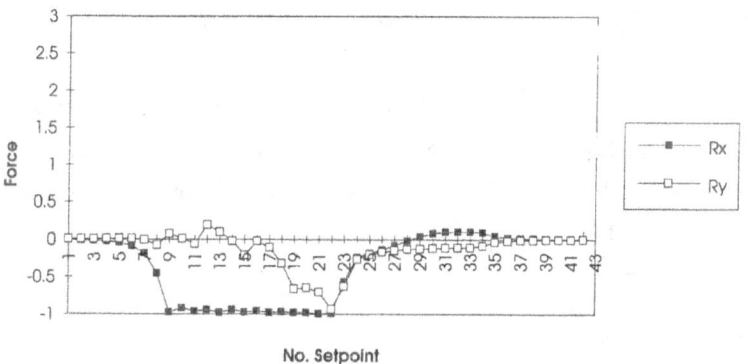

Figure 78: Repulsive Force in Simulation of Figure 76

5.2.3.3.2.5 *Tuning Go-to-goal and Avoid-static-obstacles Motor-schemas*

In the current version of the MSE only the schemas Go-to-goal and Avoid-static-obstacles are implemented. Tuning them means determining the constants u_o and u_1 to achieve the desired behaviour. The repulsive force must never be strong enough to allow the AMV penetrate an obstacle, nevertheless it should be large enough too use the full potential to move the AMV towards the goal. Reflecting this a critical distance Φ_c is defined that is the minimum distance to any obstacle the AMV must keep. For Φ_c the repulsive and the attractive force are of the same magnitude, so in the worst case where the two vectors are of opposite direction the AMV is not moving closer to the obstacle. This introduces some conservativeness in any case where the two force vectors are not of exactly opposite direction, i.e. the AMV might stay away further than necessary from obstacles which could block certain solution paths in narrow environments, e.g. doors, corridors.

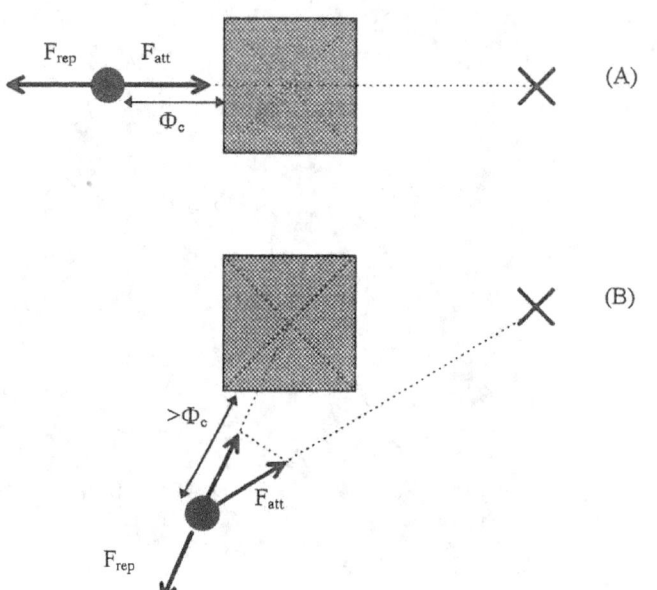

Figure 79: Tuning of the Artificial Potential Fields

Figure 79 (A) shows the worst case: the force vectors are opposite each other and the AMV (black circle) moves as close as allowed to the obstacle Φ_c. In (B) the AMV does not move closer to the obstacle at a distance greater than the critical one since the repulsive force is as large as the parallel component of the attractive force at a distance greater than Φ_c. This results in a longer path than necessary to avoid the obstacle.

Accepting this drawback and defining the attractive potential as unity the tuned field equations are for a second order repulsive field

$$\bar{F}_{att} = -\nabla U_{att}$$

$$= -1 * \left[\frac{d\bar{a}}{dx}, \frac{d\bar{a}}{dy} \right] \qquad [18.]$$

and

$$\bar{F}_{rep} = -\nabla U_{rep}$$

$$= -\frac{\Phi_c}{\Phi^2} \left[\frac{\partial \bar{b}}{\partial x}, \frac{\partial \bar{b}}{\partial y} \right] \qquad [19.]$$

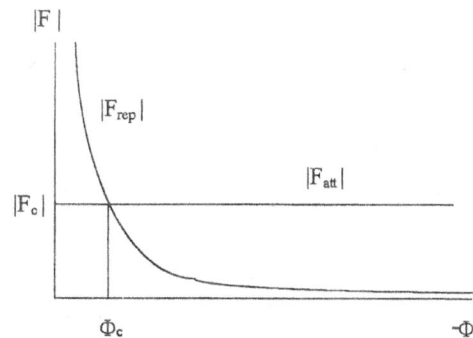

Figure 80: Tuning of Repulsive and Attractive Force

Taking the probability of the occupancy of a node into account, the worst case (Figure 79(A)) may be defined for $P=+1$, i.e. the AMV is allowed to move closer to a node with $P<+1$. The repulsive force then becomes for a second order field

$$\overline{F}_{rep} = -\frac{\Phi_c}{\Phi^2}\left[\frac{\partial \overline{b}}{\partial x}, \frac{\partial \overline{b}}{\partial y}\right] * \frac{P+1}{2}$$

[20.]

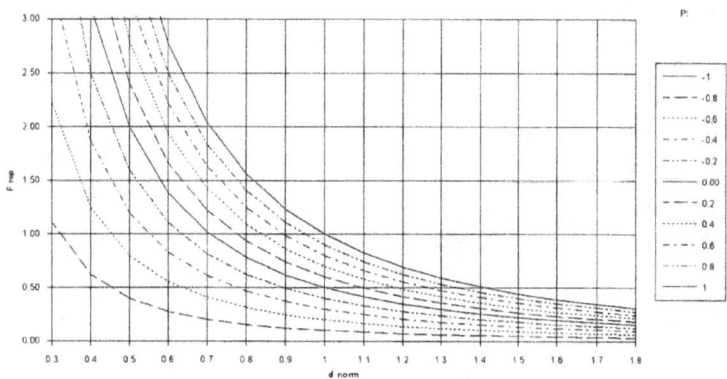

Figure 81: Second Order Repulsive Field Varying with P

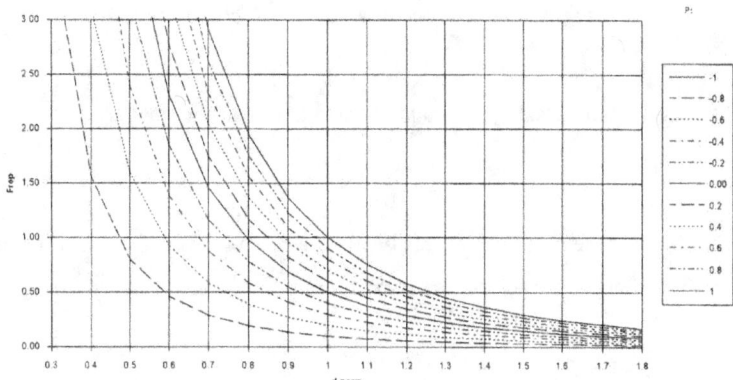

Figure 82 : Third Order Repulsive Field Varying with P

Figure 81 and 82 show the tuned repulsive Force fields according to equation 20 in second and third order. For $P=+1$ the repulsive Force equals the attractive force ($=1$) at a critical normal distance $\Phi_{c,\,norm}=1$. For decreasing P the normal critical distance reduces up to $\Phi_{c,\,norm}=0$ for $P=-1$, i.e. a node that is empty with *100%* confidence. The third order field decreases the allowable distance less quickly with decreasing P than the second order field. For $P=0$ the critical normal distance is $\Phi_{c,\,norm}=0.8$ for third order and $\Phi_{c,\,norm}=0.7$ for a second order field.

5.2.3.3.2.6 Avoid-moving-obstacles Motor-schema

The difference between static and moving obstacles is reflected in the dynamics value of the nodes D. A moving obstacle results in positive dynamics (TIPs) at positions it has just arrived and in negative dynamics at positions it has just left (TAILs).

A straightforward implementation of an Avoid-moving-obstacles schema is to create a repulsive force field at TIPs and a weak attractive force field at TAILS. Assuming a moving obstacle motion is not random but directed towards some goal positions it has just left, that are nodes with negative D, are to be preferred in the path planning. Similarly the area around the current position of a moving obstacle should be strongly avoided (compared to static obstacles) in the path generation since in the next instant of time it may move towards the AMV and violate the minimal (critical) distance. Therefore an Avoid-moving-obstacle schema would create an attractive force at nodes with negative D and a repulsive force at nodes with positive D.

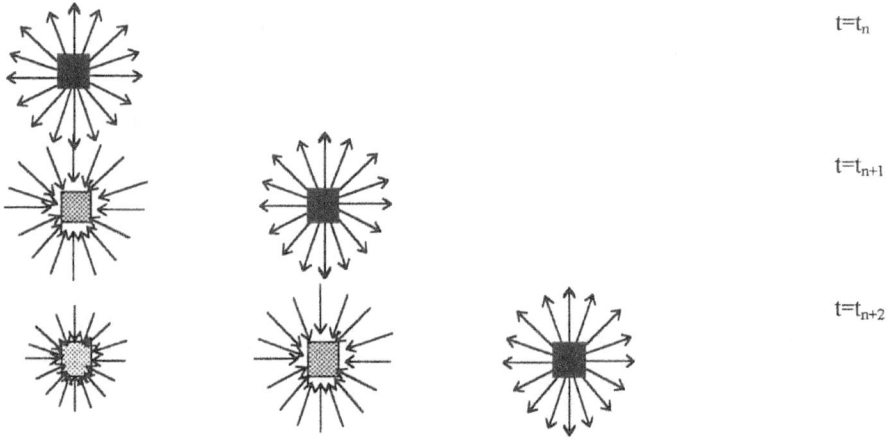

$t=t_n$

$t=t_{n+1}$

$t=t_{n+2}$

Figure 83: Avoid-moving-obstacle Schema Implementation

This increased critical distance taking the motion of an obstacle into account is

$$\Phi_{c_{dyn}} = \Phi_c + v_o * \Delta t \qquad [21.]$$

where v_o is the velocity of the obstacle and Δt is the time between sensor scans and setpoint calculation, assuming non-increasing velocity of the obstacle. The magnitude of the appropriate repulsive force is

$$F_{dyn_{rep}} = \frac{\Phi_{c_{dyn}}}{\Phi^2}$$

$$= \frac{\Phi_c + v_{o_{max}} * \Delta t_{max}}{\Phi^2} \qquad [22.]$$

where Φ is again the distance of the AMV to the node. The attractive force field can be constant with this distance.

Taking the dynamics value of the appropriate node D into account the dynamic force should be designed as shown in Figure 84 for a certain distance.

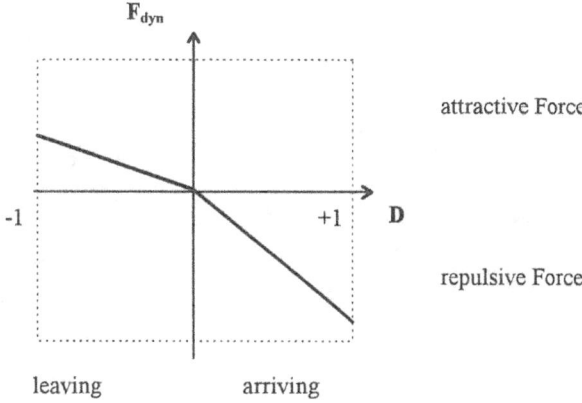

Figure 84: Dynamic Force as Function of Dynamics

An implementation of this characteristic would be

$$F_{dyn} = \begin{cases} F_{dyn_{rep}} = \dfrac{\Phi_c + v_{o_{max}}*\Delta t_{max}}{\Phi^2} * D & \forall \quad D >= 0 \\ F_{dyn_{att}} = -u_3 * D & \forall \quad D < 0 \end{cases} \qquad [23.]$$

5.2.3.3.2.7 Stay-on-path Motor-schema

The purpose of a Stay-on-path schema is to keep the AMV on a straight line path of the Elastic Band, i.e. to control the stiffness of the Elastic Band. This can be realised with a line force field that points towards the Elastic Band.

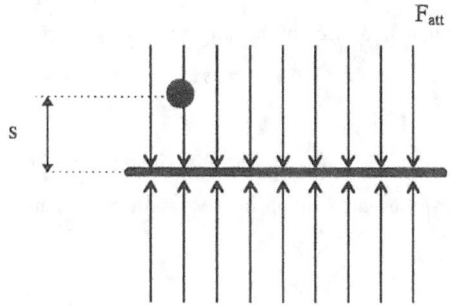

Figure 85: Stay-on-path Force Field

5.2.3.3.2.8 Combining Repulsive Forces

Each obstacle (node) with positive P has one repulsive force at the AMV's position as result. Usually these forces are simply added in order to find the combined effect. However, this leads to additional conservativeness as is apparent in Figure 86.

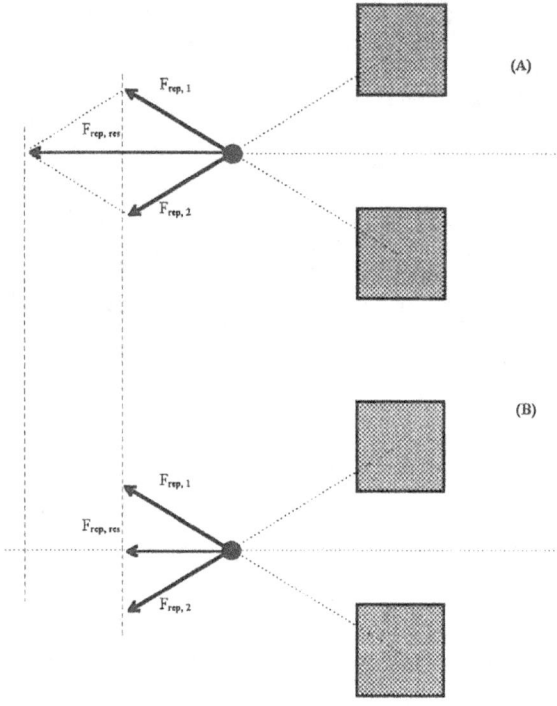

Figure 86: Combining Repulsive Forces

The AMV is approaching a door consisting of two nodes. Each node creates one repulsive force of the same magnitude. In (A) these two forces are simply added using the vector summation

$$\overline{F}_{rep} = \sum_i \overline{F}_{rep,i} \qquad\qquad [24.]$$

Decomposing each of the repulsive forces into a component parallel and perpendicular to the door, the parallel components cancel out since they are of opposite sign. The resultant force is therefore of twice the magnitude of the perpendicular force component of each of the single repulsive forces. The effect of the perpendicular components pointing away from the door is contained twice in the resultant force, however, only one of these components fulfils the requirements of both nodes.

Picture (B) shows a different way of combining forces. The resultant force is considering only the maximum component of all repulsive forces in negative and positive x and y coordinates:

$$\overline{F}_{rep} = \left[F_{rep_x}, F_{rep_y} \right]$$

$$= \left[\max_i\left(F_{rep_{x_i}} \middle| F_{rep_{x_i}} > 0\right) + \min_i\left(F_{rep_{x_i}} \middle| F_{rep_{x_i}} < 0\right), \max_i\left(F_{rep_{y_i}} \middle| F_{rep_{y_i}} > 0\right) + \min_i\left(F_{rep_{y_i}} \middle| F_{rep_{y_i}} < 0\right) \right]$$

$$[25.]$$

The parallel components still disappear as desired, the AMV does not move to either side of the door. Only one of the two perpendicular components is considered. The resultant force is of the same direction as in (A) but of smaller magnitude. Doors of the minimum size, i.e. diameter of the AMV plus twice a security distance, are passable only with this combination rule of maximum effect.

It is apparent in Figures 87 and 88 that the magnitude of the repulsive force vectors are smaller for this rule of maximum effect. The direction of the repulsive vectors are the same as in a vector summation. In Figures 89, 90, 91, and 92 an attractive force at two different goal positions is introduced. It can be seen that the vector summation is of higher conservativeness than the rule of maximum effect.

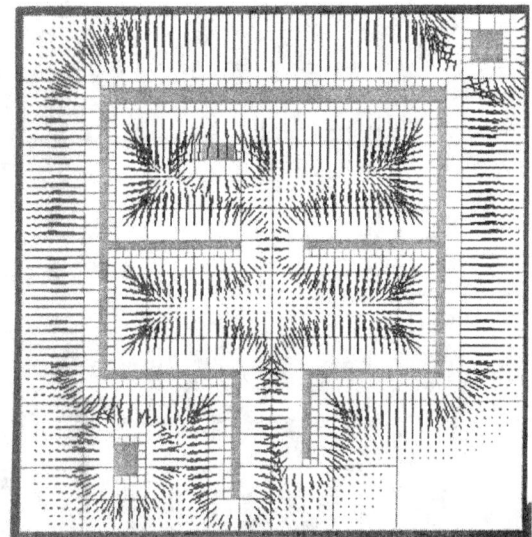

Figure 87: Repulsive Force Vectors for Simple Force Addition

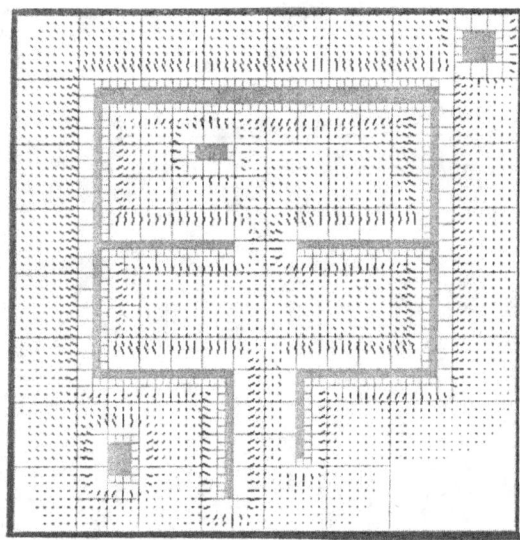

Figure 88: Repulsive Force Vectors for Force Addition Using Maximum Effect Rule

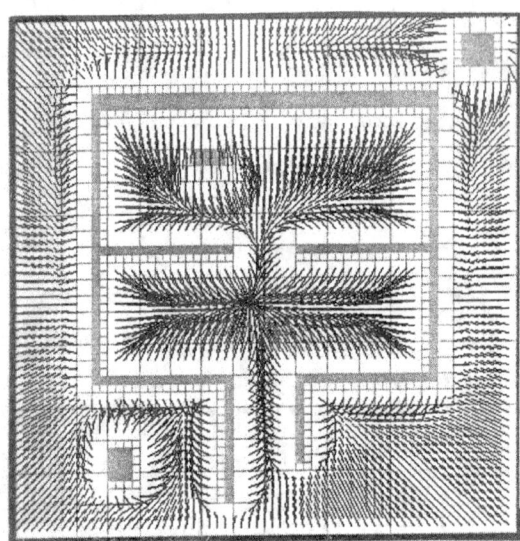

Figure 89: Resultant Force Vectors for Force Addition, Goal in Middle

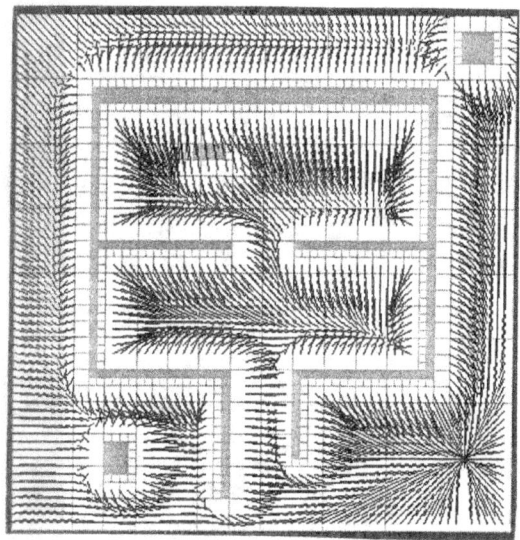

Figure 90: Resultant Force Vectors for Force Addition, Goal in Lower Right-Hand Corner

Figure 91: Resultant Force Vectors for Force Addition Using Maximum Effect Rule, Goal in Middle

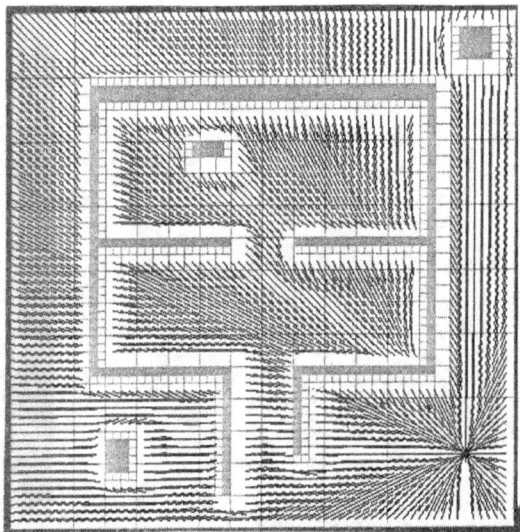

Figure 92: Resultant Force Vectors for Force Addition Using Maximum Effect Rule, Goal in Lower Right-Hand Corner

Implementing the rule of maximum effect the resulting forces and position setpoints when trying to pass three doors of different widths in simulations are shown in Figures 93 to 101. The data used in this simulation are

- AMV diameter: 0.5 m
- Security distance: 0.5 m
- Door widths: (A) 3 m, (B) 1.5 m, (C) 0.75 m

The coordinate directions in the maps are x to the right and y upwards. The critical width of the door is 1.5 m and the AMV is supposed to pass the door in cases (A) and (B).

The path in (A), Figure 93, is a single straight line as desired, the repulsive force in y direction is zero, and the one in x direction is slightly negative when the AMV is in front of the door, i.e. it is repelling it slightly, and slightly positive for positions behind the door. The resultant force is always close to *1*, which is the magnitude of the attractive force of the goal behind the door.

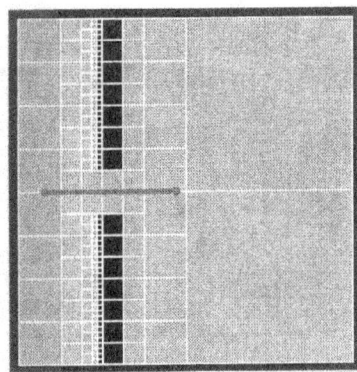

Figure 93: Path for Simulation (A)

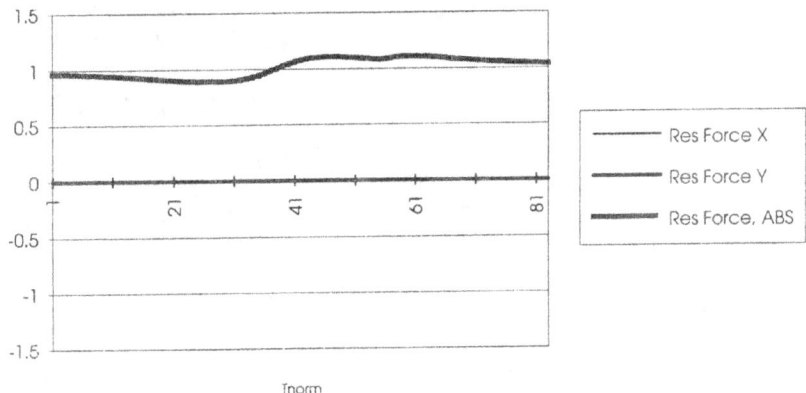

Figure 94: Repulsive Force Components for Simulation (A)

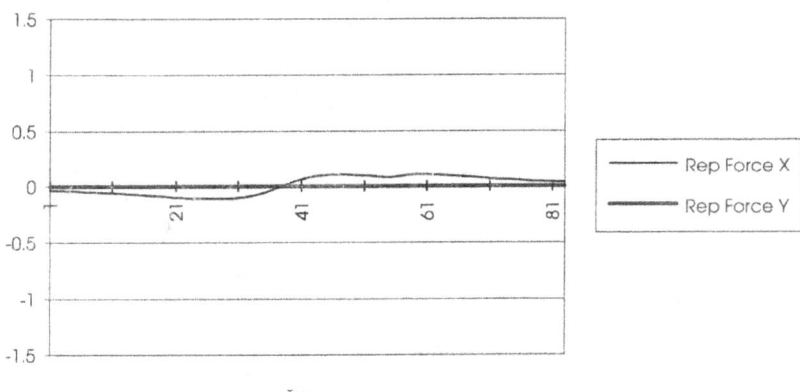

Figure 95: Resultant Force Components and Absolute Value for Simulation (A)

The path in simulation (B) is equivalent to the one in (A), Figure 96. The magnitude of the repulsive force in x direction is much larger, though, and the resultant force magnitude is as low as *0.5*, half the attractive force in front of the door.

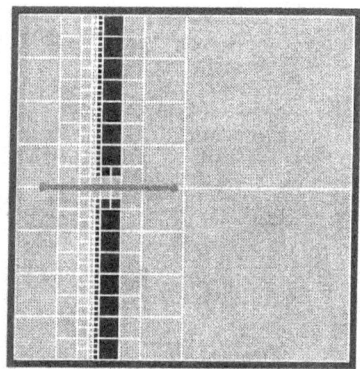

Figure 96: Path for Simulation (B)

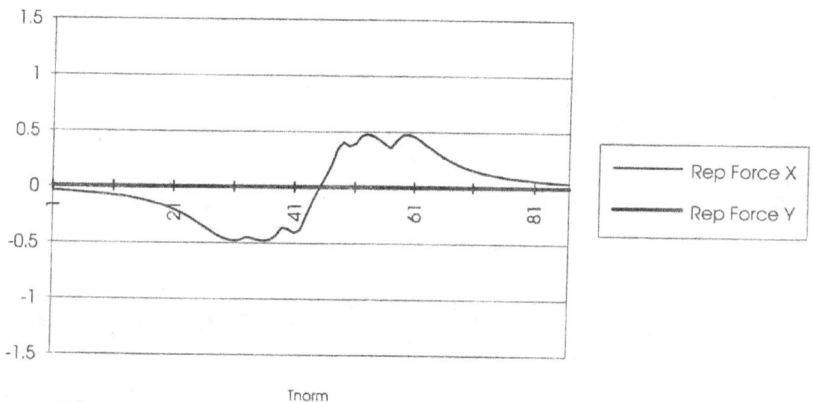

Figure 97: Repulsive Force Components for Simulation (B)

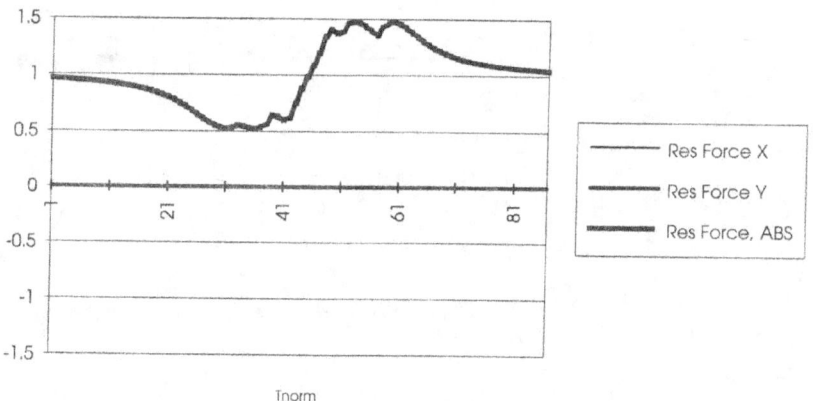

Figure 98: Resultant Force in Simulation (B)

In simulation (C) the AMV is stuck in front of the door, since the obstacles are too close together, which results in too large repulsive forces and a resultant force of literally "0", Figures 99 to 101.

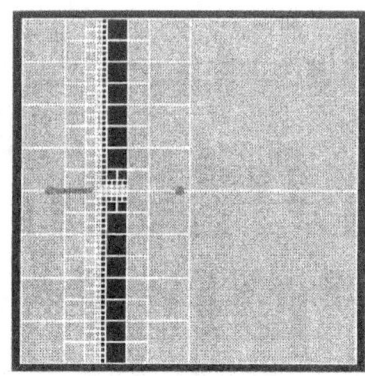

Figure 99: Path for Simulation (C)

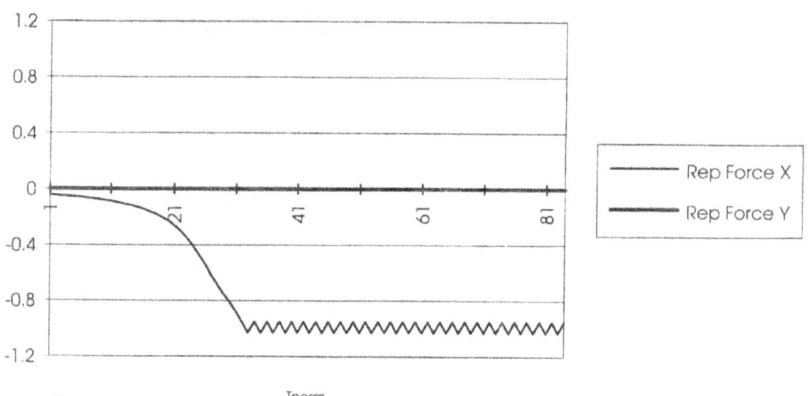

Figure 100: Repulsive Force Components for Simulation (C)

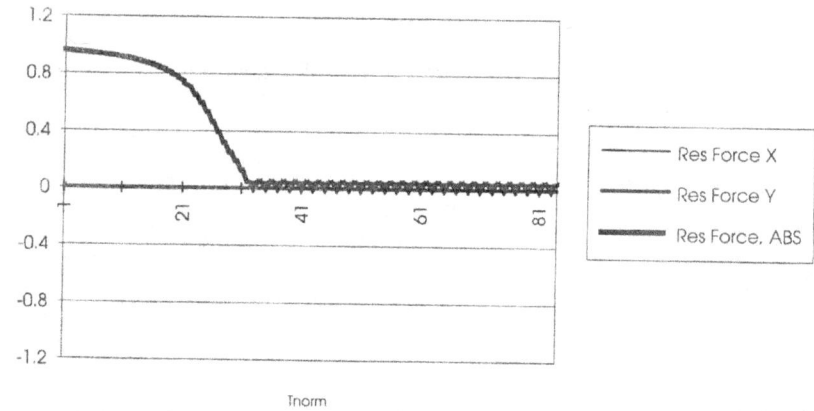

Figure 101: Resultant Force in Simulation (C)

5.2.3.3.2.9 Resultant Force

The total force on the AMV is determined as the vector sum of the combined repulsive forces and the attractive force:

$$\overline{F}_{res} = \overline{F}_{rep} + \overline{F}_{att}$$

[26.]

To implement different priorities for the different schemas appropriate scalar factors have to be introduced when combining the forces.

5.2.3.3.2.10 Implementing Elastic Bands

As mentioned earlier the MSE uses Elastic Bands in order to the calculate position setpoints. An Elastic Band is defined with a start and a target point. When moving on a path subsequently Elastic Bands are calculated by the PILOT and passed to the MSE. To ensure a smooth path it is important to decide when a new Elastic Band should be used by the MSE. It is not required that a target point of an Elastic Band is reached exactly unless this is the endpoint of a motion command. The next Elastic Band is used when the remaining distance from the AMV to the target point of the current Elastic Band is half the length of this Elastic Band. Attractive potential fields are always created at the start and target point of the Elastic Band. The magnitude of these fields are scaled such that the gain of the field at the start point is *1* at the beginning and *0* when the AMV has passed it. The field of the target point is *0* at the beginning and is ramped up to *1* when the start gain is *0*, see Figure 102.

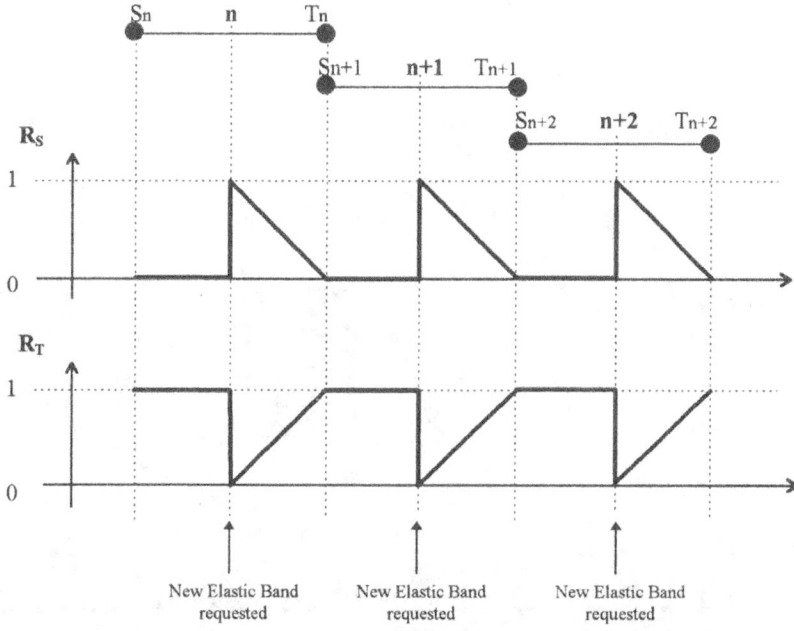

Figure 102: Start and Target Ramp Values for Attractive Potential Fields

The sum of the start and target field gains is always *1*, such that the total attractive force is never greater than *1* and the worst case scenario of chapter 5.2.3.3.2.5 is still valid.

5.2.3.3.2.11 Calculating Position Setpoints

Once all single forces and the resultant force are determined the resultant force is used to determine the next position setpoint. The position at which all forces are calculated is always the last setpoint in the list of position setpoints, assuming the AMV will reach this position. Errors in the position controller of the AMV are not considered in the CA²MOV architecture, the position control is closed loop only in the motion controller of the AMV. The direction from the current position to the next setpoint is the direction of the resultant force. The nominal distance to the next setpoint $l_{sp, max}$ is specified beforehand according to the requirements of the motion controller, the desired path accuracy, and the desired reactivity. Of course it is limited by the available computational power. The nominal distance is adjusted according to the magnitude of the resultant force to smoothen the path. A constant position stepsize causes the forces and the path to oscillate around the critical distance. These oscillations are shown in Figure 103 and 104 for a constant position step size of *0.2 m*. In Figure 105 the step size was varied between *0.1 m* and *0.3 m*, and the resulting path is smooth.

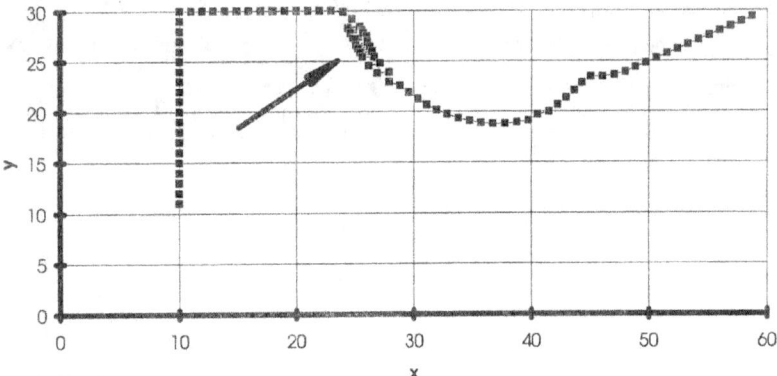

Figure 103: Oscillating Path with Constant Position Step Size

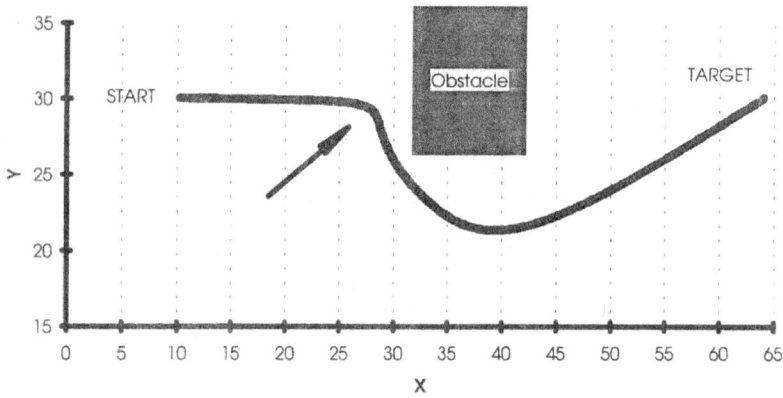

Figure 104: Smooth Path with Various Step Size

The function used to determine the step size is

$$l_{sp} = F_{res} * \frac{l_{sp_{max}}}{F_{att}}$$

[27.]

and is displayed in Figure 105.

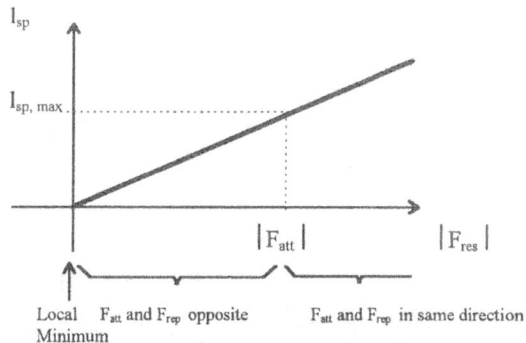

Figure 105: Position Step Size as Function of the Resulting Force Magnitude

If the resulting force magnitude is large the navigational situation is "clear" and safe for the AMV, the position setpoint can be relatively far away from the current position (lower reactivity). Is the resultant force smaller, the reactivity of the path is enhanced by a smaller position step size, i.e. the pat is re-evaluate earlier. Smaller resultant forces occur when the AMV is approaching an obstacle.

The calculation time for position setpoints in dependency of the number of occupied nodes in the Local Map has been determined:

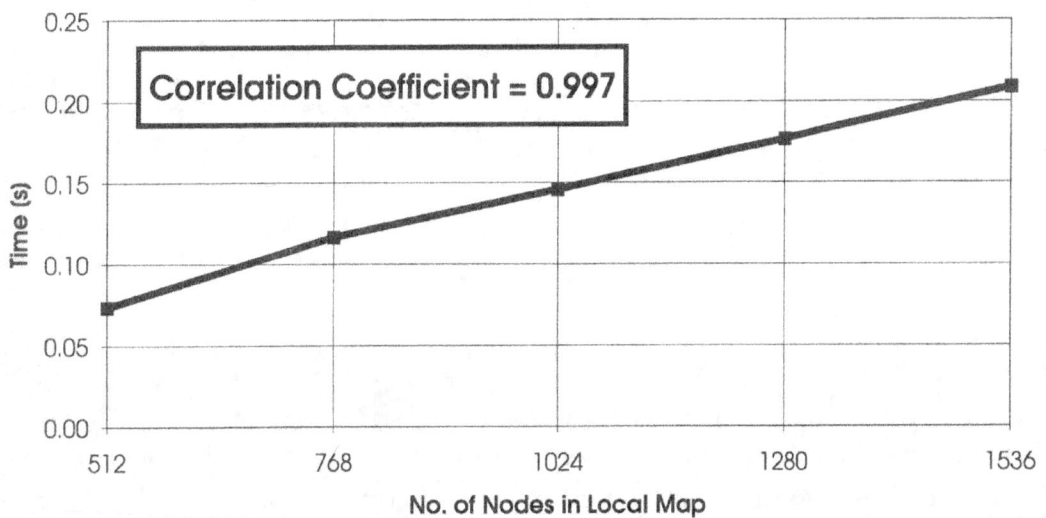

Figure 104b: Calculation Time for Position Setpoints

This excludes local re-planning and is only a guideline.

5.2.3.3.2.12 Local Minima

If the MSE encounters a local minimum a new position setpoint cannot be calculated; the MSE status is set to "local failure" and returns to the PILOT for local Re-planning.

It is essential, however, to identify clearly when the AMV is at a local minimum. Mathematically at a local minimum the resultant force disappears. Since the position is evaluated discontinuously a local minimum might not be reached exactly. The resulting path in this case is an oscillation between the two same positions. This is shown in a simulation where the AMV is stuck in a local minimum before a wall, the goal is unreachable, Figure 106. Figure 107 shows the oscillation in the forces.

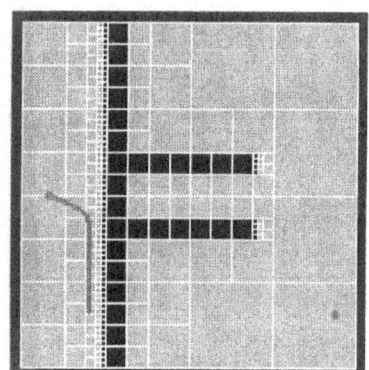

Figure 106: AMV is Stuck Before Wall

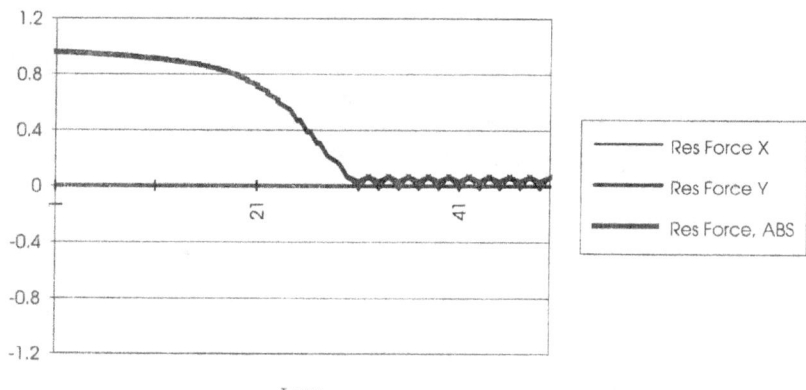

Figure 107: Oscillating Forces When Stuck

The easiest way to determine whether a local minimum is reached is by defining a threshold magnitude for the resulting force. Is the resulting force below this limit a local minimum is assumed. In simulations however this threshold was determined and a significant overlap between the force magnitude in a local minimum and a small resultant force outside a local minimum was found. Taking this into account, a second method has to be introduced.

As discussed earlier, at a local minimum the position setpoints are oscillating. Calculating the angle between the connections of three position setpoints enables the MSE to detect such oscillations geometrically. A requirements is, of course, that at least three position setpoints are contained in the list of position setpoints. The change in angle $\Delta\alpha$ is calculated as

$$\Delta\alpha = |\alpha_1 - \alpha_2| \qquad\qquad [28.]$$

using the definitions in Figure 108.

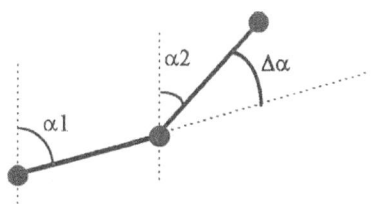

Figure 108: Definition of Angles between Position Setpoints

A local minimum is assumed when $\Delta\alpha$ is greater a threshold angle α_{th}.

Summarising the two conditions to detect a local minimum are:

$$|F_{res}| < F_{th} \qquad \text{(A)}$$
$$\Delta\alpha > \alpha_{th} \qquad \text{(B)}$$

[29.]

The threshold values are to be determined in simulations or experiments, respectively. The values used in the CA^{2}MOV architecture in the current implementation are

- $F_{th}=0.4$
- $\alpha_{th}=175°$

5.2.3.3.2.13 Velocity Calculation

As mentioned earlier a position consists of its global coordinates and the desired velocity to be reached at this position setpoint expressed as percentage of the maximum velocity of the vehicle. This is the only time CA^{2}MOV considers the vehicle dynamics. The velocity depends on two factors: the angle between setpoints and the remaining distance to the goal of a motion command where the AMV has to stop (breaking).

In narrow curves of the path the AMV might have to slow down to reduce the overshoot. Curvature of the path is assessed calculating the angle between the links of three setpoints $\Delta\alpha$ as introduced in the previous chapter. The velocity function is shown in Figure 109, it is simply defined using a critical change in angle where the velocity must be zero, i.e. the AMV stops at this position setpoint before using the next one. This simple function is chosen to calculate the velocity fast..

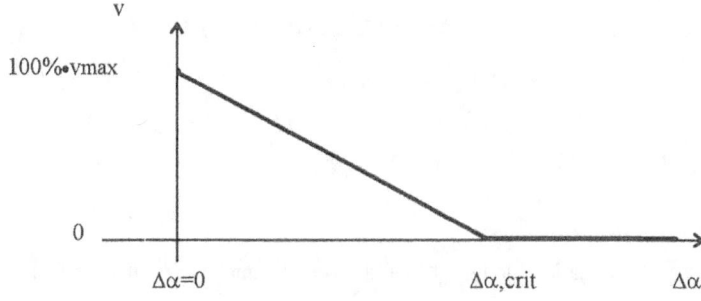

Figure 109: Velocity as Function of Path Curvature

Considering the remaining distance to the mission goal is done by calculating the maximum allowable velocity at the next setpoint for the AMV to be able to break at the endpoint with maximum deceleration. The velocity lowered to this value if the user specified a larger velocity.

5.2.3.3.2.14 MSE Flow Diagram

The functions of the MSE are summarised in the following flow-diagram:

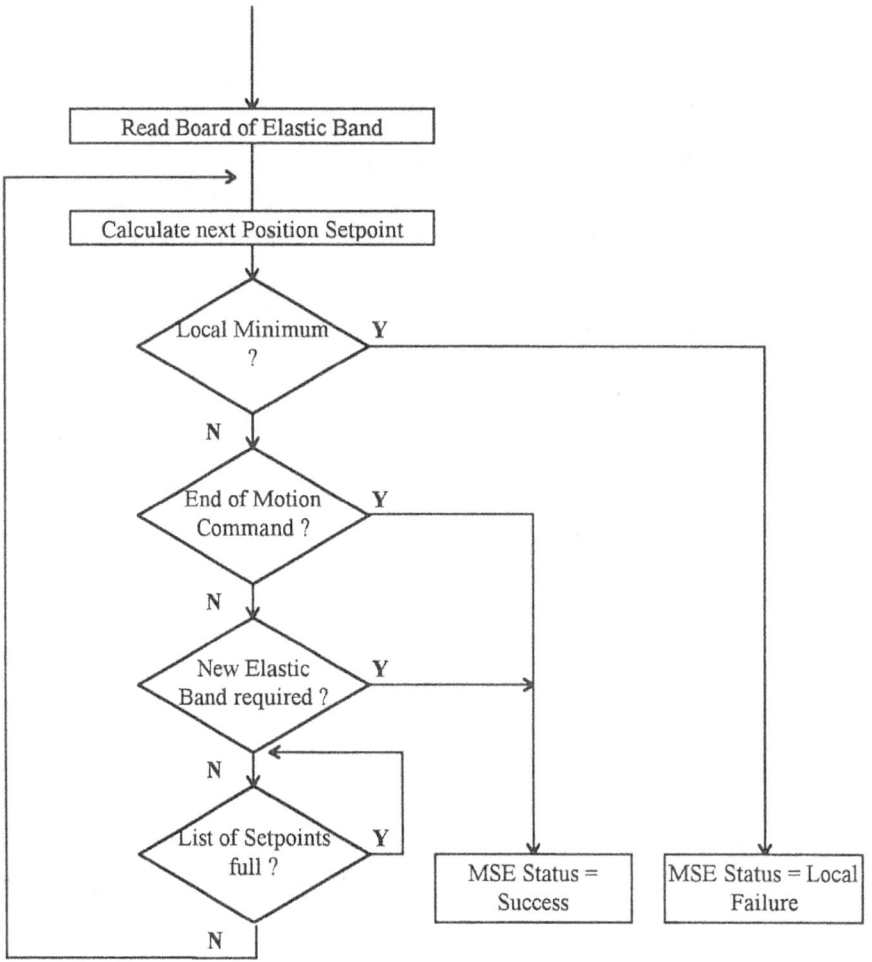

Figure 110: Flow Diagram MSE

5.2.3.3.3 Simulation of Sample GOTO - Missions

5.2.3.3.3.1 Description

To evaluate the Local Navigation Module (LNM) a series of simulations is made. The path of 14 missions is determined using the LNM and the Vertex Graph method (see chapter 5.2.2.1). The Vertex Graph method will find the shortest Euclidean path and is used as a benchmark to assess the quality of the path of the LNM. The environment in the simulations is always static, such that the reactive quality of the LNM is not assessed. The parameters used for both navigation techniques are

- Sidelength of the Local Map: 10000 mm

- Diameter of the AMV: 500 mm

- Security distance to obstacles: 500 mm

- Maximum velocity of the AMV: 1 m/s

- Maximum deceleration of the AMV: 0.5 m/s^2

- Maximum distance between position setpoints: 300 mm

Characteristics of a "good" path are

- go straight to goal

- curve only when necessary to reach the goal

- use AMV effectively, i.e. try to set a high velocity

- do not waste computing power

The missions use the following environments:

Mission Number	Environment
1	Corridor
2	Corridor
3	Door
4	Door
5	Door
6	Door
7	Door
8	Corner, open
9	Corner, closed
10	1 Obstacle
11	2 Obstacles
12	4 Obstacles
13	U shaped Obstacle
14	I shaped Obstacle

The resulting paths are shown in the Figures of the next chapter. The start point is always on the left-hand side of the map, the goal point on the right-hand side. Each position setpoint is displayed as a white circle of the diameter of the AMV.

5.2.3.3.3.2 Resulting-Paths

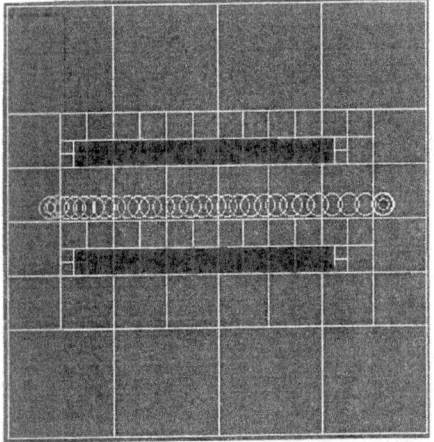

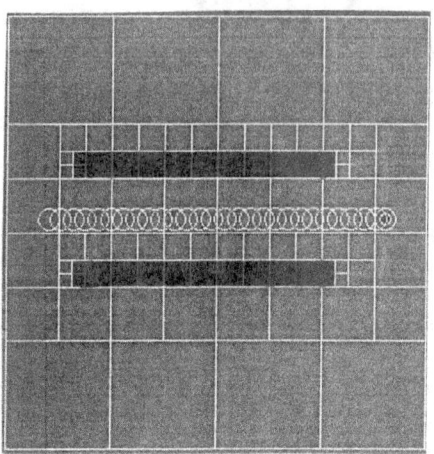

Figure 111: Path for Mission 1: LNM   -   *Vertex Graph*

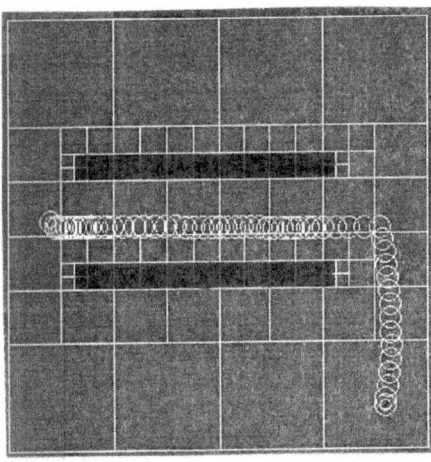

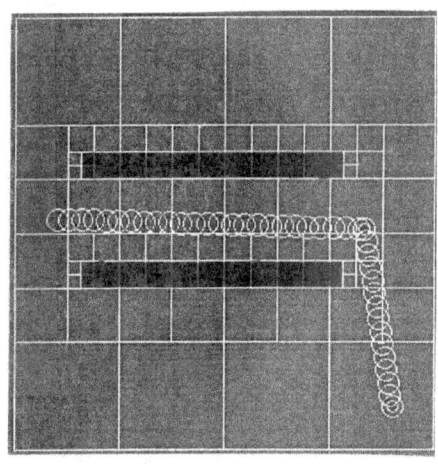

Figure 112: Path for Mission 2: LNM   -   *Vertex Graph*

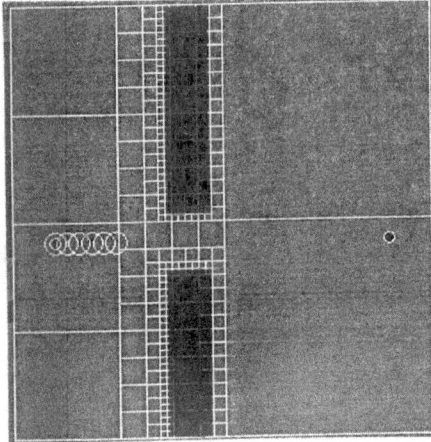

N/A

Figure 113: Path for Mission 3: LNM   -   *Vertex Graph*

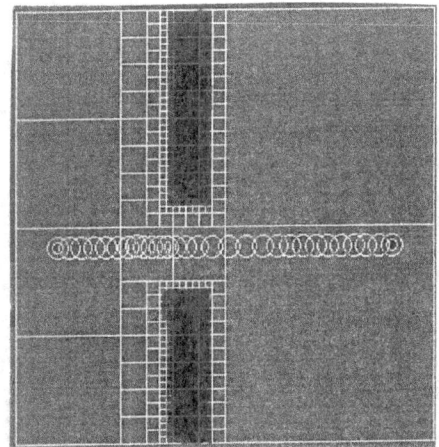
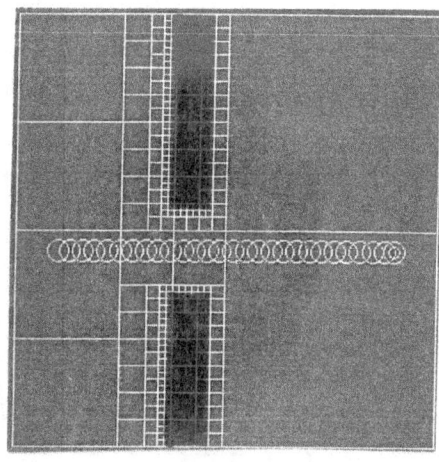

Figure 114: Path for Mission 4: LNM - *Vertex Graph*

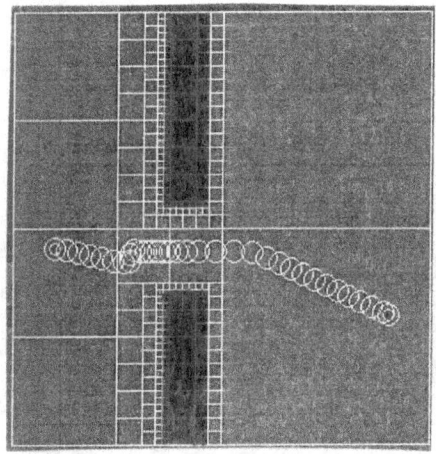
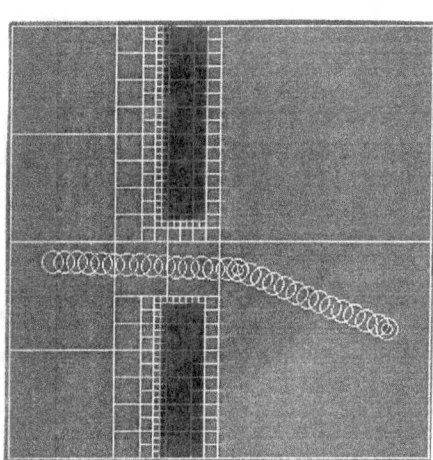

Figure 115: Path for Mission 5: LNM - *Vertex Graph*

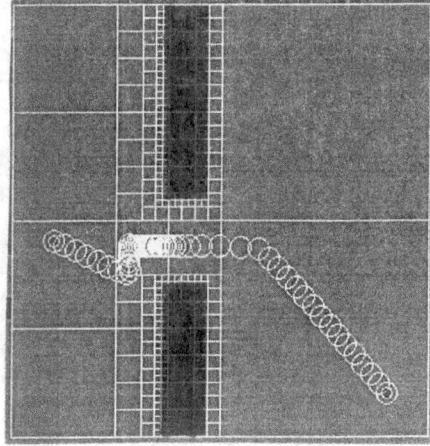
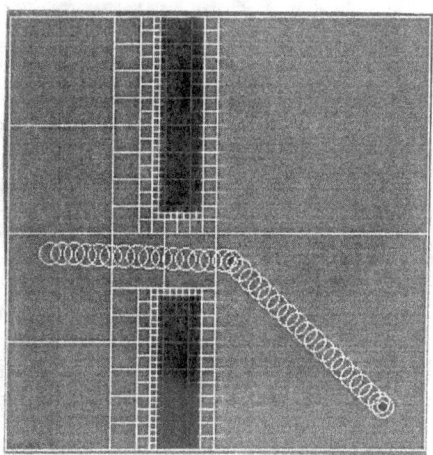

Figure 116: Path for Mission 6: LNM - *Vertex Graph*

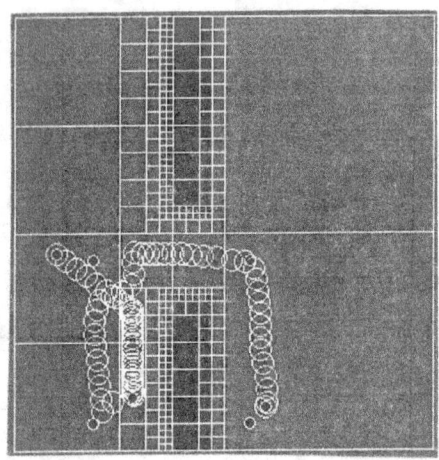
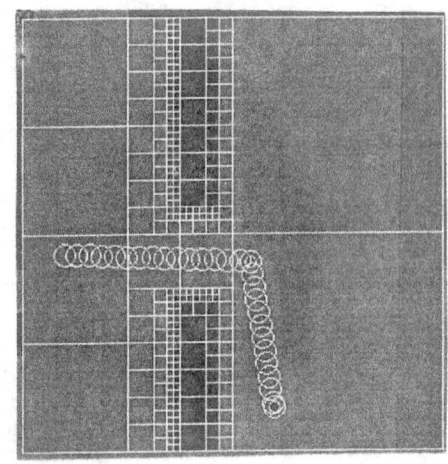

Figure 117: Path for Mission 7: LNM - *Vertex Graph*

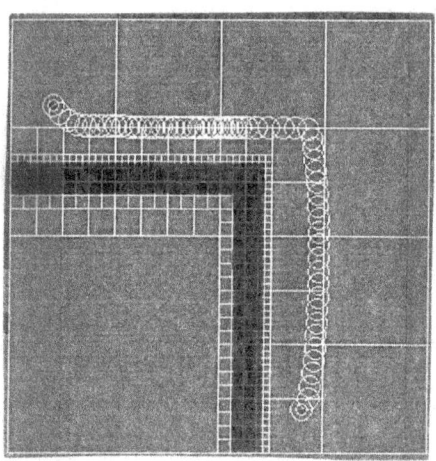
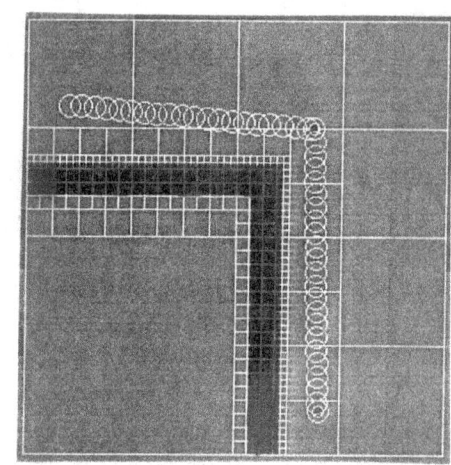

Figure 118: Path for Mission 8: LNM - *Vertex Graph*

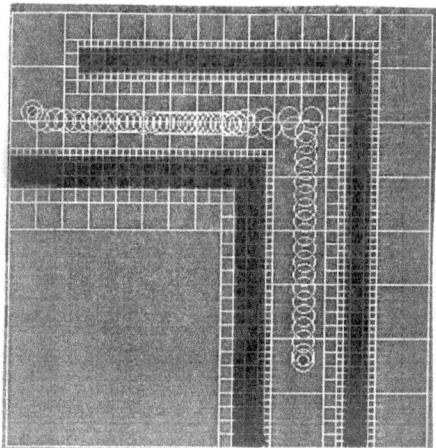
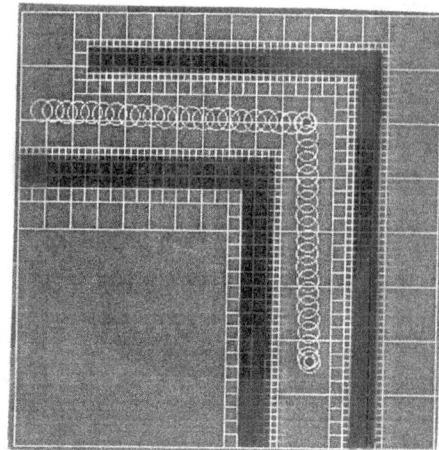

Figure 119: Path for Mission 9: LNM - *Vertex Graph*

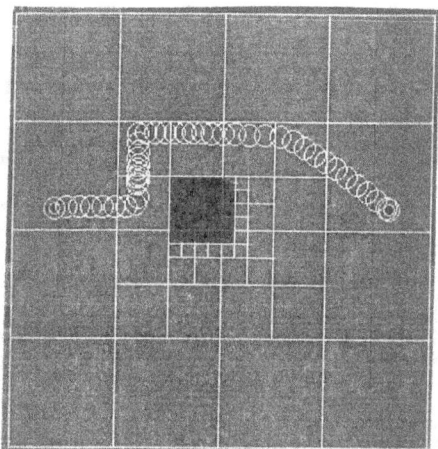
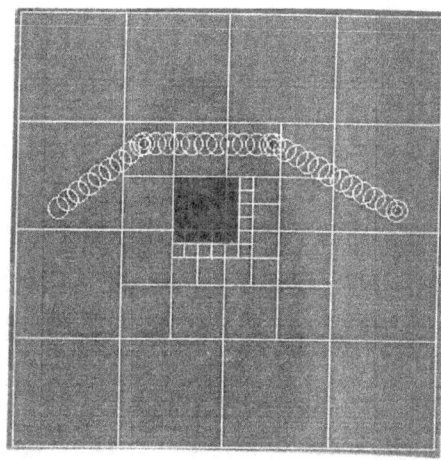

Figure 120: Path for Mission 10: LNM - *Vertex Graph*

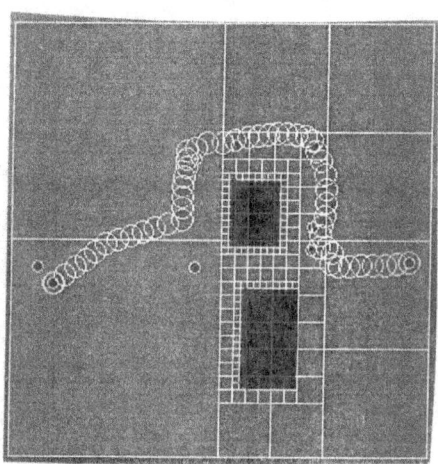
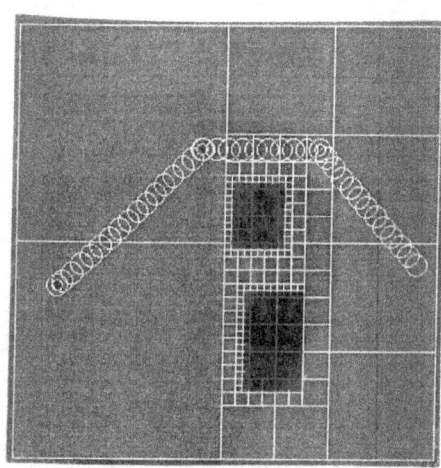

Figure 121: Path for Mission 11: LNM - *Vertex Graph*

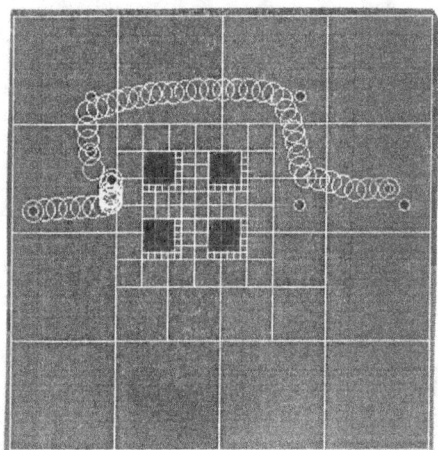
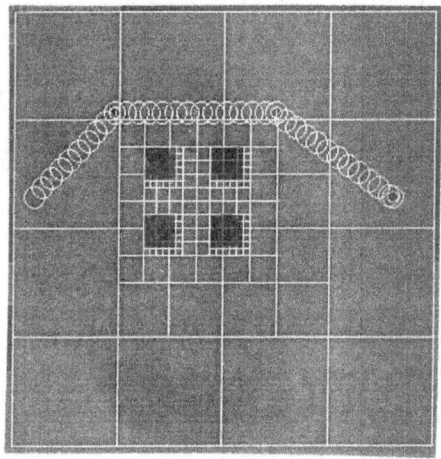

Figure 122: Path for Mission 12: LNM - *Vertex Graph*

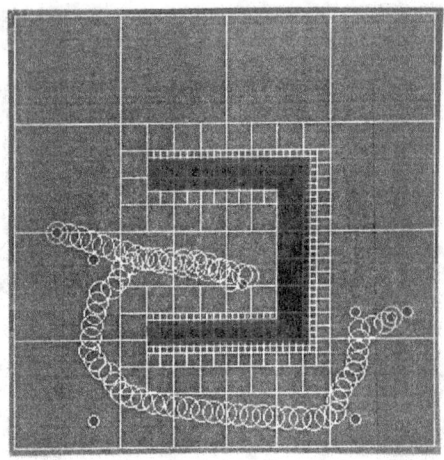 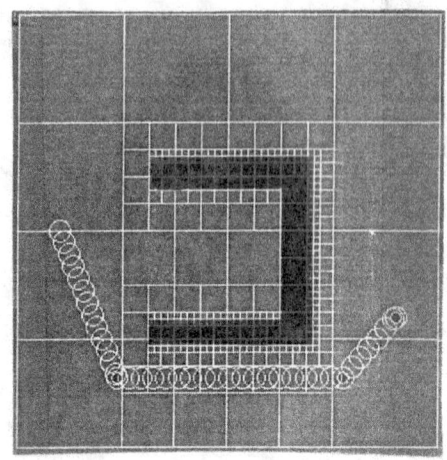

Figure 123: Path for Mission 13: LNM   -   *Vertex Graph*

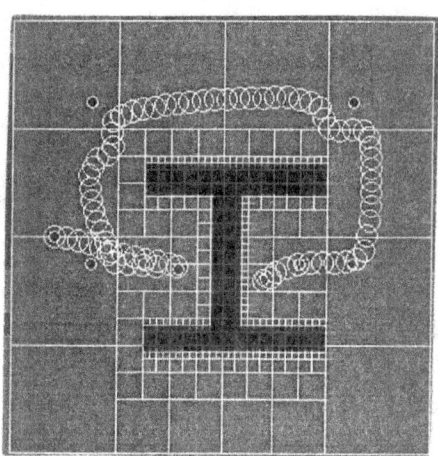 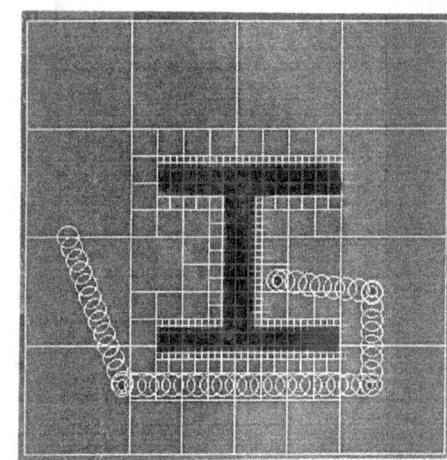

Figure 124: Path for Mission 14: LNM   -   *Vertex Graph*

5.2.3.3.3 Evaluation

Examining the solution path some positive and some negative aspects are apparent:

Mission No.	+	−
1	• No deviation from direct path to goal	• Distance between setpoints is not always maximal
2	• Almost direct path to goal	• Distance between setpoints not always maximal while in corridor • Unnecessary deviation after leaving corridor
3	• Stops in front of too narrow door, no deviation to either side	
4	• Almost no deviation from direct path to goal • Distance between setpoints smaller before door (more reactive), larger behind door (less reactive)	
5	• Almost no deviation from optimal path • Distance between setpoints smaller in front of door (more reactive)	
6	• Close to optimal path	• Distance between setpoints very small in front of door (reactive, but too much effort in communication with AMV)
7	• Local re-planning successful	• Path too long
8	• Almost no deviation from optimal path	• Distance between setpoint small where no increased reactivity necessary
9	• Security distance in narrow corridor always kept	• Oscillating path at corner • Distance between setpoints too close in first part of path
10	• Close to optimal path	
11	• Local re-planning successful • Close to optimal path	
12	•Local re-planning successful	• Many close setpoints before local minimum is detected
13	• Local re-planning successful	• Path too long • Narrow curve at end
14	• Local re-planning successful • Re-planned path almost optimal	

A number of parameters is now defined in order to assess the quality of the paths numerically:

- Angle between the straight line segments of three consecutive position setpoints ξ
- Distance between two consecutive position setpoints d_{sp}
- Change in the remaining direct straight line distance to the goal point Δd_g
- Effectivity of a position setpoint $e_{sp} = \dfrac{\Delta d_g}{d_{SP}}$
- Total travelling time of the AMV when following the path t_m
- Total length of path l_t
- Computing time per position setpoint t_c
- Average effectivity of path generation $e_g = \dfrac{Average\left[e_{sp}\right]}{Average\left[t_c\right]}$

For each of the missions the velocity of the AMV (issued with the position setpoint by the LNM), the distance between setpoints d_{sp}, and the effectivity of the position setpoints e_{sp} are shown for the LNM in the Figures 125 to 162. Mission 3 is excluded from this evaluation since the mission could not be completed.

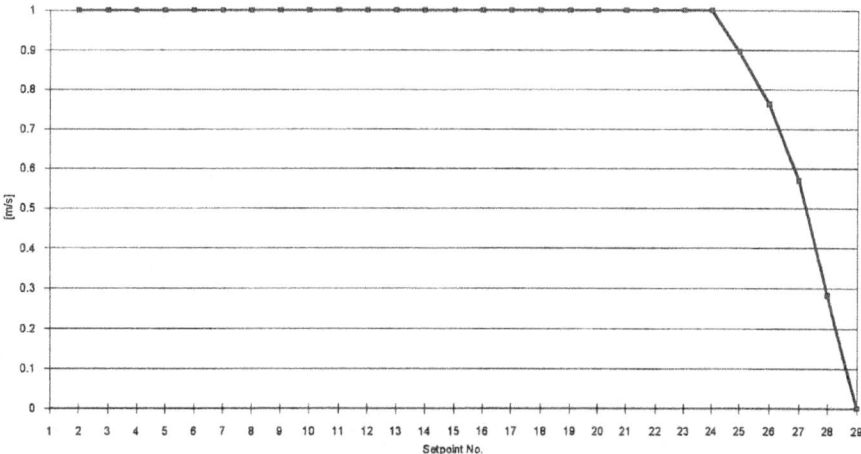

Figure 125: MISSION 1 - Velocity

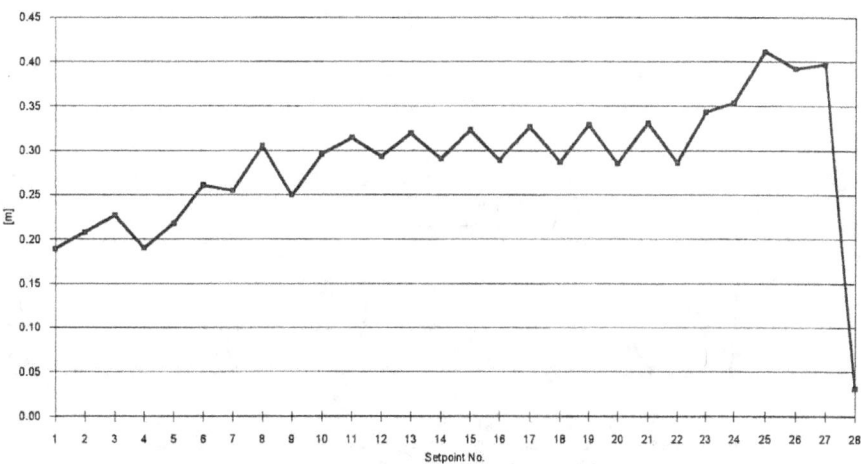

Figure 126: MISSION 1 - Distance between Position Setpoints d_{sp}

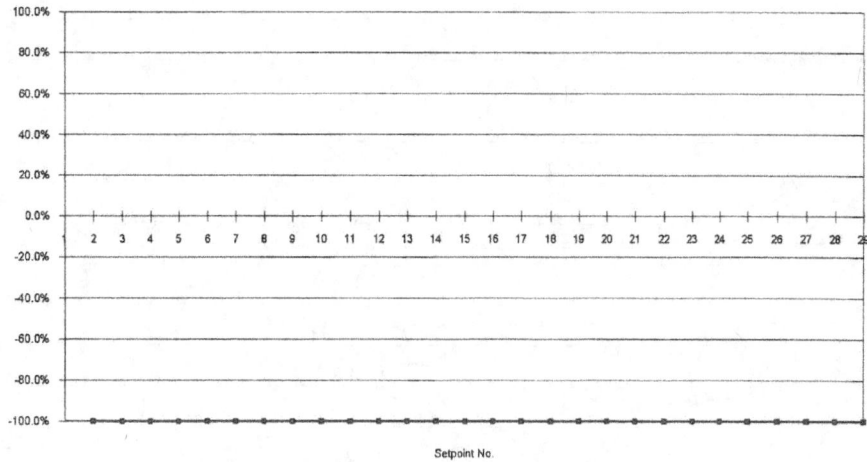

Figure 127: MISSION 1 - Effectivity of Position Setpoints e_{sp}

Figure 128: MISSION 2 - Velocity

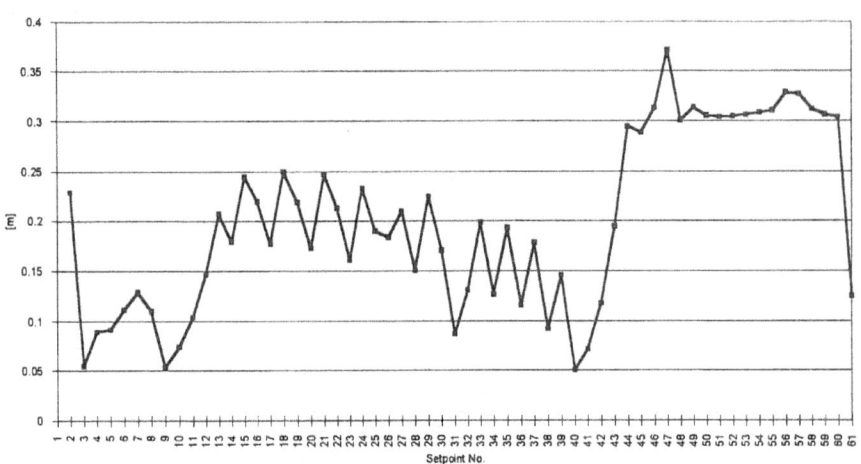

Figure 129: MISSION 2 - Distance between Position Setpoints d_{sp}

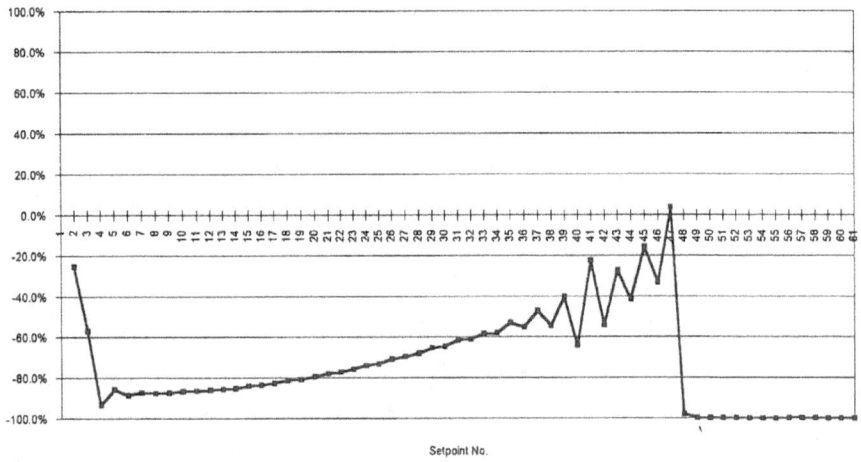

Figure 130: MISSION 2 - Effectivity of Position Setpoints e_{sp}

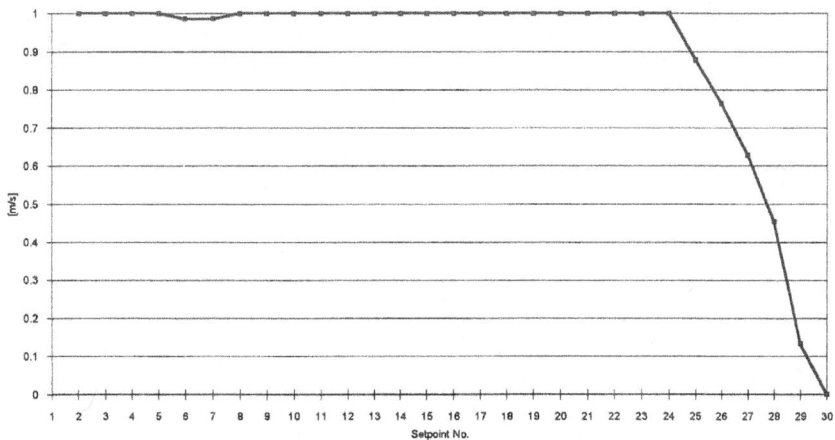

Figure 131: MISSION 4 - Velocity

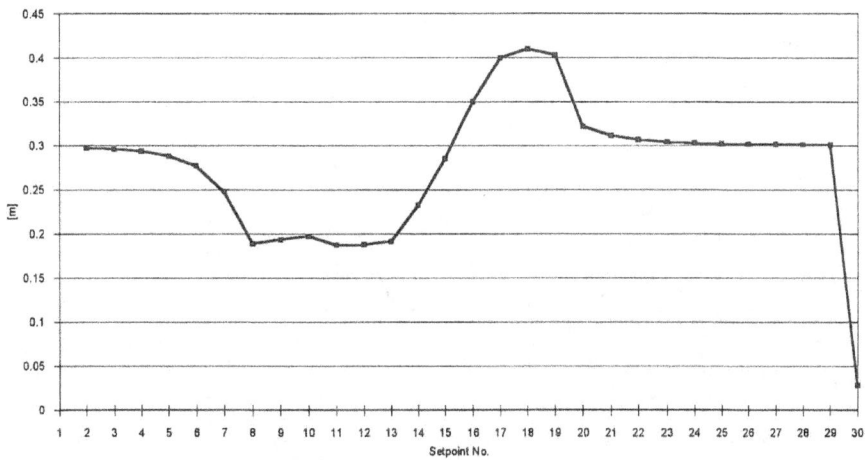

Figure 132: MISSION 4 - Distance between Position Setpoints d_{sp}

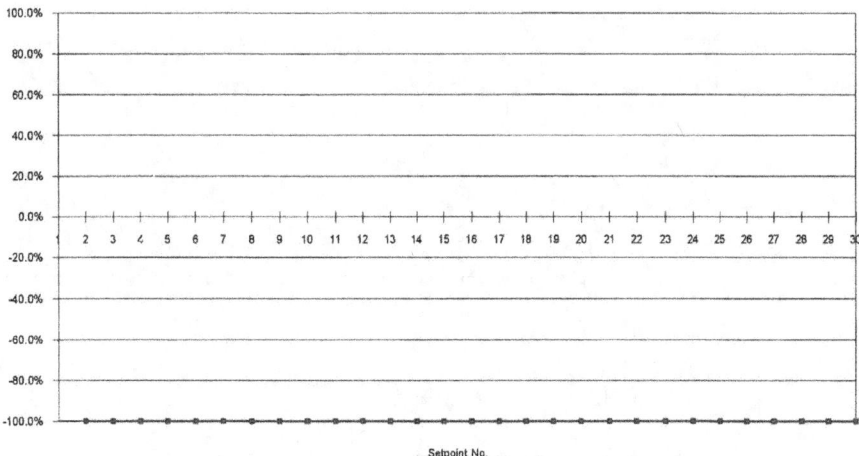

Figure 133: MISSION 4 - Effectivity of Position Setpoints e_{sp}

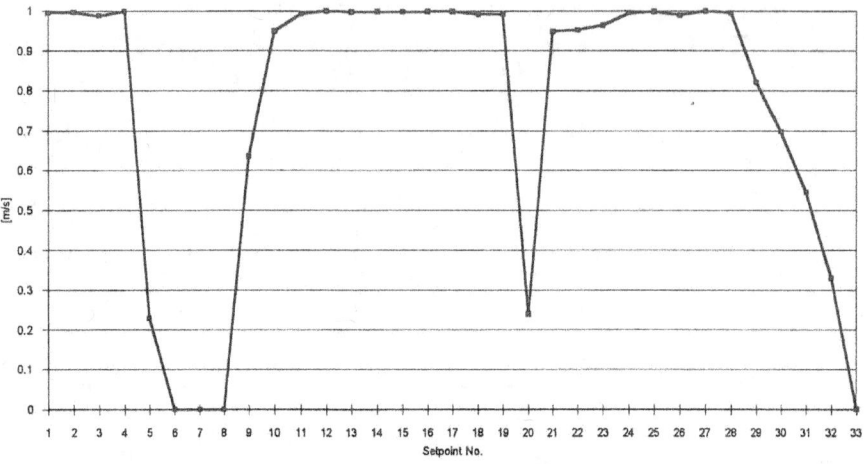

Figure 134: MISSION 5 - Velocity

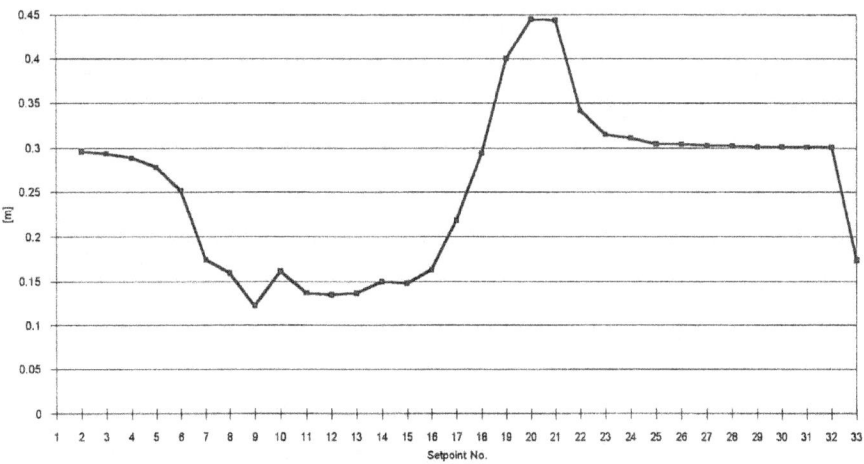

Figure 135: MISSION 5 - Distance between Position Setpoints d_{sp}

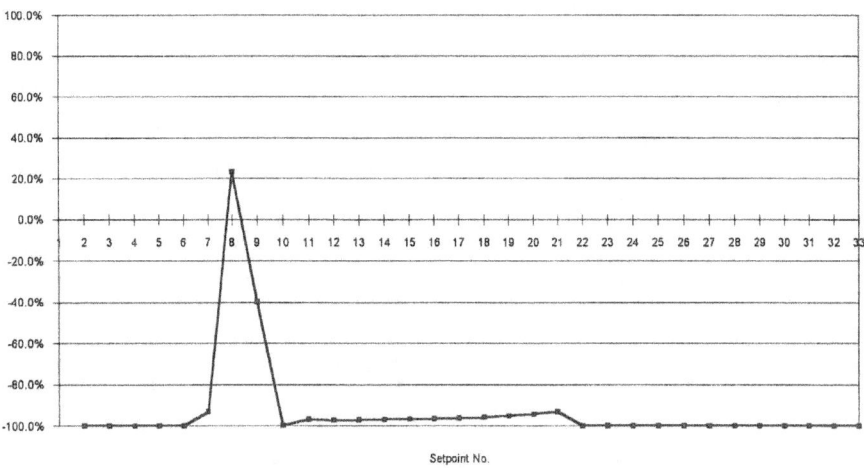

Figure 136: MISSION 5 - Effectivity of Position Setpoints e_{sp}

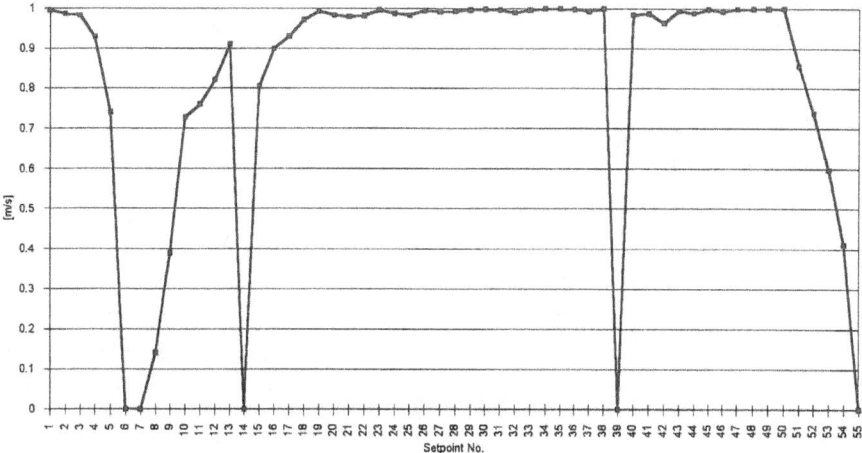

Figure 137: MISSION 6 - Velocity

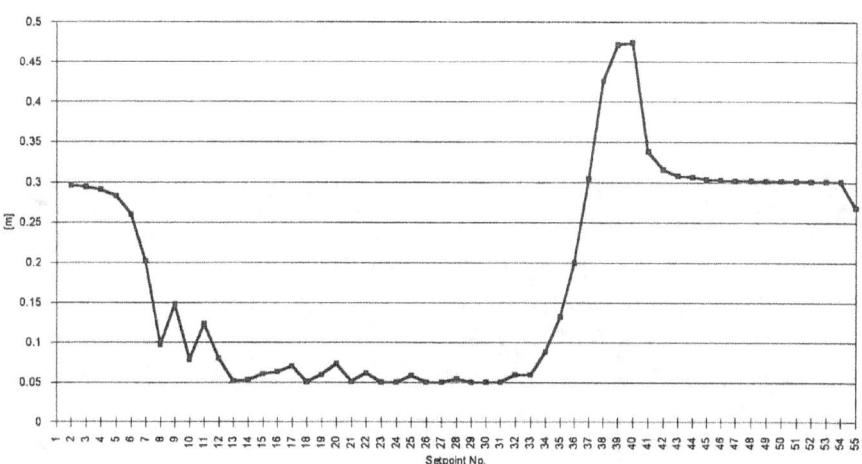

Figure 138: MISSION 6 - Distance between Position Setpoints d$_{sp}$

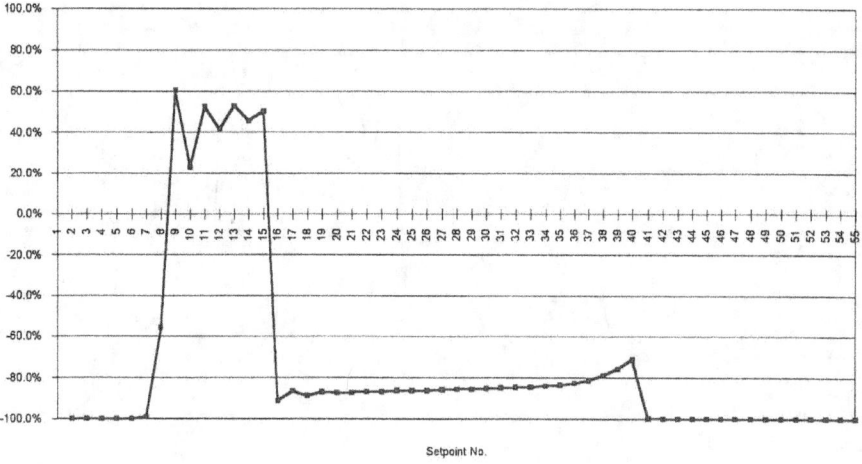

Figure 139: MISSION 6 - Effectivity of Position Setpoints e$_{sp}$

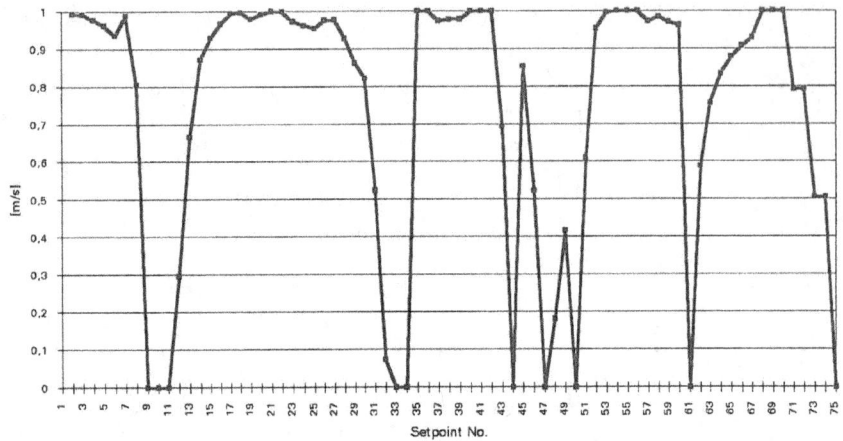

Figure 138a: MISSION 7 - Velocity

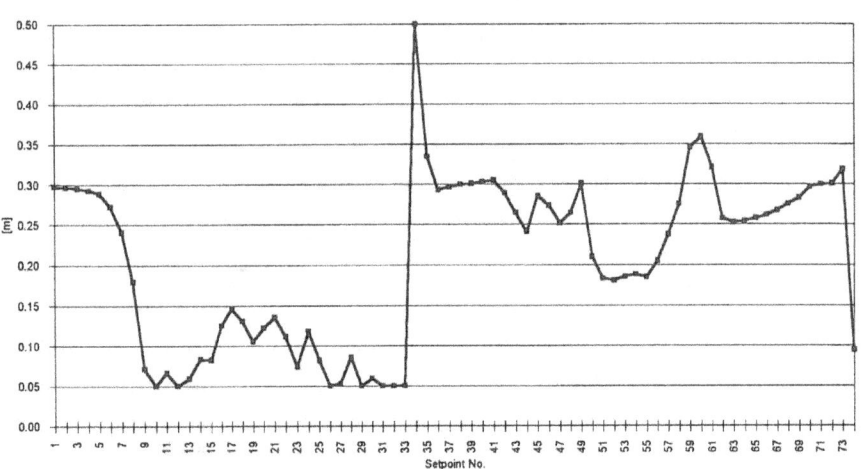

Figure 140: MISSION 7 - Distance between Position Setpoints d$_{sp}$

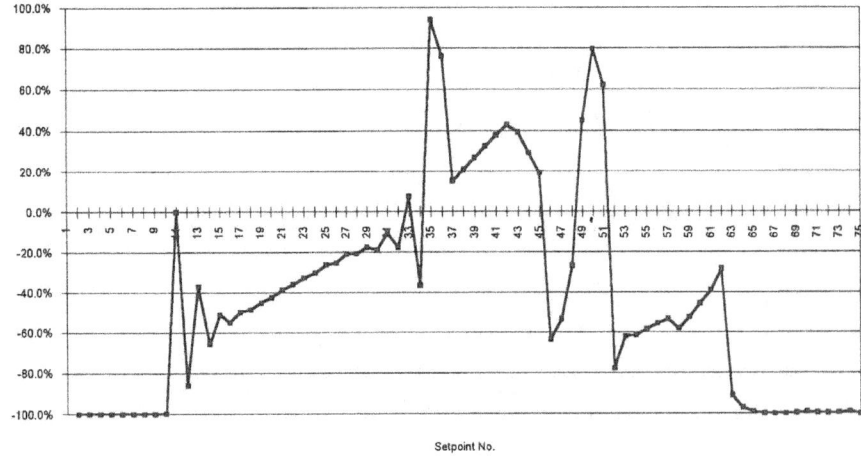

Figure 141: MISSION 7 - Effectivity of Position Setpoints e$_{sp}$

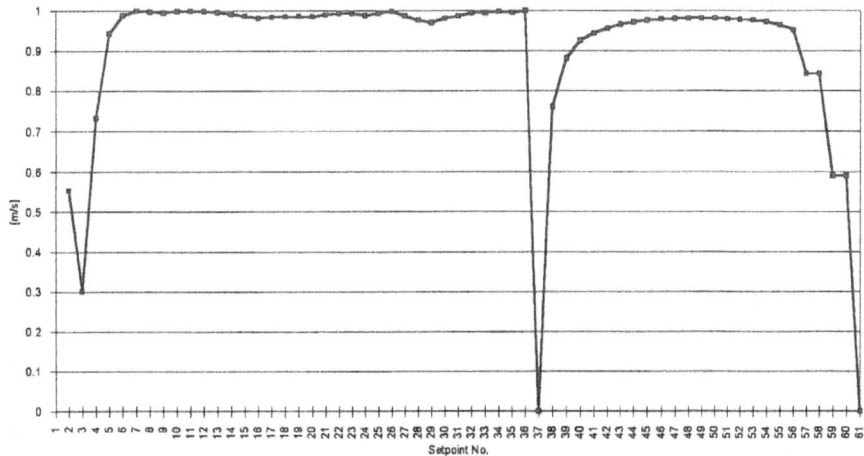

Figure 142: MISSION 8 - Velocity

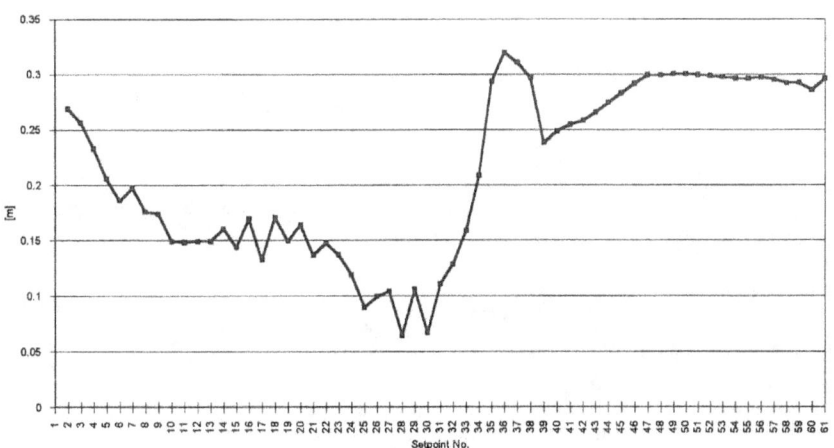

Figure 143: MISSION 8 - Distance between Position Setpoints d$_{sp}$

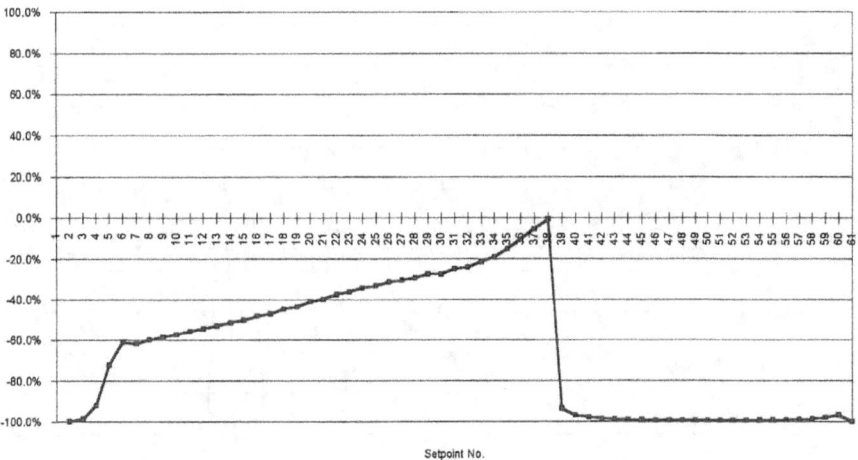

Figure 144: MISSION 8 - Effectivity of Position Setpoints e$_{sp}$

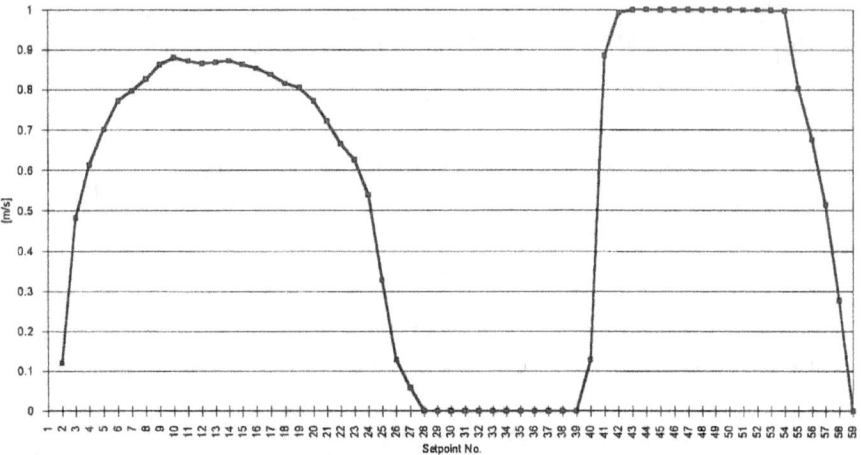

Figure 145: MISSION 9 - Velocity

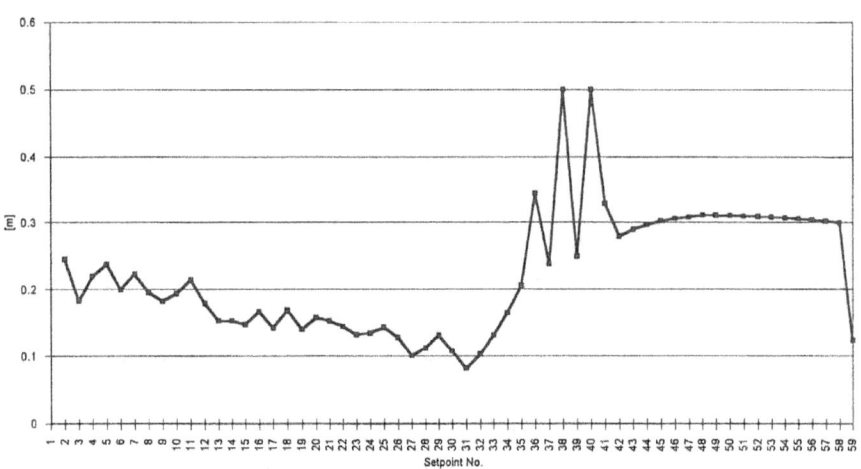

Figure 146: MISSION 9 - Distance between Position Setpoints d_{sp}

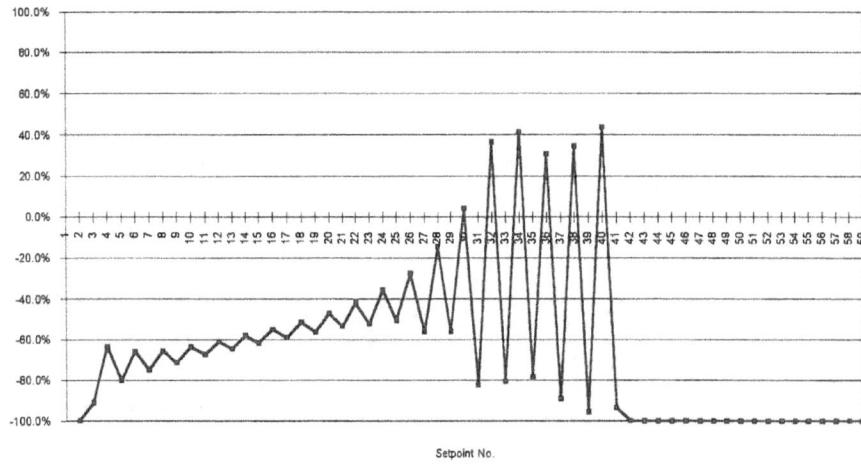

Figure 147: MISSION 9 - Effectivity of Position Setpoints e_{sp}

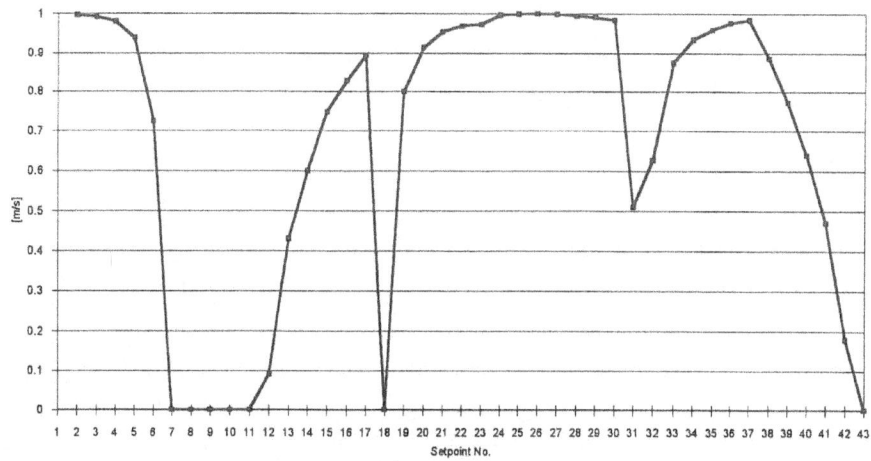

Figure 148: MISSION 10 - Velocity

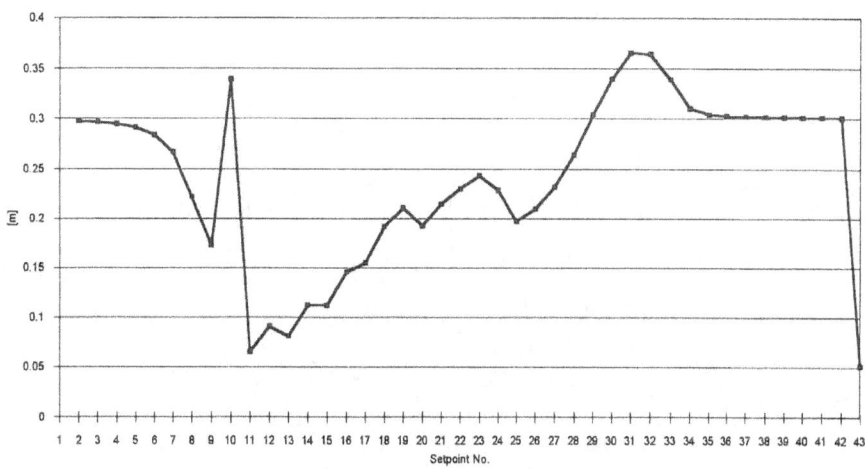

Figure 149: MISSION 10 - Distance between Position Setpoints d$_{sp}$

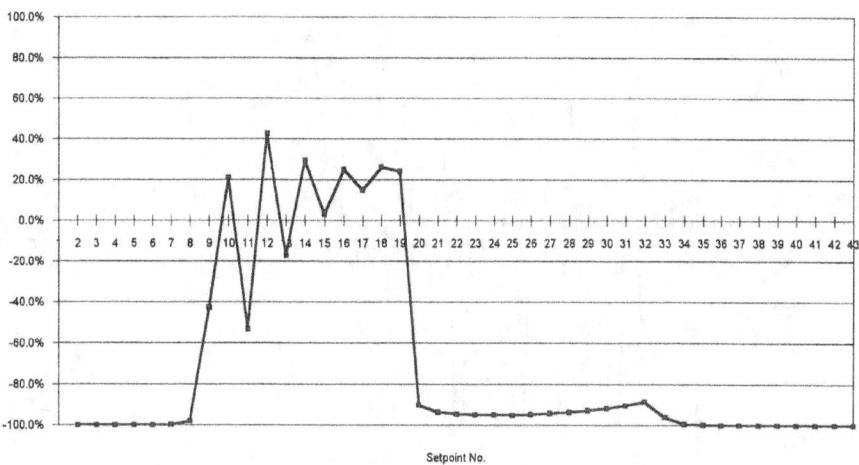

Figure 150: MISSION 10 - Effectivity of Position Setpoints e$_{sp}$

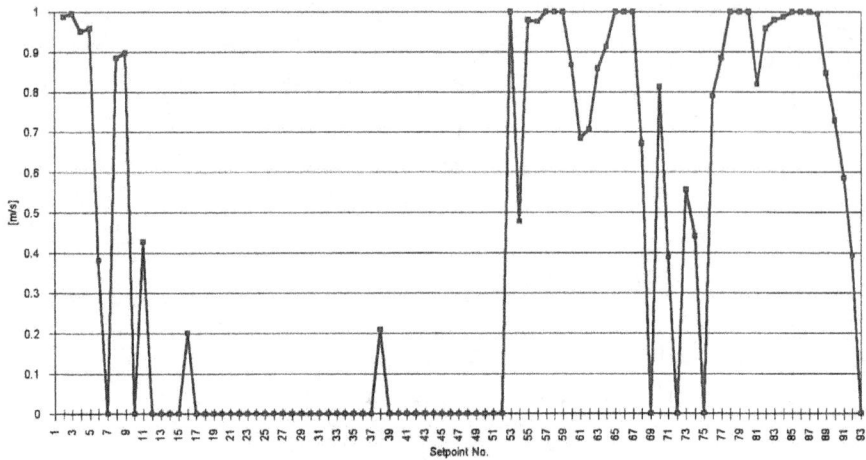

Figure 151: MISSION 11 - Velocity

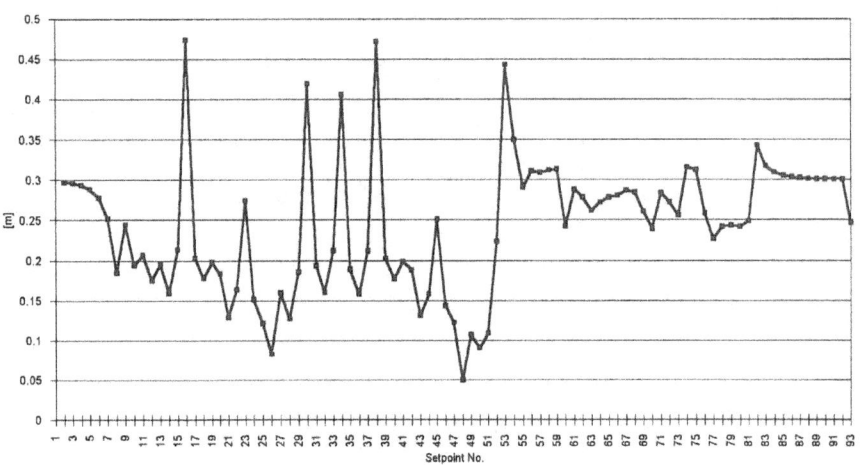

Figure 152: MISSION 11 - Distance between Position Setpoints d_{sp}

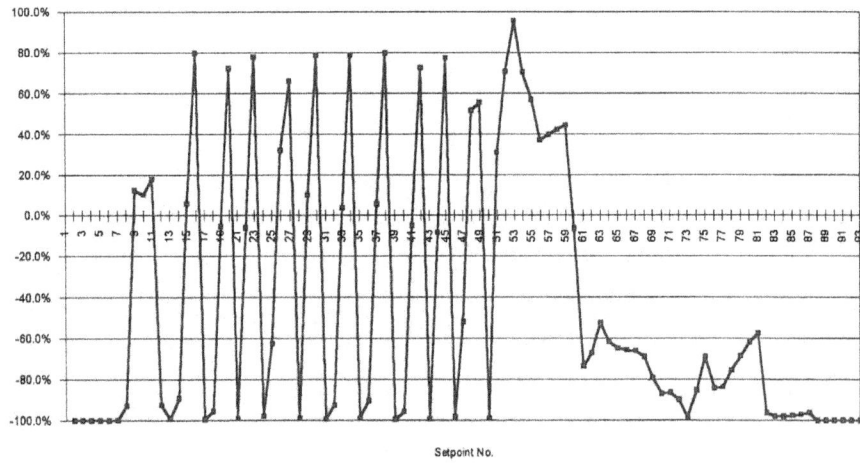

Figure 153: MISSION 11 - Effectivity of Position Setpoints e_{sp}

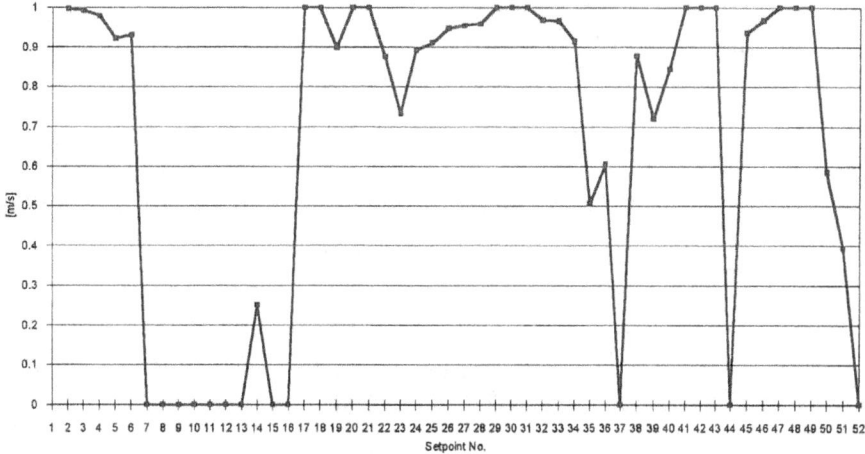

Figure 154: MISSION 12 - Velocity

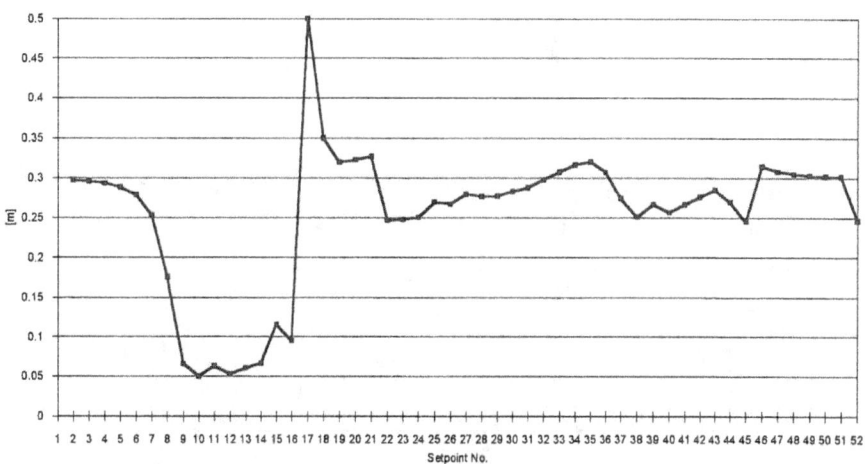

Figure 155: MISSION 12 - Distance between Position Setpoints d$_{sp}$

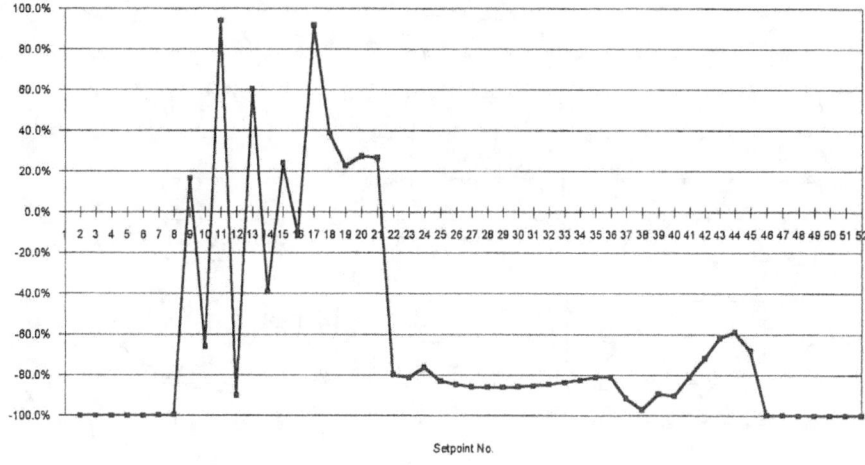

Figure 156: MISSION 12 - Effectivity of Position Setpoints e$_{sp}$

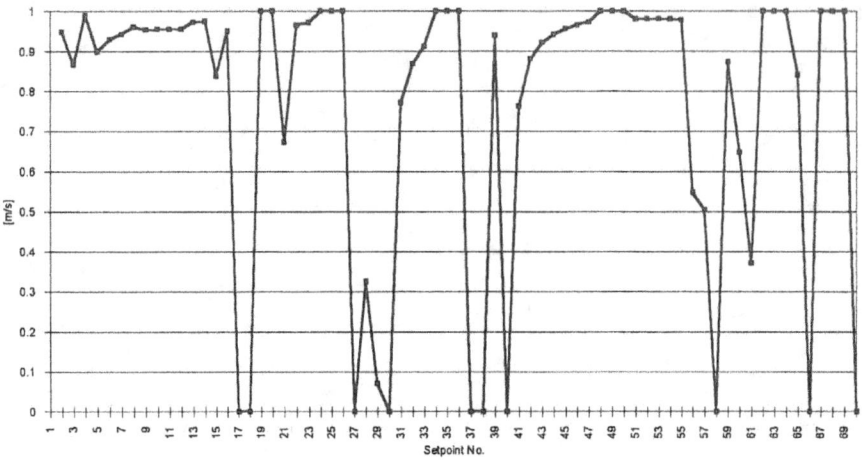

Figure 157: MISSION 13 - Velocity

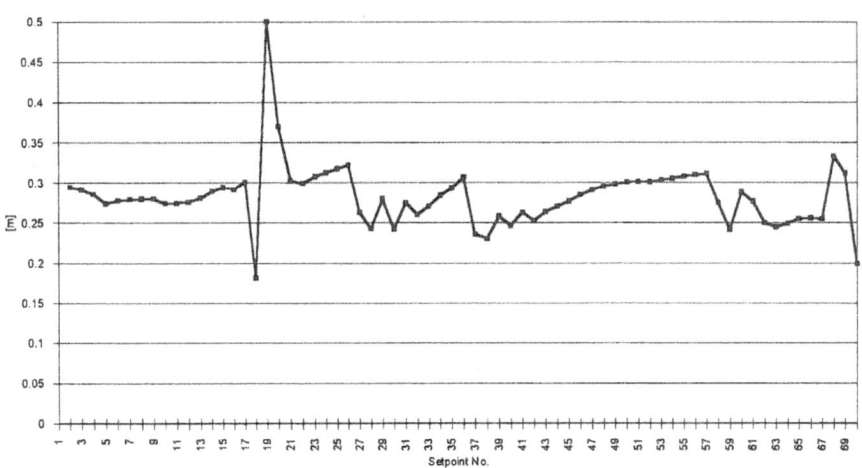

Figure 158: MISSION 13 - Distance between Position Setpoints d_{sp}

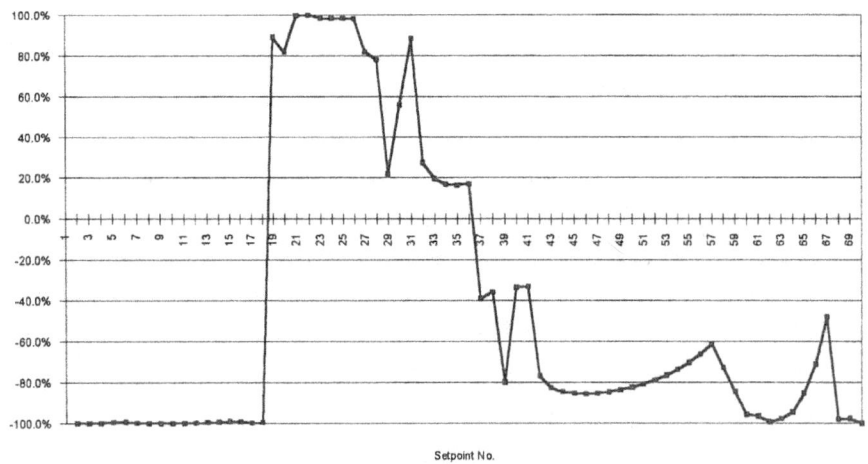

Figure 159: MISSION 13 - Effectivity of Position Setpoints e_{sp}

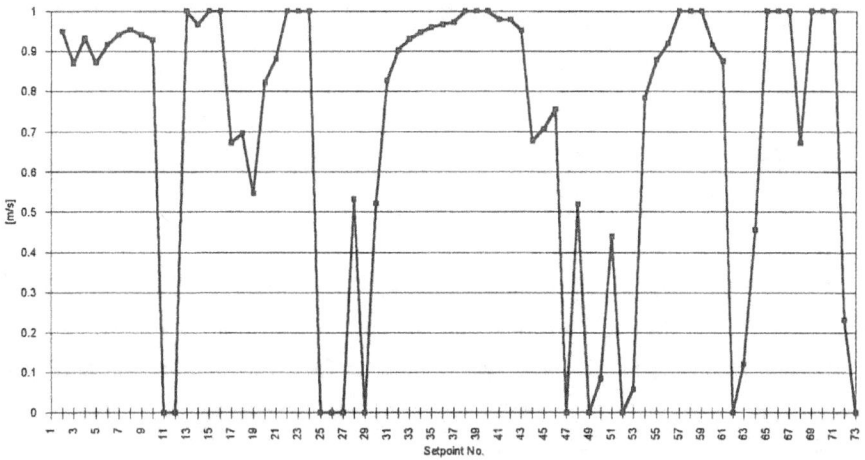

Figure 160: MISSION 14 - Velocity

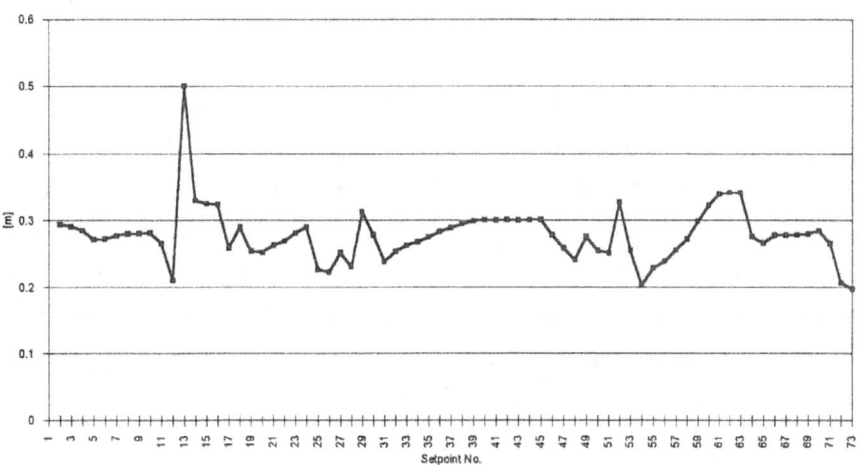

Figure 161: MISSION 14 - Distance between Position Setpoints d_{sp}

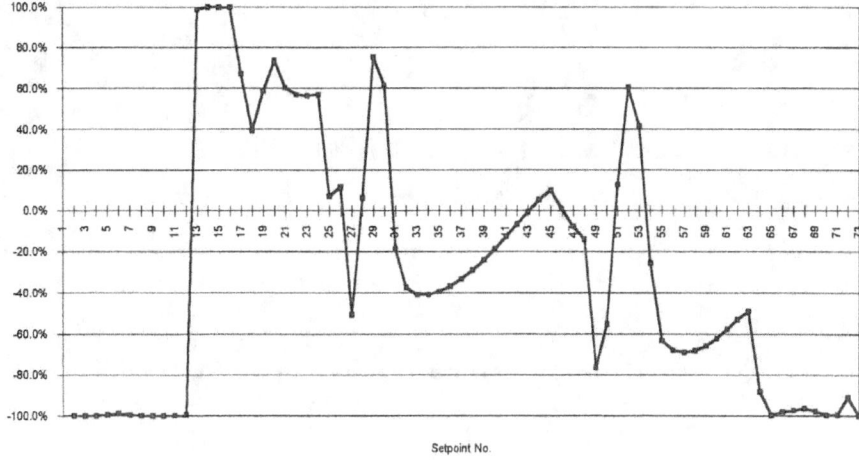

Figure 162: MISSION 14 - Effectivity of Position Setpoints e_{sp}

The breaking function at the end of the mission goal as described in chapter 5.2.3.3.2.13 works as desired, e.g. Mission 1, Figure 125. The decreasing of the velocity in corners of the path is apparent e.g. in Mission 2, Figure 127. However, in many cases the velocity tends to react too sensible to changes in the angle between setpoints. Sudden changes of the velocity to 0 and back to a higher value as in the Missions 5, 6, and 8, Figures 134, 137, and 143, are not traceable by the AMV. This also causes oscillations in the velocity setpoint as in Missions 11, 12, 13, and 14, Figures 152, 155, 158, and 161.

The distance between the position setpoints oscillates in Missions 1 and 2 due to the parallel force components in the corridor that tend to „decelerate" and „accelerate" the AMV, Figures 126 and 129. When the AMV approaches an obstacle, the setpoints are place closer to enhance the reactivity of the path generation as described in chapter 5.2.3.3.2.11 which is obvious in mission 4, Figure 132, in front of the door. Behind the door the distance is larger than the nominal distance of *300mm*.

The effectivity of the position setpoints is 100% for missions 1 and 4 where the path is a straight line towards the goal, Figures 127 and 133. In missions 5 and 6 single inefficient setpoints occur at the corners of obstacles were the AMV is „pushed around", Figures 136 and 139.

Comparing the path parameters of the 14 missions of the LNM the maximum change in the angle between the setpoints and the average distance between the setpoints are similar for all missions, Figures 171 and 172. The average change in the angle is larger for missions 9 and 11 as shown in Figure 173. This is due to the oscillation in the corner in mission 9, and the oscillations close to the obstacle when moving on the re-planned path in mission 11, respectively. All missions come at least close to 100% (=-300mm) effectivity of the setpoints in their minimum value, Figure 166. The worst values for this effectivity occur for the missions that include Local Re-planning, and the average depends again on the necessity for Local Re-planning. The average processing time, i.e. the computational efforts for the path generation, depends on the complexity of the environment, Figure 167, and so does the effectivity of the path generation in Figure 168.

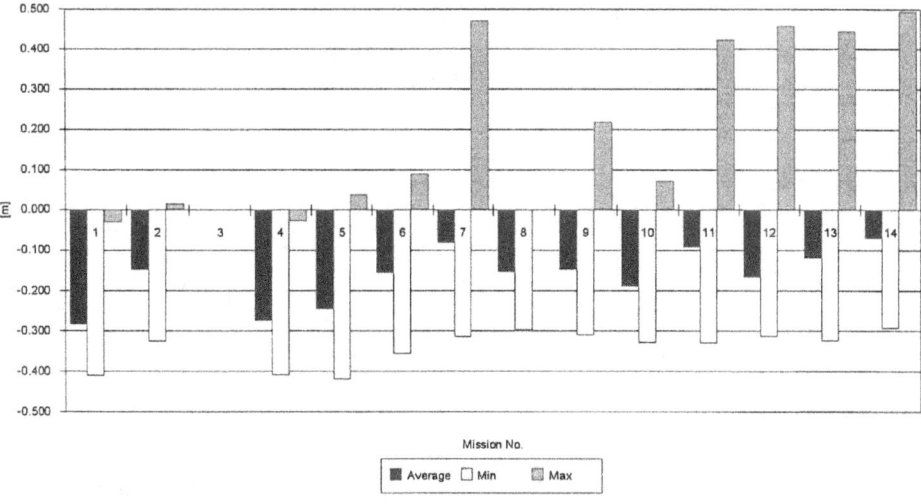

Figure 163: Effectivity of Setpoints e_{sp} for LNM Path

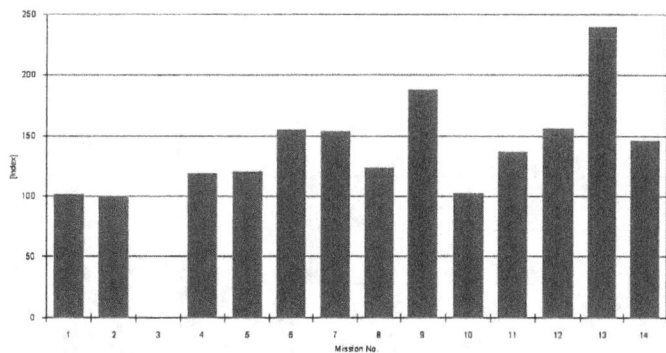

Figure 164: Average Processing Time per Setpoint of LNM Path

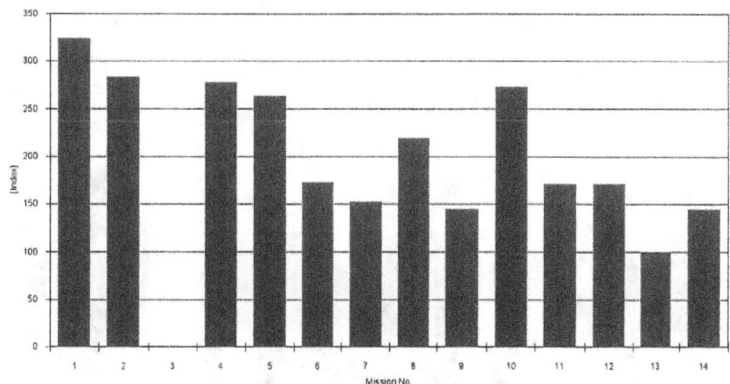

Figure 165: Average Effectivity of Path Generation of LNM Path

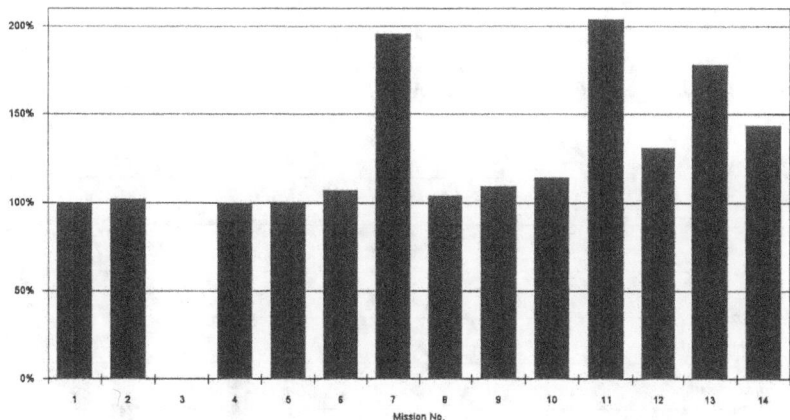

Figure 166: Total Length of LNM Path Compared to Vertex Graph

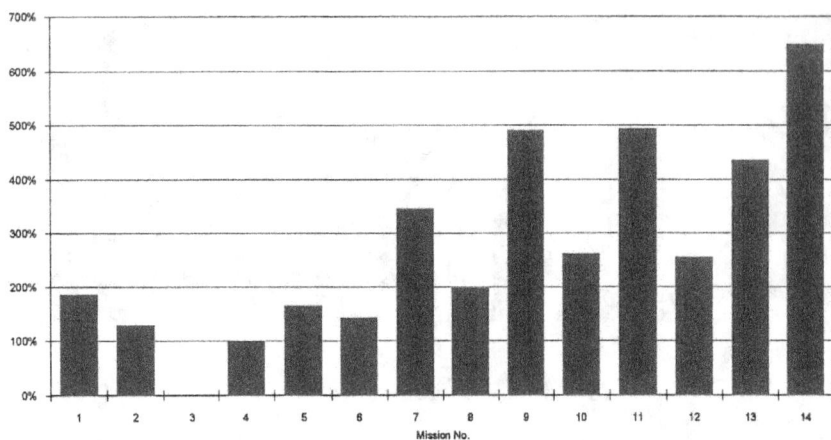

Figure 167: Total Mission Execution Time of LNM Path Compared to Vertex Graph

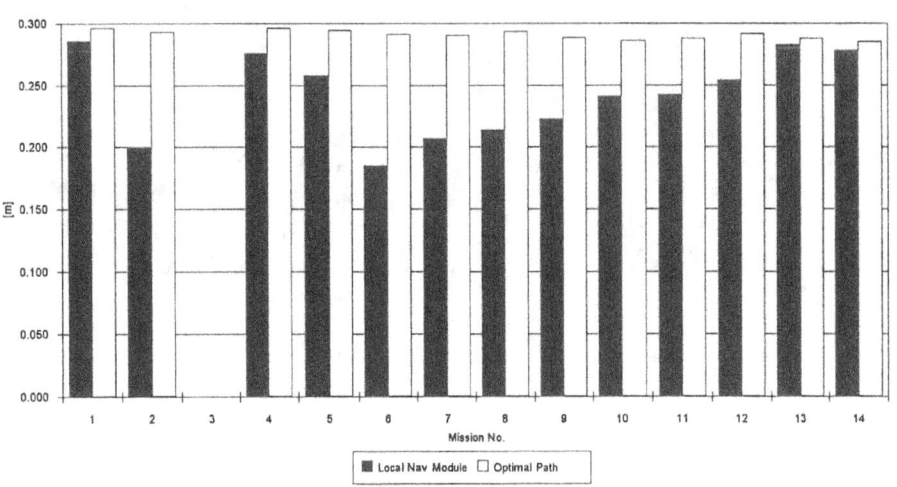

Figure 168: Average Distance between Setpoints d_{sp}

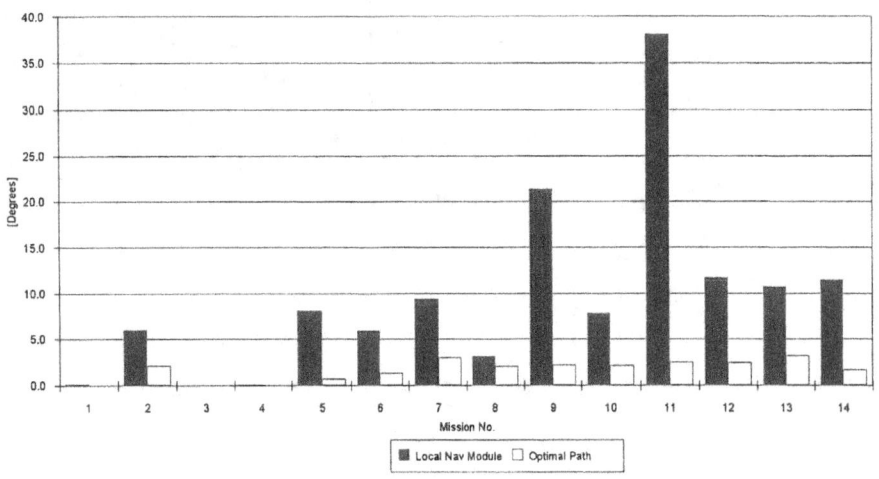

Figure 169: Average Change in Angle between Setpoints

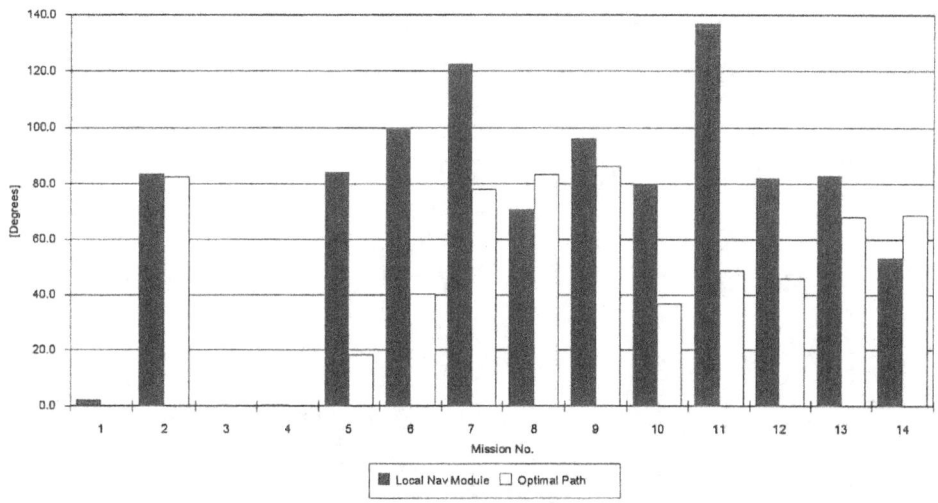

Figure 170: Maximum Change in Angle between Setpoints

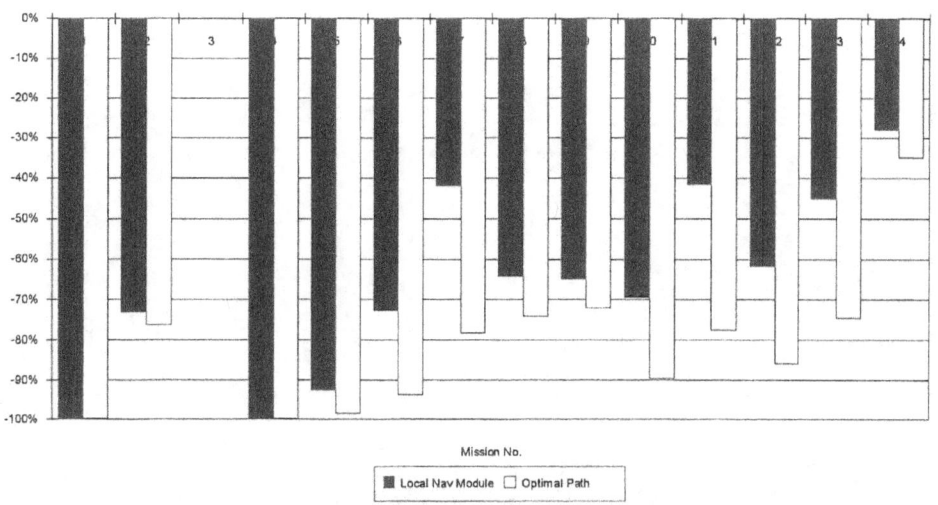

Figure 171: Average Effectivity of Setpoints e_{sp}

The LNM path is of course longer than the Vertex Graph path when Local Re-planning was necessary as in missions 7, 11 and 13, see Figure 169. The mission time (= time the AMV would need to complete the mission if it could follow the desired velocity exactly) is longer for the LNM when the total path length is longer, missions 7, 11, 13, and 14, and if the path is more curvy, i.e. the average change in angle is high like in mission 9, see Figure 169.

The oscillating path in mission 9 at the corner leads to an interesting result: in chapter 5.2.3.3.2.4.1 the shape of the repulsive force field was determined such that oscillations would not occur when a path along a straight wall is determined. This does apparently not guarantee a smooth path when passing a corner. It seems more appropriate to decompose the repulsive force vector generally in a component parallel to the current moving direction and a component perpendicular as sketched in Figure 172. The first component's effect is an „acceleration" or

„deceleration" of the AMV, respectively, i.e. a larger of smaller distance between the position setpoints, the latter would influence the direction of the path.

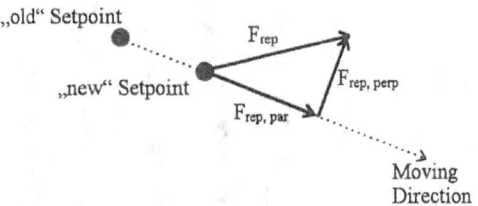

Figure 172: Decomposition of the Repulsive Force

The condition for a straight line path would then be a disappearing perpendicular force component.

5.3 Sensor Model and Map Building

5.3.1 Sensor Model

5.3.1.1 Sensors for Map Building

Many sensor types are used in AMVs to collect information about the environment: Radar, infrared (IR), ultrasonic (US), single-camera-vision, stereo-vision, touch, torque, pressure, etc. sensors. Some sensor data can be used to measure physical properties directly, e.g. temperature, pressure, distance, some is used to get higher level information, e.g. feature extraction/ recognition. Using different types of sensors to measure the same property can enhance the information significantly. Ambiguous, inaccurate or missing sensor data can be filtered and improved. Many different techniques have been discussed to combine signals of various sensors: Flynn [53] describes rules to fuse IR and US sensor readings, Thomopoulos [54] presents a general approach for data fusion independent from any particular sensor types, and Shafer et al. [55] use a whiteboard for sensor data fusion in their NAVLAB vehicle. Beckermann [56] describes the application of a Bayes-Maximum-Entropy method for the fusion of US and vision sensor data.

In map building for navigation purposes it is essential to detect obstacles, their size and position. Two common methods can be distinguished: measuring a relatively large are at once and extracting features, their size and position (Figure 173) or measuring the distance to the closest distance in a sensor beam in several directions with higher angular resolution (Figure 174).

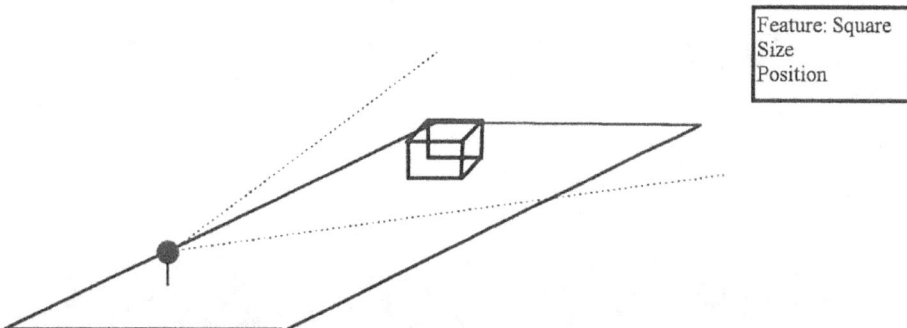

Figure 173: Obstacle Determination through Feature Extraction

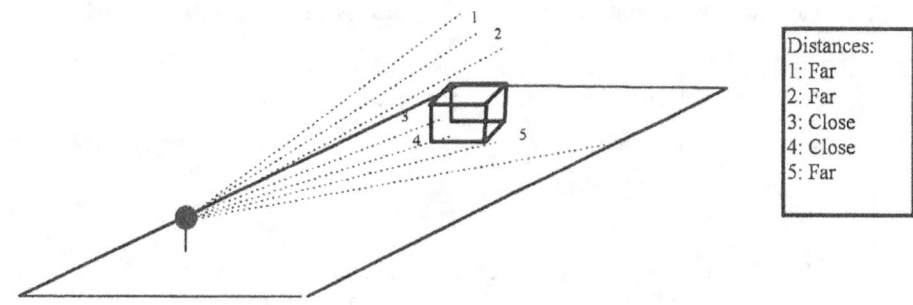

Figure 174: Obstacle Determination through Multiple Distance Measurements

The second method using range sensors is most common since feature extraction and identification is computationally very expensive. Map building and maintenance is a task that has to be done in real-time. Among range finders ultrasonic sensors are widely, they are relatively cheap and easy to use. SUAVE is equipped with ultrasonic range sensors (see chapter 5.3.1). These sensors operate at a sound frequency of 40 kHz and their beams form an angle of 22.5°.

5.3.1.2 Ultrasonic Sensor Modelling

Ultrasonic sensors use time-of-flight measurements (ToF) of the return echo of a sound impulse to measure the distance to the nearest sound reflecting object in the beam [57]. If no return echo s detected no sound reflecting object is in the beam up to the distance of the sensing range (which is limited due to the sensitivity of the receiver and the decreasing intensity of the sound impulse due to resistance in the air). The accuracy of this measurement depends on the accuracy of the anticipated speed of sound, and therefore on the air temperature, pressure, etc. Its resolution depends in a digital implementation on the frequency of the digital counter.

The sensors used in SUAVE assume a speed of sound of

$$v_{soiund} = 343 \frac{m}{s}$$

and operate at a counter frequency of

$$f_c = 1 \text{ MHz}$$

with a variation of approximately

$$\Delta f_c \approx \pm 0.5 \text{ KHz}$$

This results in a resolution of

$$\Delta d_{min} = \frac{1}{2} * \frac{v_{sound}}{f_c}$$

$$= 0.175 \text{ mm}$$

[30.]

and an accuracy due to the variation of f_c of ± 0.1 % of the measured distance d.

After an ultrasonic sensor is triggered and the distance to the nearest object is measured this information has to be translated into information useful for the map building process, i.e. in P and D values for the Local Map. This requires two steps:

- Determining which nodes are affected by this sensor reading
- Determining a probability value P_s for each node that reflects the probability that this node is occupied according to this sensor reading

The first task is relatively easy. Nodes outside the sensor beam are not affected. Nodes inside the beam are empty between the sensor and the measured distance to the obstacle. At the measured position of the obstacle the nodes are occupied, and nodes behind the obstacle can not be affected, again. Incorporating probabilistic behaviour of the sensors, a normal distribution of the variation of the distance measurements is assumed. This normal distribution is described by the measured distance as the mean, and the standard deviation is assumed to be known as a linear function of the measured distance:

$$\sigma_s = f(d_s)$$

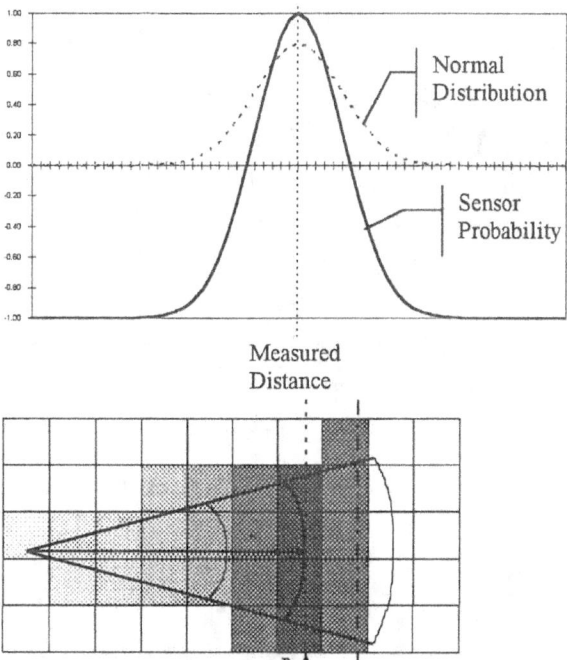

Figure 175: From Normal Distribution to Sensor Probability P_s

The probabilities of the normal distribution is then translated into P_s, the node probability with a range of *-1* to *+1* as outlined in Figure 175; the darker the nodes the higher the probability.

The normal distribution might be stretched symmetrically around the mean value by half the sensor resolution in each direction. This change in the model is more correct, but does not lead to major changes in the result and requires additional computational efforts.

The functional dependency of the standard deviation of the measured distance $\sigma_s = f(d_s)$ was determined in a series of experiments under the following conditions:

- Air temperature approximately 20°
- Air pressure approximately 1atm
- Measured distance to a brick wall at approximately 1000/ 2000/ 3000/ 4000/ 5000 mm
- 1 measurement every 0.8 s
- 1000 measurements for each distance

The measured distance, the mean and the standards deviation are shown for each of the five series in Figures 176 to 180.

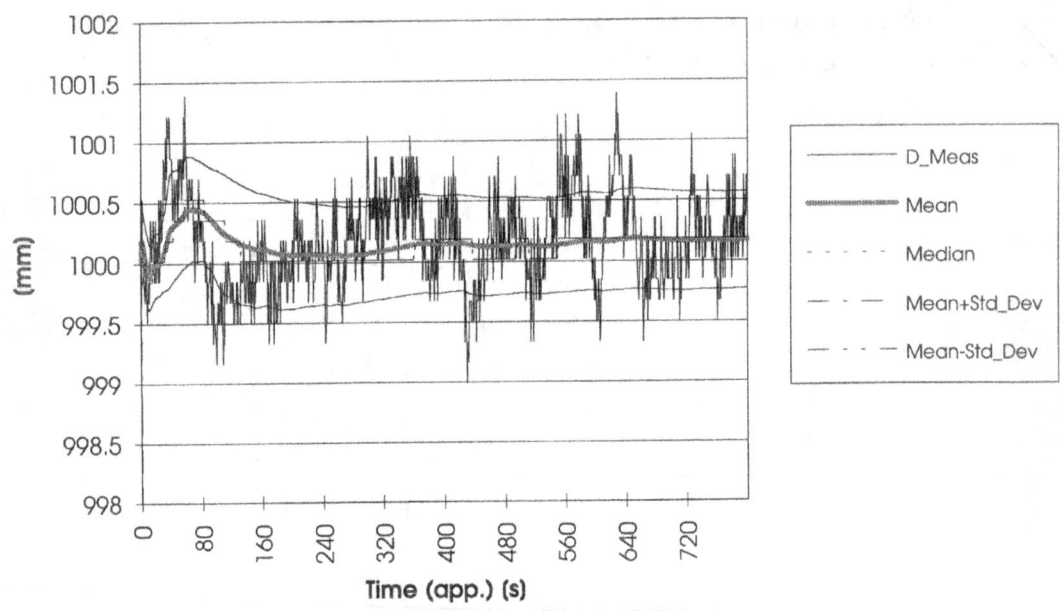

Figure 176: Distance Measurements at 1000 mm

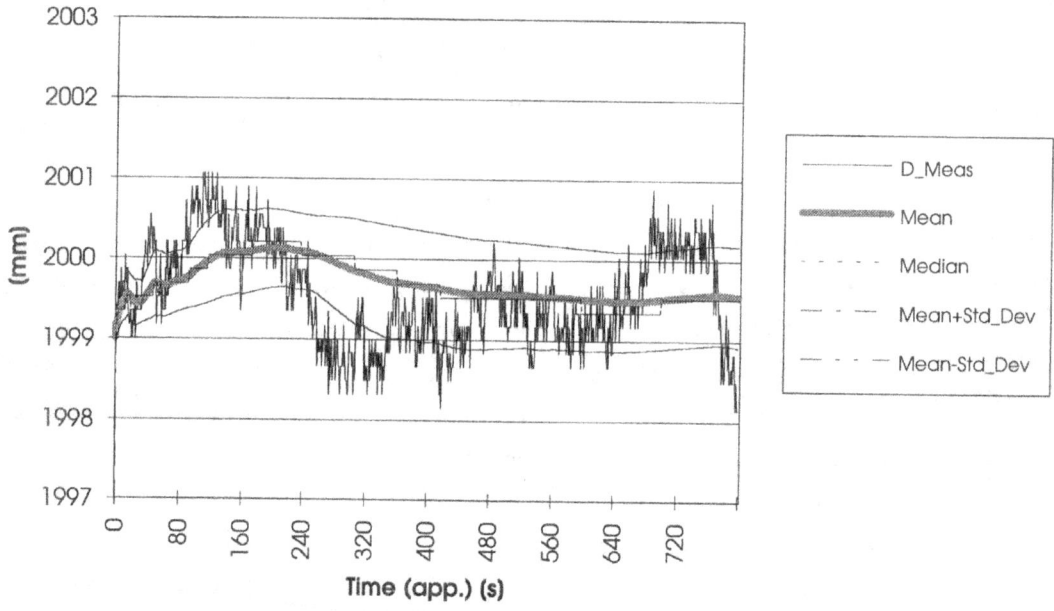

Figure 177: Distance Measurements at 2000 mm

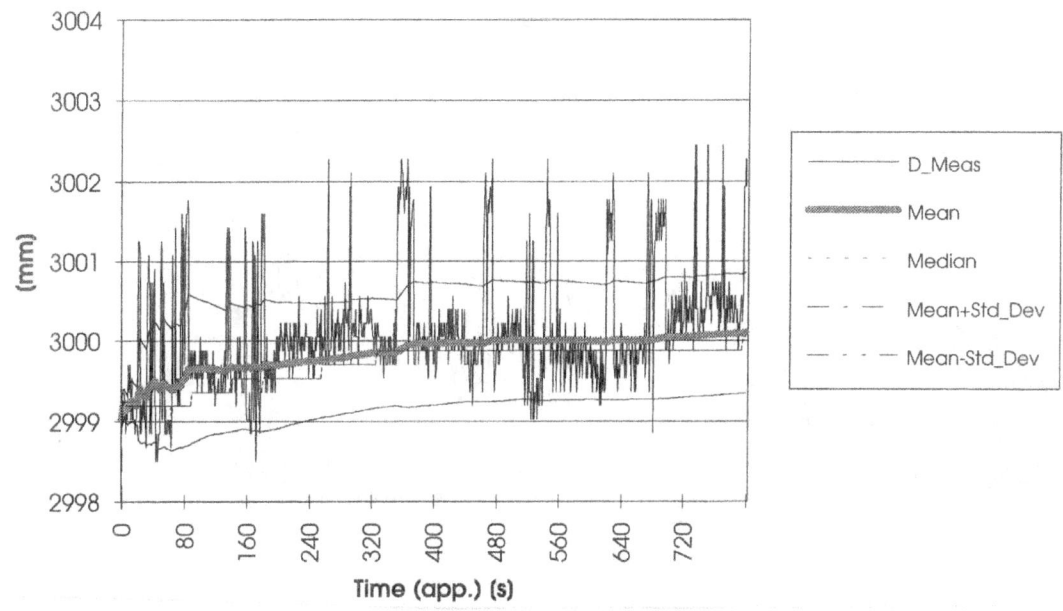

Figure 178: Distance Measurements at 3000 mm

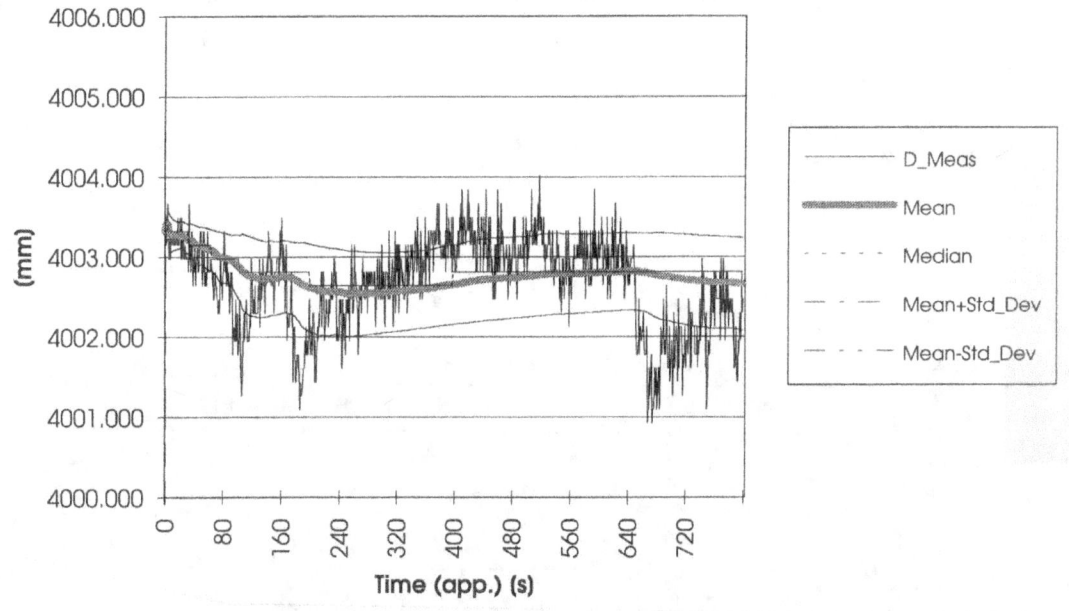

Figure 179: Distance Measurements at 4000 mm

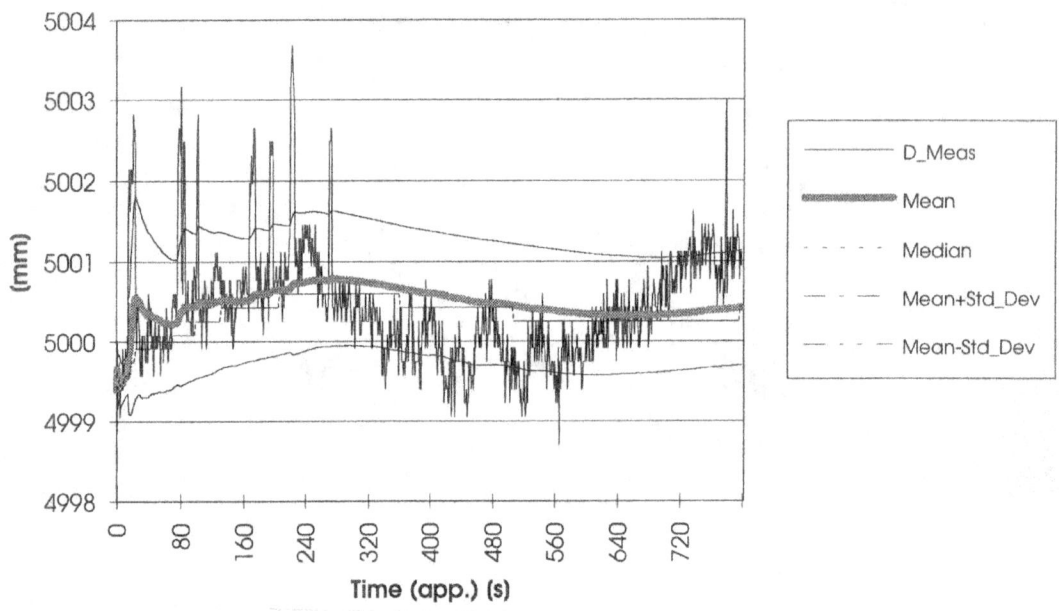

Figure 180: Distance Measurements at 5000 mm

The desired function is determined in a linear regression with regression coefficient *0.66* to

$$\sigma_s = 5.85 * 10^{-5} \, \frac{1}{mm} \, * d + 0.440042 \text{ mm} \qquad [31.]$$

which is shown in Figure 181.

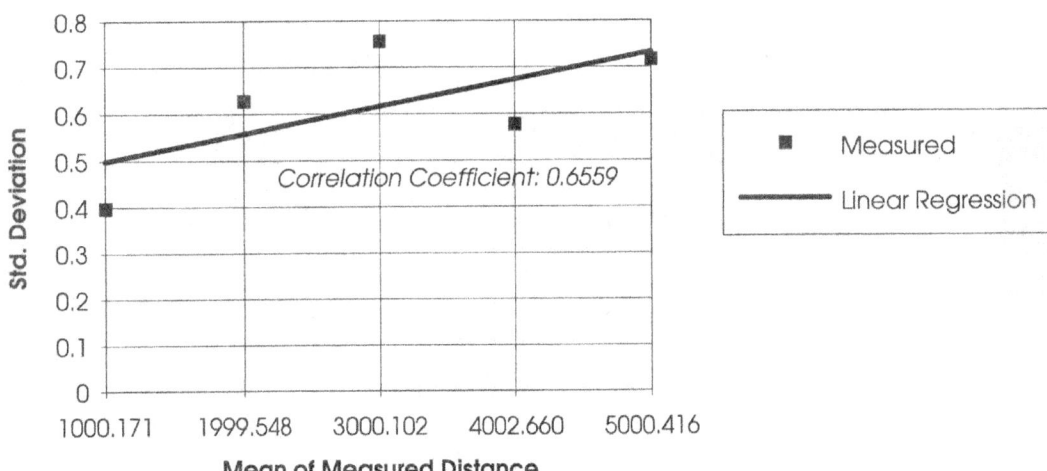

Figure 181: Standard Deviation as Function of Distance

In order to judge if the assumption of normally distributed distance values is feasible the measured values for the distance of *4000mm* are used to determine the real probability and are compared to the theoretical normal distribution (Figure 182).

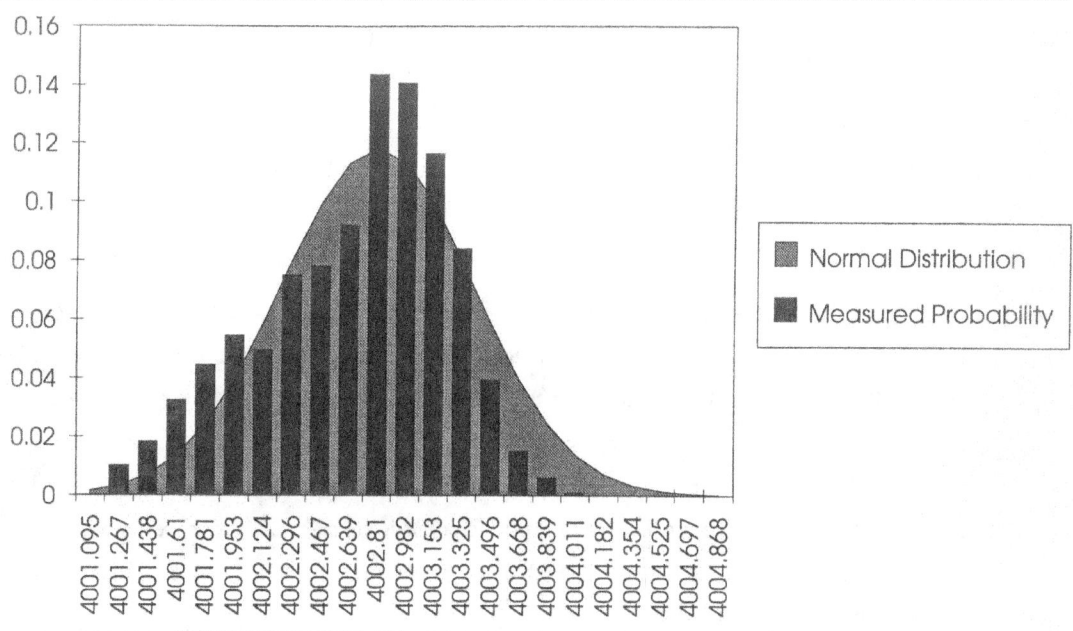

Figure 182: Normal Distribution Compared with Measured Values

5.3.2 Map Building Module

5.3.2.1 Introduction

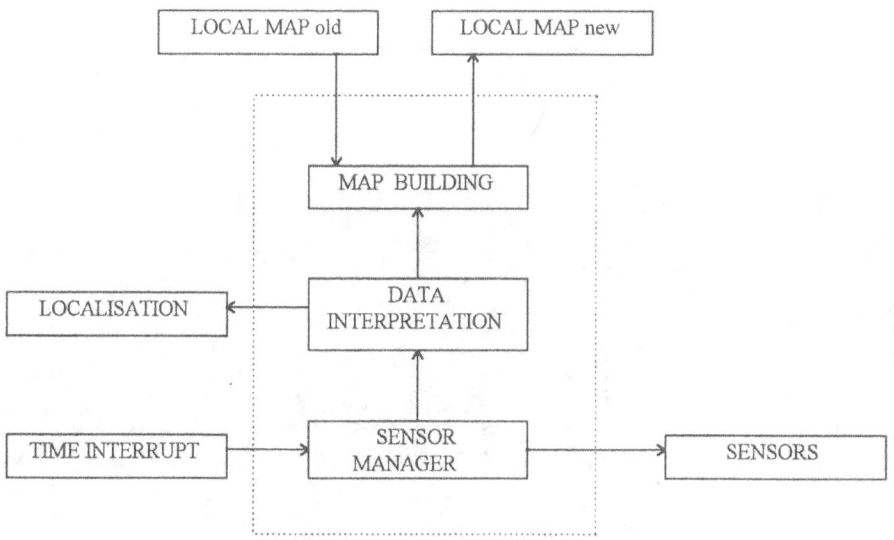

Figure 183: Map Building

Map Building is the link between the sensor system and the Local Map. It uses the current state of the Local Map and the collected sensor data in order to update the Local Map. Inputs to the Map Building module are

- Local Map probability $P_{m,\,old}$
- Local Map dynamics $D_{m,\,old}$
- Sensor probability P_s
- Sensor dynamics D_s

for each node in the Local Map.

In the current implementation a time-interrupt triggers all 24 sensors subsequently to obtain a *360°* scan. After each sensor has been triggered and the raw data has been collected (distance measurement) Map Building searches the entire Local Map for nodes that lie within the beam of the sensor. For these node P_s and D_s are determined as described in chapter 5.3.1.2, and the updated values $P_{m,\,new}$ and •are written to the Local Map. If necessary the nodes are splitted at the edge of the sensor beam. After the Local Map values have been updated the QDS is compressed, i.e. quadruples of nodes with the same parent node are deleted if they have the same probability and dynamics value and these values are transferred to their parent node. For detailed information about these QDS tree operations the reader is referred to [59].

The Map Building should at all times maintain a Local Map that is sufficient in accuracy and that models changes in the environment quickly. The direct use of the sensor probability and dynamics for each node P_s and D_s would result in a very reactive map, thus does not account for noise in the distance reading and false readings due to multiple specular reflections of the sensor beam. These are the two main problems when using ultrasonic sensors for map building. Multiple specular reflections of the ultrasonic sensor beam result in a longer ToF measurement and lead to "virtual holes" as shown in Figure 184.

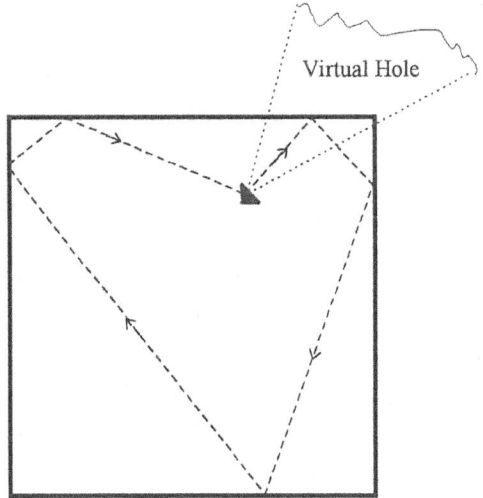

Virtual Hole

Figure 184: Virtual Hole due to Multiple Specular Reflection

Noise in the distance reading leads to noise in the sensor probability and dynamics for the affected nodes. This noise can be filtered with a Kalman Filter. Kalman Filters are widely and successfully used to filter noisy measurements. The Kalman Filter makes use of a node model that describes the behaviour of the node values P_m and D_m.

In order to filter sensor readings that seem very unlikely, e.g. the sudden disappearance of a static obstacle due to multiple specular reflections, a prediction model is be used. Sensor readings that oppose the prediction can be used for map building with reduced weight or might be rejected entirely.

Figure 185 shows an overview of the map building modules.

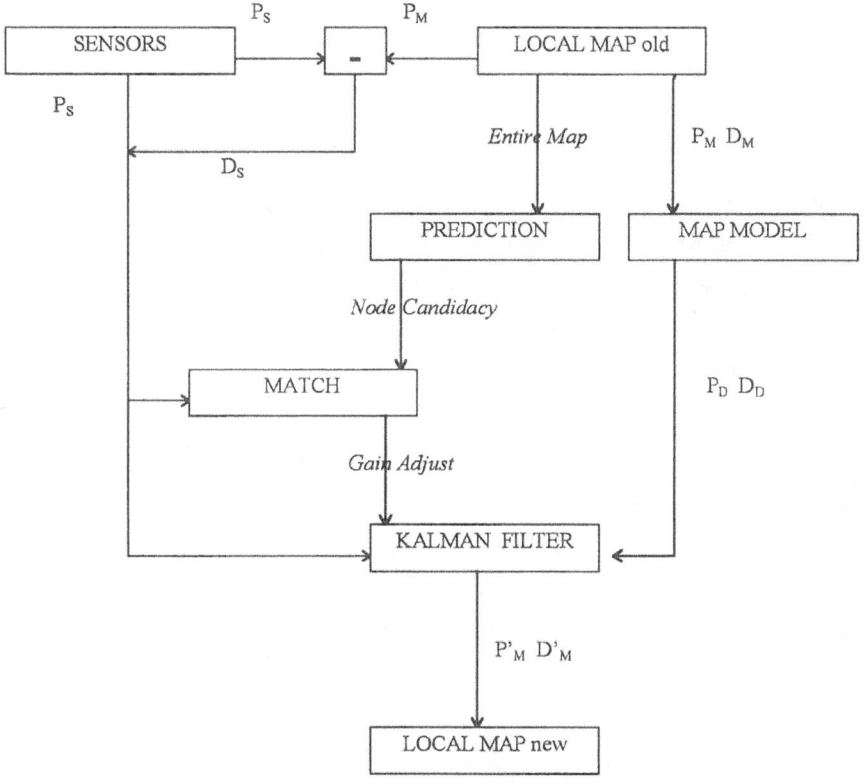

Figure 185: Overview Map Building Modules

The procedure in Figure 185 is to be done for each node affected by a sensor reading, i.e. that is in the sensor beam. The state vector of the sensor data

$$x_S = \begin{bmatrix} P_S \\ D_S \end{bmatrix} \quad [32.]$$

contains the sensor probability P_s determined according to chapter 5.3.1.2 and is completed with a pseudo measurement D_s with

$$D_S = P_S - P_M \quad [33.]$$

The map state vector

$$x_M = \begin{bmatrix} P_M \\ D_M \end{bmatrix} \quad [34.]$$

is the input for the map model. The entire Local Map is used to predict the behaviour of the nodes by defining a "candidacy" for each node. According to the match of the sensor data with the candidacy of the node the gain of the Kalman Filter is adjusted. Other inputs to the Kalman Filter are the sensor and the model state vector.

5.3.2.2 Map Model
The model describes the behaviour of the map state vector

$$x_M = \begin{bmatrix} P_M \\ D_M \end{bmatrix} \qquad\qquad [35.]$$

However, compared to a mechanical system whose behaviour depends on physical laws it is much harder to find general rules for the node state. Three models are proposed:

Model (I) assumes a static environment that does not change:

$$x_D = \begin{bmatrix} 1 & 0 \\ 0 & 1 \end{bmatrix} * \begin{bmatrix} P_M \\ D_M \end{bmatrix} \qquad\qquad [36.]$$

model (II) assumes a constant change in probability values, i.e. constant dynamics:

$$x_D = \begin{bmatrix} 1 & 2 \\ 0 & 1 \end{bmatrix} * \begin{bmatrix} P_M \\ D_M \end{bmatrix} \qquad\qquad [37.]$$

and model (III) defines a nonlinear relationship between map and model state vector:

$$X_D = \begin{bmatrix} P_D \\ D_D \end{bmatrix}$$
$$= \begin{bmatrix} \begin{cases} 2(P_M + D_M) + P_M D_M & \forall & 2(P_M + D_M) + P_M D_M \ >= -1 \wedge 2(P_M + D_M) + P_M D_M \ <= 1 \\ 1 & \forall & 2(P_M + D_M) + P_M D_M \ > 1 \\ -1 & \forall & 2(P_M + D_M) + P_M D_M \ < -1 \end{cases} \\ D_M \end{bmatrix}$$

$$[38.]$$

These three models are compared in a simulation. A node at a distance of 5 m from the sensor is considered. The node is considered empty for the first 13 measurements and occupied thereafter. The sensor measuring signal is corrupted with noise as shown in Figure 186.

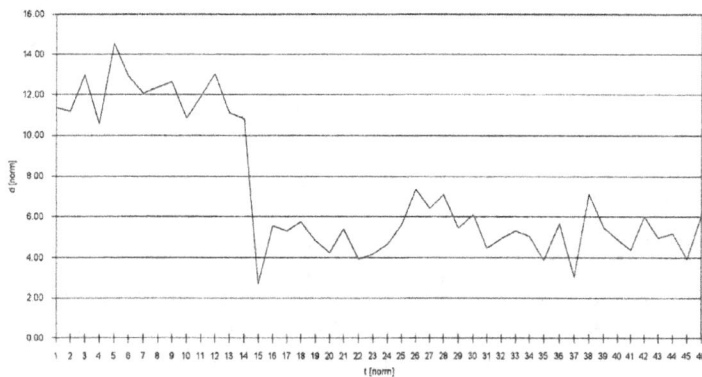

Figure 186: Simulated Distance Readings

The distance measurements are converted into sensor probabilities for this node as described in chapter 5.3.1.2, see Figure 187.

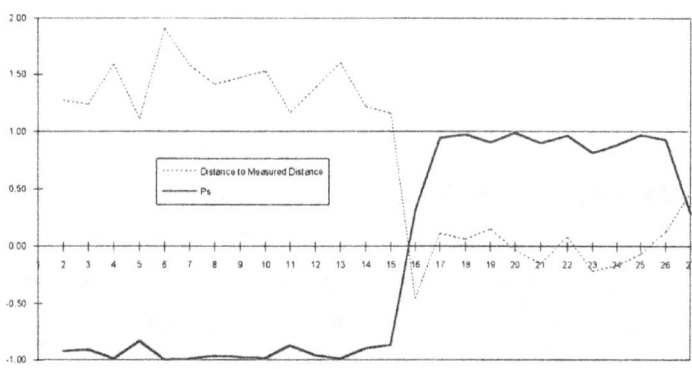

Figure 187: Generated Sensor Probability

This is used to update the state vector of the node and to determine the model state vector in Figure 188.
The node state vector is calculated as the simple average of sensor and model probability for this simulation.

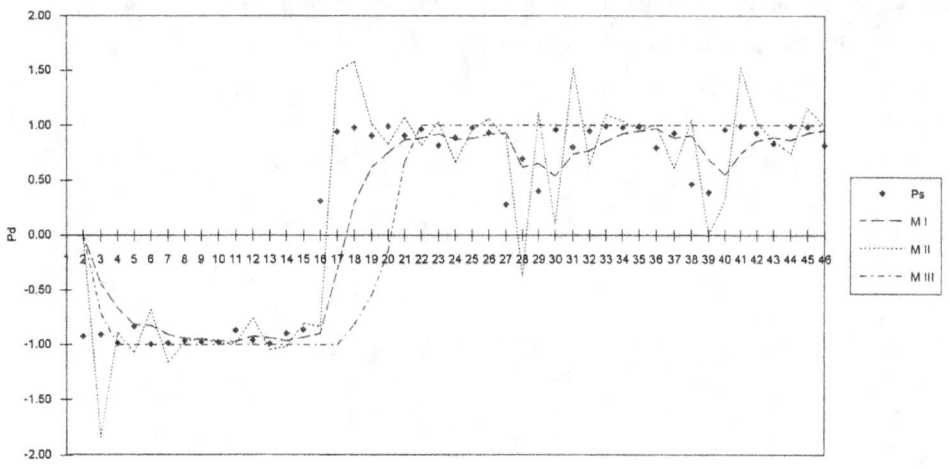

Figure 188: Map Probability for the Three Models

[127]

Model (I) filters part of the noise in the sensor signal. However, it follows the valid change in the sensor reading in measurement 16 with delay, since it assumes a static environment. Model (II) is more reactive, but exhibits obviously a more noisy signal than the original sensor probability. Model (III) is almost noise free, but shows an even greater delay than model (I).

To decide which model to use it is important to consider the task of the model in the map building process. Noise reduction is mainly the task of the Kalman Filter, it seems more important that the reactivity of the map building process is not limited by the model itself. Furthermore if the model is linear the Kalman Filter evaluation is much easier. Additionally the calculation of the model itself should be no more expensive than necessary since this has to be done for each node in the sensor beam.

Considering these factors model (II) is chosen. Model (II) is

- very reactive
- computationally cheap
- linear
- noise amplifying

5.3.2.3 Kalman Filter

Nebot et al. [65] show that for time invariant systems under certain conditions [58] the Kalman Gain G_K approaches a constant value. This is especially important when considering the necessity to perform the map building process on-line. A continuous evaluation of the Kalman Gain would be impossible. Therefore the approximation of a constant Kalman Gain is made. The updating equations become

$$P_{M,new} = P_D + K_G(P_S - P_D)$$
$$D_{M,new} = D_D + K_G(D_S - D_D) \hfill [39.]$$

In this experiment only one sensor is fired towards a straight wall of cardboard in a distance of 5000 mm. The Local Map is initialised as completely unknown ($P_m = D_m = 0$). The map is of a sidelength of 5424 mm. The sensor is placed at the edge of the Local Map, 40 mm from the edge. The map has a maximum resolution of 128 x 128 nodes, i.e. the sidelength of the smallest nodes is 42.4 mm.

The sensor is triggered 50 times and the node probability values are recorded for a slice through the middle of the map.

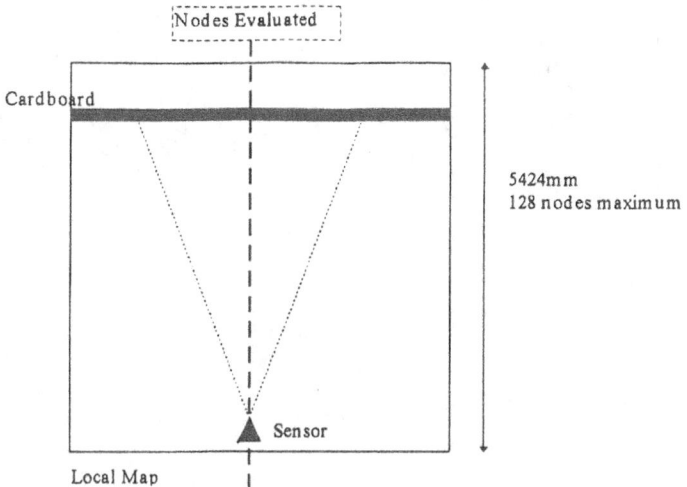

Figure 189: Experimental Setup

The experiment is repeated with different Kalman Gains of *0.1, 0.3, 0.5, 0.7,* and *0.9.*

Figure 190 shows an example of the sensor probability P_s, its variation over all 50 scans can be seen for one of runs in Figure 191. The map probability P_m is shown after 50 scans for one of the runs in Figure 192, and the change in P_m for the 50 scans is shown for $K_G=0.1$ in Figure 193. The learning process of the map from unknown to empty in front of the wall and to full at the wall is shown in Figure 194.

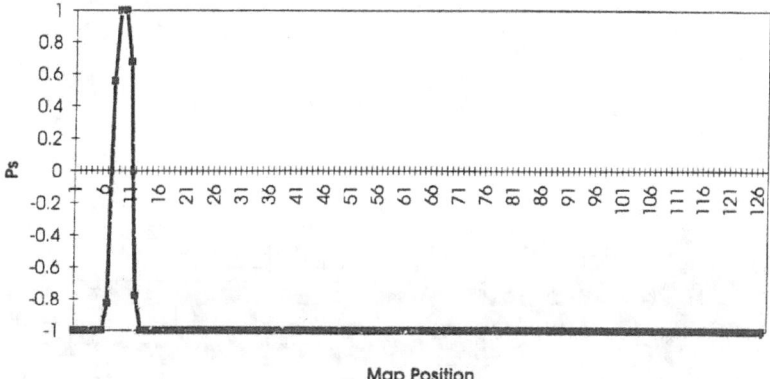

Figure 190: Example for Sensor Probability P_S

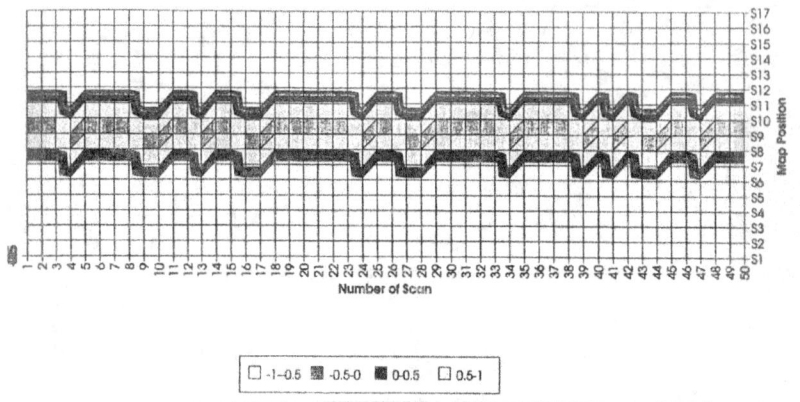

Figure 191: Change of Sensor Probability, Example

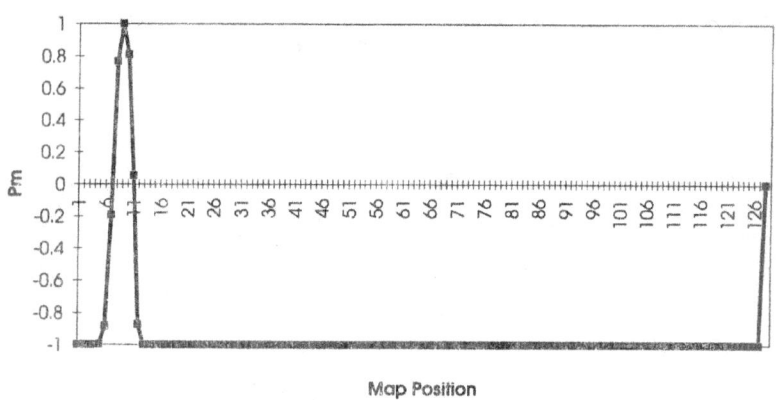

Figure 192: Map Probability after 50 Scans, Example

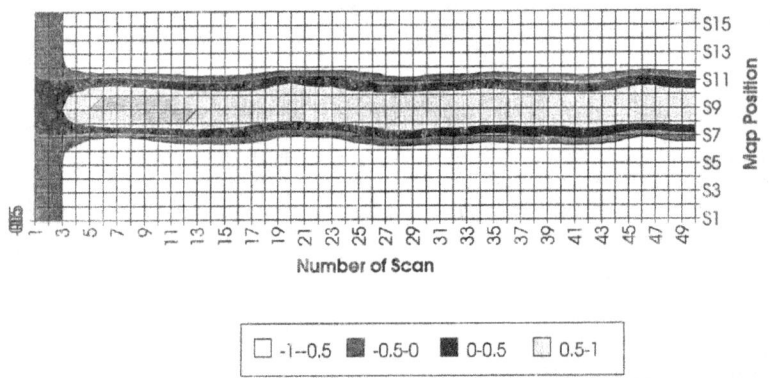

Figure 193: Change of Map Probability, Example

Figures 194 to 201 show the map probabilities for the nodes in the vicinity of the wall for the different Kalman Gains. It can be seen how the map learns the wall and how noise affects the map.

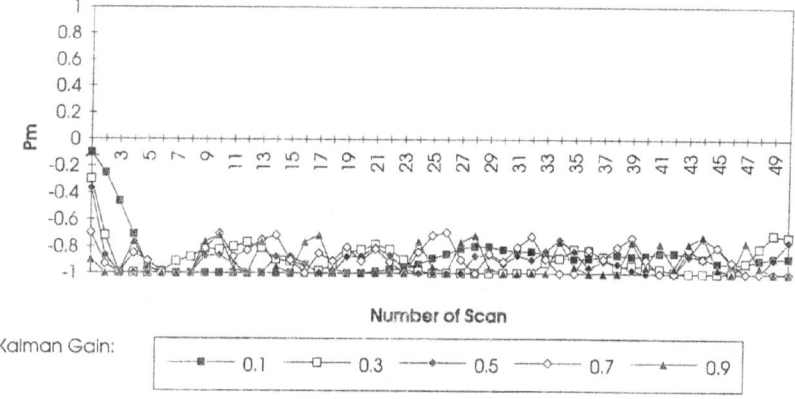

Figure 194: Map Probability for Map Position 6

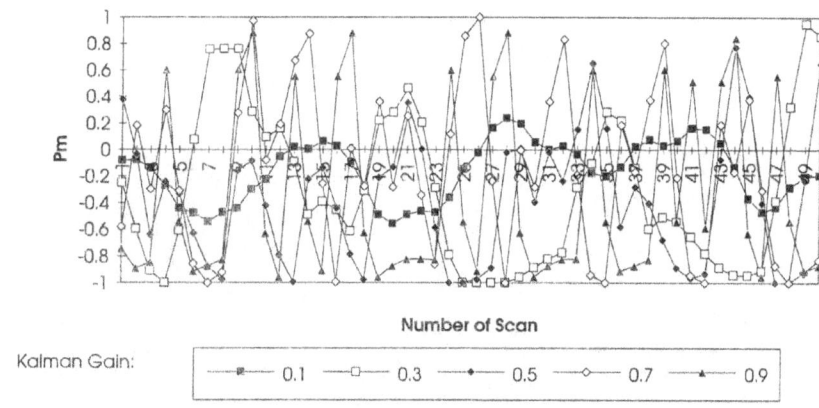

Figure 195: Map Probability for Map Position 7

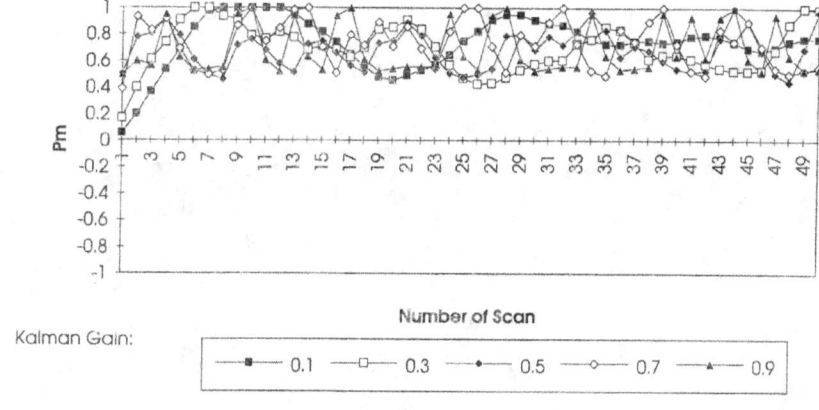

Figure 196: Map Probability for Map Position 8

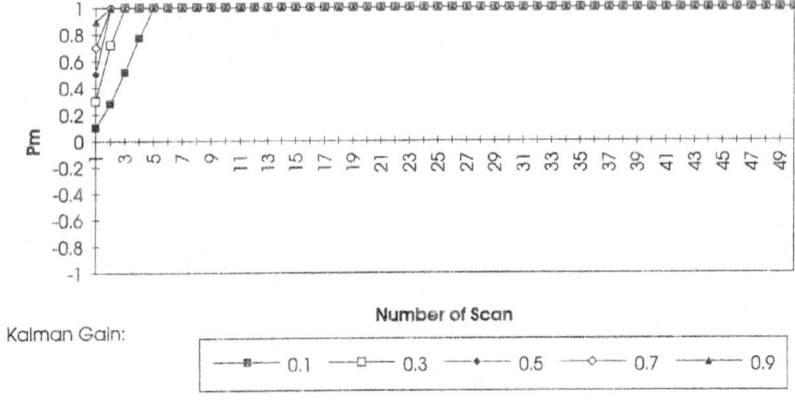

Figure 197: Map Probability for Map Position 9

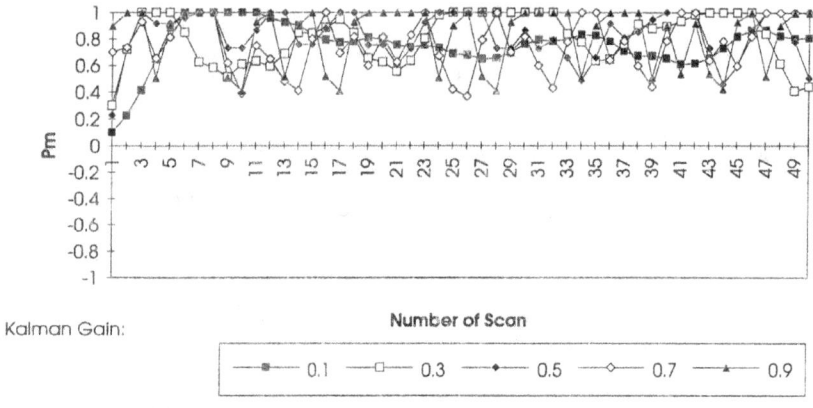

Figure 198: Map Probability for Map Position 10

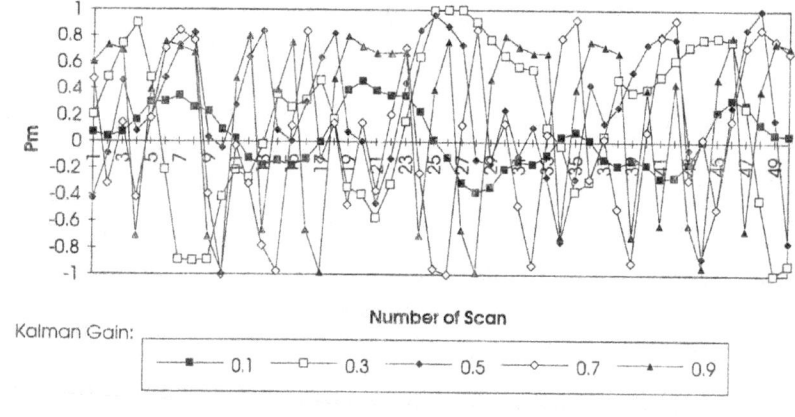

Figure 199: Map Probability for Map Position 11

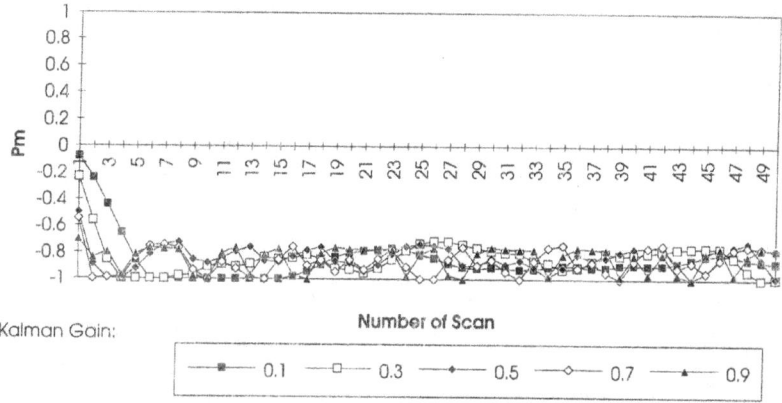

Figure 200: Map Probability for Map Position 12

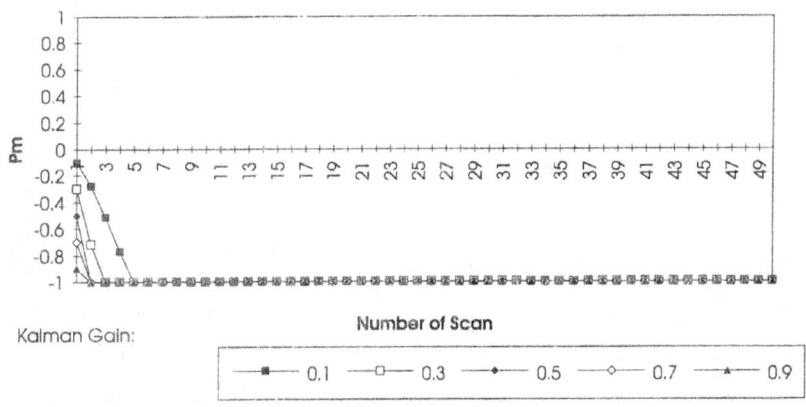

Figure 201: Map Probability for Map Position 13

Map position 13 refers to a node in front of the wall. As expected the larger the Kalman Gain the more quickly the map learns that this node is empty. The Kalman Gain *0.1* needs 5 scans, with *0.9* two scans are sufficient in order to change the map probability to *-1*. Once established the probability does never change from *-1*. The sensor noise has no influence on this node.

Node 12 is close to the wall, thus the noise is of greater influence. The probability varies between -1 and -0.7 for all Kalman Gains.

Node 11 is subject to large variations, the sensor noise could not be filtered sufficiently. The node is undetermined. The probability for $K_G=0.1$ oscillates around a value of approximately *0.1*. For $K_G=0.9$ the probability exhibits almost random behaviour between *-1* and *+1*.

At node 10 the probability is clearly in the positive part of the state space plane. The probability for $K_G=0.1$ varies little around $P_m=0.8$.

Node 9 is right at the position of the wall, its probability rises quickly to *+1* and stays there for all Kalman Gains. Again higher gain leads to a more quickly learning process.

Nodes 8, 7, and 6 behave similar to nodes 10, 11, and 12 due to the symmetry of the sensor model.

In summary a larger Kalman Gain leads to

- quicker learning
- larger variations

of the map probability.

Figure 202 shows the standard deviation of the map probability.

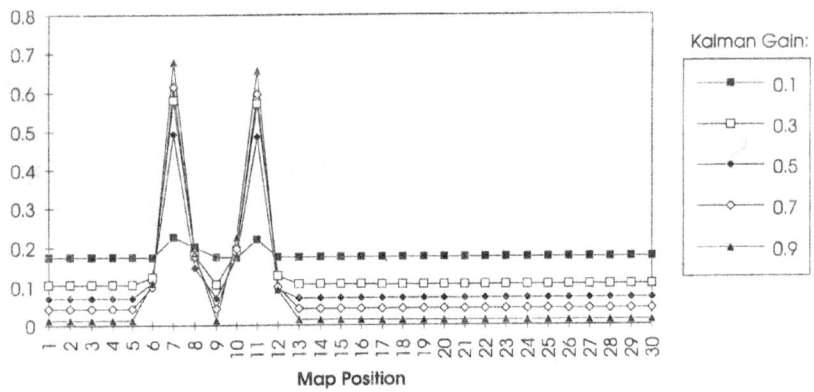

Figure 202: Standard Deviation of the Map Probability P_m

Obviously the standard deviation is minimal for nodes 1 to 6, 9, and 12 to 30 for all Kalman Gains. The lower standard deviation for larger K_G is due to the quicker learning process in the first few scans. The critical nodes are nodes 7 and 11 as observed before. The standard deviation reaches values of up to *0.68* for $K_G = 0.9$. It is surprising that the K_G *0.1* is subject to much less variations than the other values for these nodes. The filtering of the noise is obviously only effectful for $K_G = 0.1$ in this experiment. To assess the noise reduction effect better the ratio of the standard deviation of the sensor probability to the standard deviation of the map probability $\dfrac{\sigma(P_s)}{\sigma(P_M)}$ is shown in Figure 203.

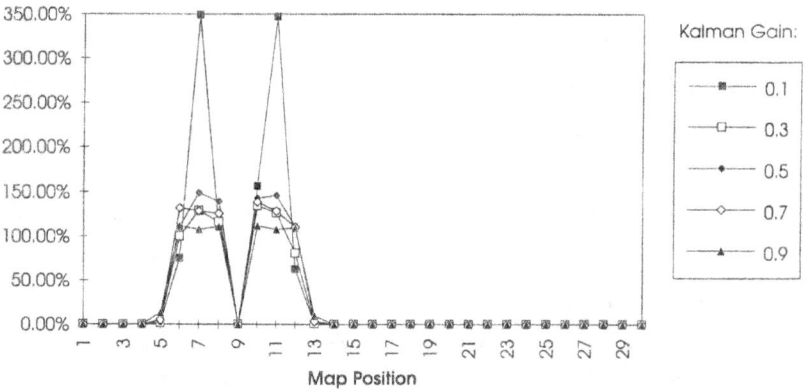

Figure 203: Ratio $\dfrac{\sigma(P_s)}{\sigma(P_M)}$

[134]

Disregarding the zero values, there is no noise to be filtered, the ration lies most of the times above the threshold of 100%, where the noise of the sensor is larger in the sensor signal than in the map probability. Interesting is the fact that the extremes values are both for $K_G = 0.1$.

5.3.2.4 Prediction

Prediction is the only part of the map building module that takes more than one node into account. Prediction should eliminate or weaken observations that are unlikely to be true. Examples are extremely quick changes in the environment configuration, e.g. disappearing objects, that usually are created by multiple specular reflections. Prediction also improves the reactivity of the map building process if moving obstacles can be detected as such and their path can be predicted.

All nodes in the Local Map become a candidacy assigned which determines possible changes in their state that are likely. Possible candidacies are

- Change of P_M unlikely, P^0
- Increasing P_M possible, P^+
- Decreasing P_M possible, P^-
- Increasing or Decreasing P_M possible, P^{+-}

One attempt to determine these candidacies is to detect possible paths of moving obstacles by connecting TIP and TALE nodes. The candidacies are then defined as shown in Figure 204 where one TAIL-TIP corridor is omitted for simplicity.

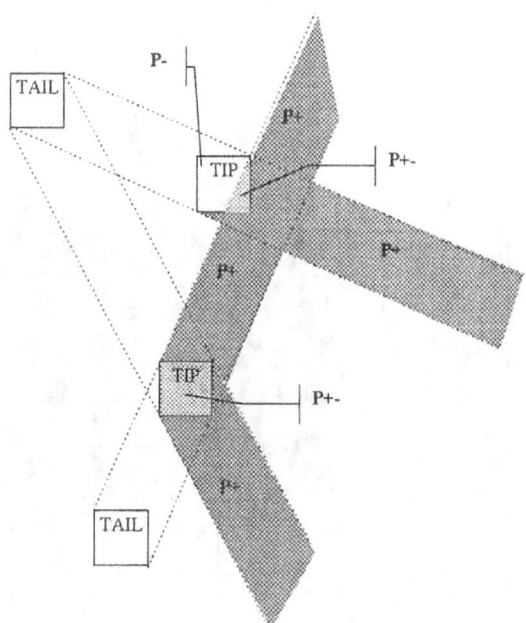

Figure 204: Definition of Candidacies for Prediction

A prediction model has not been implemented yet.

5.3.3 Map Building Experiments

5.3.3.1 *Mapping a Static Environment*

5.3.3.1.1 Sensor Probability Map

In this experiment a squared room built of cardboard is mapped. The Local Map has here a maximum resolution of 128x128 nodes. The map printouts show the sensor probability of the nodes as

WHITE	$P_S \approx 0$
BLACK	$P_S > 0.7$
DARK GREY	$P_S < -0.7$
LIGHT GREY	$-0.7 \leq P_S \leq 0.7$

In Figure 205 the sensor was placed in the middle of the room, in Figure 206 in the upper right-hand corner, in Figure 207 in the upper left-hand corner, and in Figure 208 in the lower right-hand corner of the room. In Figure 209 a door at the bottom of the room was opened, the sensor was placed in the middle of the room.

The arcs of the sensor beam a clearly visible. Corners of the room are not sharp due to limited angular resolution (beam width). Multiple reflections are obvious as "holes" in the walls.

The efficiency of the QDS is apparent: the area of free space in the middle of the room can be represented with only a few nodes. At the walls where a higher resolution is necessary, the resolution is increased as necessary.

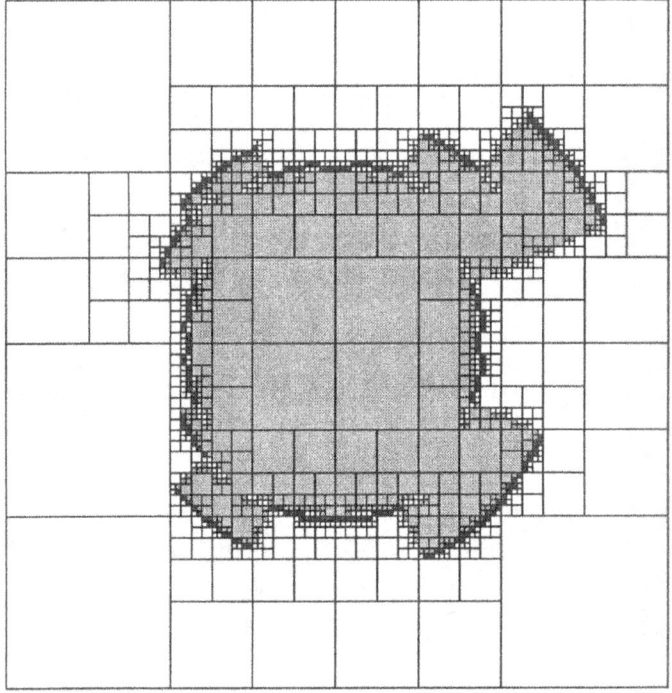

Figure 205: P$_s$ Mapping a Squared Room, Sensor in Middle

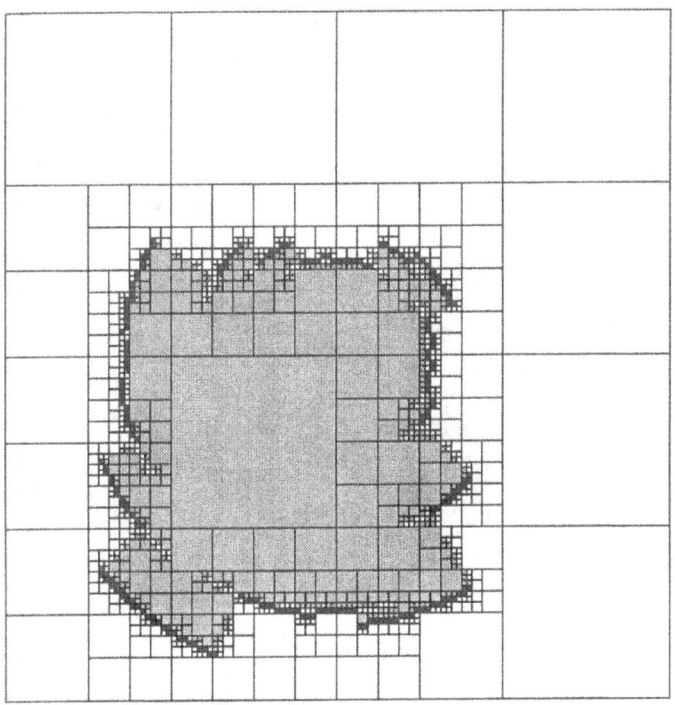

Figure 206: P$_s$ Mapping a Squared Room, Sensor in Upper Right-Hand Corner

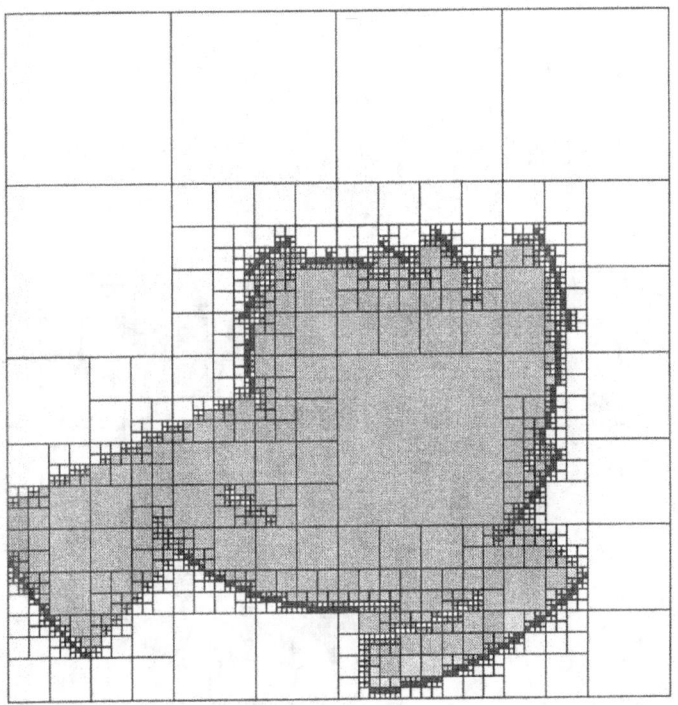

Figure 207: P$_s$ Mapping a Squared Room, Sensor in Upper Left-Hand Corner

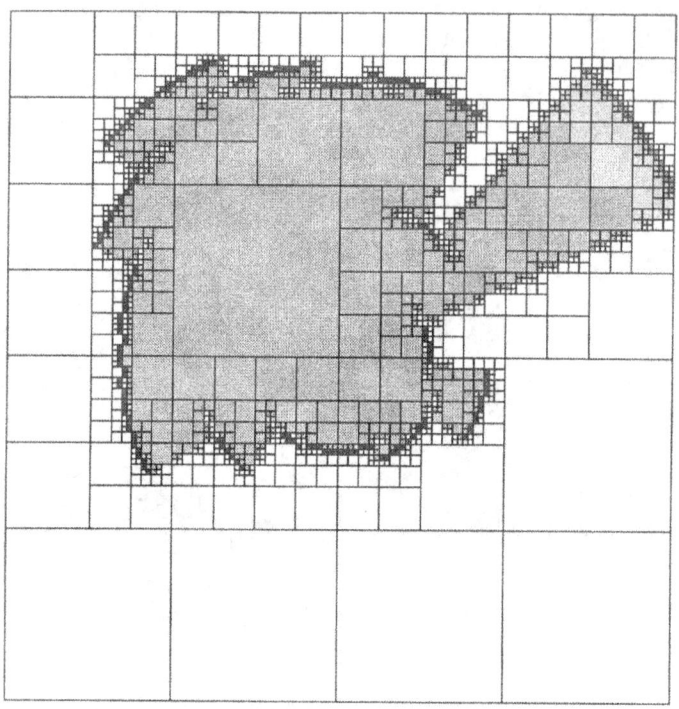

Figure 208: Pₛ Mapping a Squared Room, Sensor in Lower Roght-Hand Corner

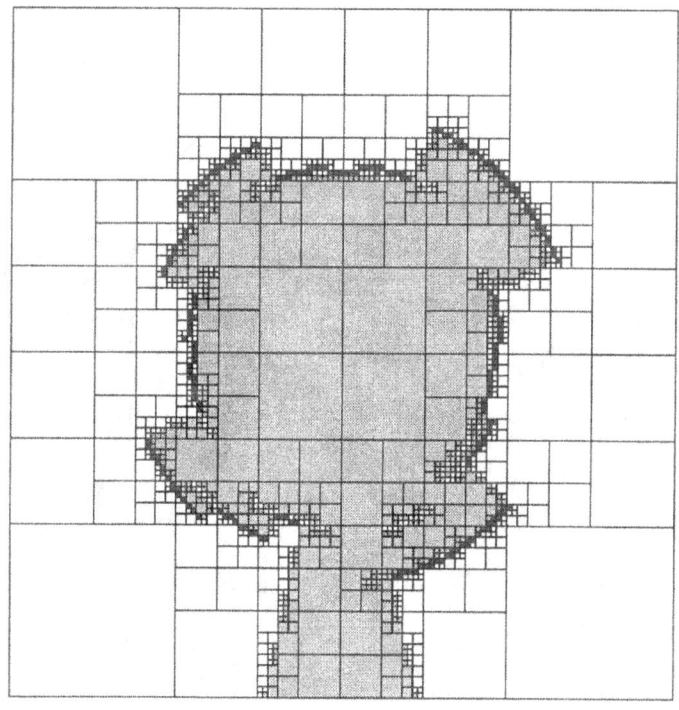

Figure 209: Pₛ Mapping a Squared Room With an Open Door, Sensor in Middle

The arcs resulting from the sensor model as part of the sensor beam are forming the walls of the room. In Fog. 204 straight walls are composed of many of these arcs that are all detected the wall at the same position. The corners are reflected by larger parts of an arc. The efficiency of the QDS is apparent: the middle area of the room for example is covered by only four nodes of the fourth level (the entire tree has eight levels for this map). At the walls a higher resolution is necessary and these nodes are of the eighth level. In figure 207 and 208 the effect of multiple specular reflections is shown: a "hole" in the wall appears.

5.3.3.1.2 Node State Map

Again a squared room is mapped. The room is built of cardboard with a sidelength of *3000mm*. The sensor is placed in the middle, the Local Map resolution is limited to 64x64 nodes. The Kalman Gain is chosen as $K_G=0.6$, and the threshold for the dynamic node states is chosen as $D_{th}=0.2$. Distance values that are larger than the diagonal of the room are rejected since they must clearly originate from multiple reflections.

The printouts of the Local Map show the state of the nodes. The following coding is used:

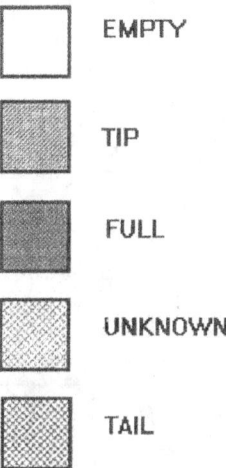

Figure 210: Legend of Node States

Figure 211 shows the initial state of the map: all nodes are UNKNOWN.

Figure 211: Initially: All Nodes are Unknown

After the first scan the nodes of free space are TAILs, nodes at walls are TIPs and nodes out of the reach of the sensors remain UNKNOWN.

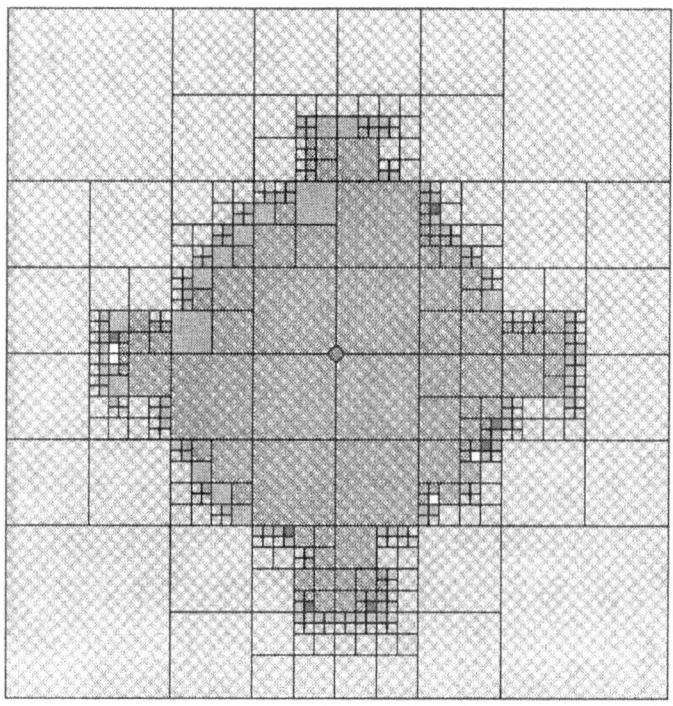

Figure 212: Scan 1: Learning the Environment

In scan three the learning process is not yet completed, the nodes remain dynamic.

After three scans most nodes are static: FULL at walls, EMPTY at free space. The nodes that remain dynamic have not clearly been identified, yet. This is due to multiple reflections or sensor noise. Two multiple reflections are clearly present in Figure 213.

One of the multiple reflections is removed after the fourth scan where the echo could be received correctly.

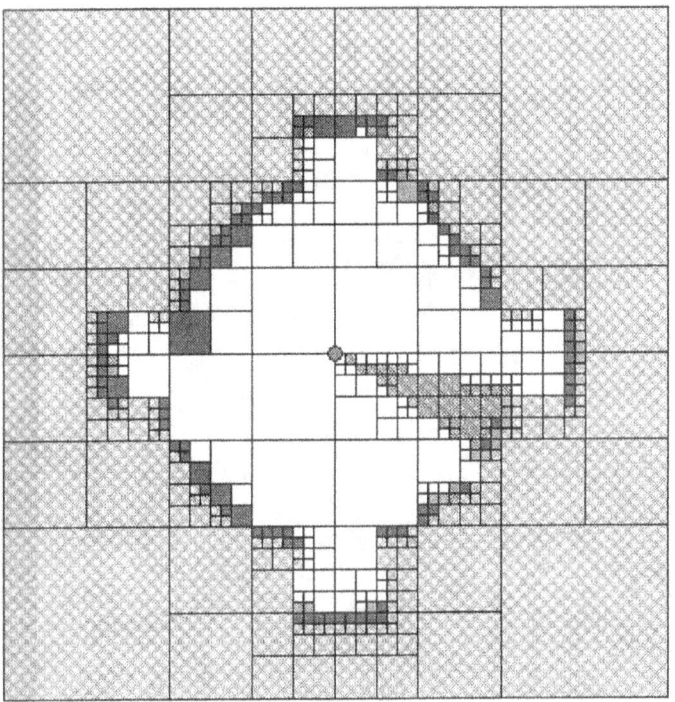

Figure 213: Scan 4: Most Parts of the Environment are Known

In Figure 214 after the fifth scan the second multiple reflection is removed, but a new mis-measuremend in the lower left-hand part of the room has caused these nodes to change from static to dynamic values.

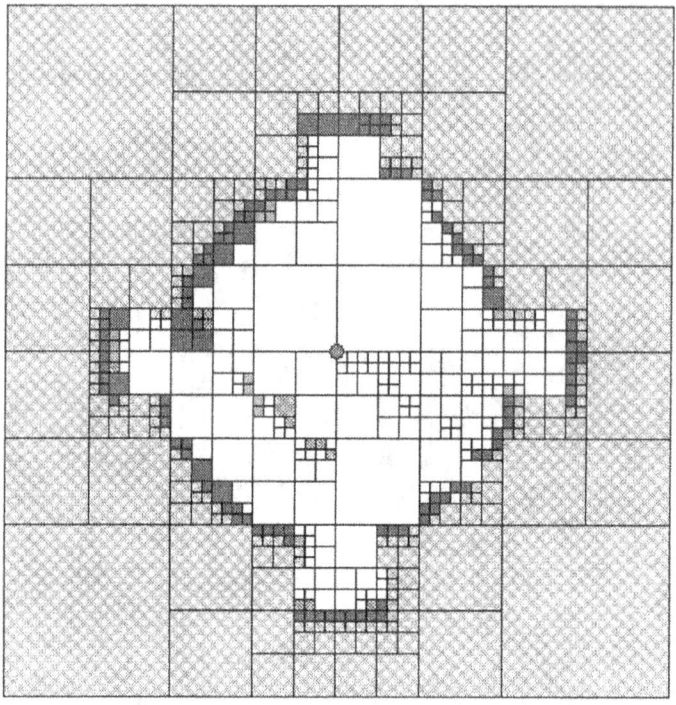

Figure 214: Scan 5: Only Slight Changes in the Map

Again the sensor arcs are visible. The node state show how the map "learns" the environment: a completely
UNKNOWN map in figure 211 is transformed into the map in figure 214. The nodes that were covered by a
sensor beam and get a probability of less than *0* assigned have negative dynamics and are TAILs. The ones with a
probability of higher than *0* at the walls are TIPs. In figure 214 this learning process is mostly completed. The
majority of the nodes is static, either FULL, EMPTY or UNKNOWN.

5.3.3.2 Mapping a Dynamic Environment

5.3.3.2.1 Moving Obstacle in Free Space

In an otherwise empty environment a cylindrical moving obstacle of a diameter of approximately *45 cm* is mapped
in a static and empty environment. The obstacle moves with a relative velocity of *30cm* per scan from the left to
the right in the map. The maximum resolution of the Local Map is set to *64 x 64* nodes, its sidelength is *4500mm*.
The Kalman Gain is set to *0.9* to increase the reactivity of the map, the state threshold is set to $D_{th}=0.1$.

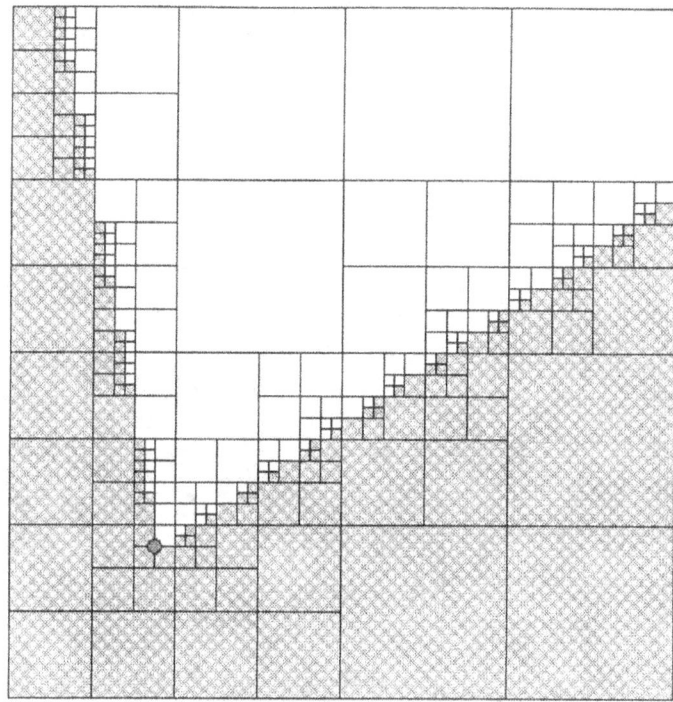

Figure 215: Scan 1

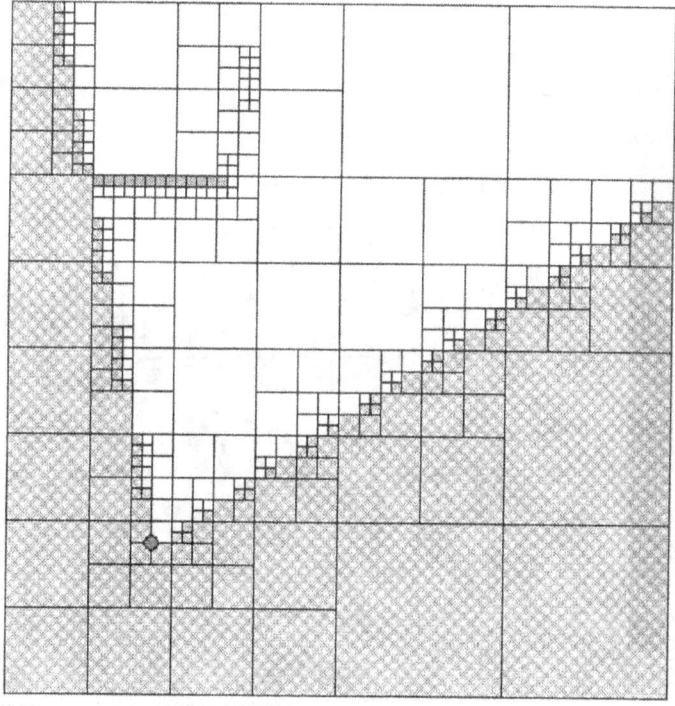

Figure 216: Scan 2

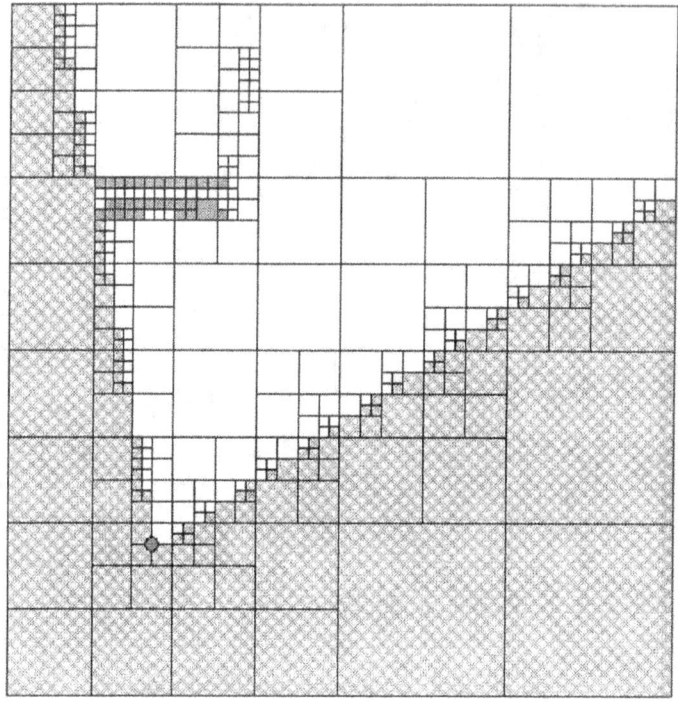

Figure 217: Scan 3

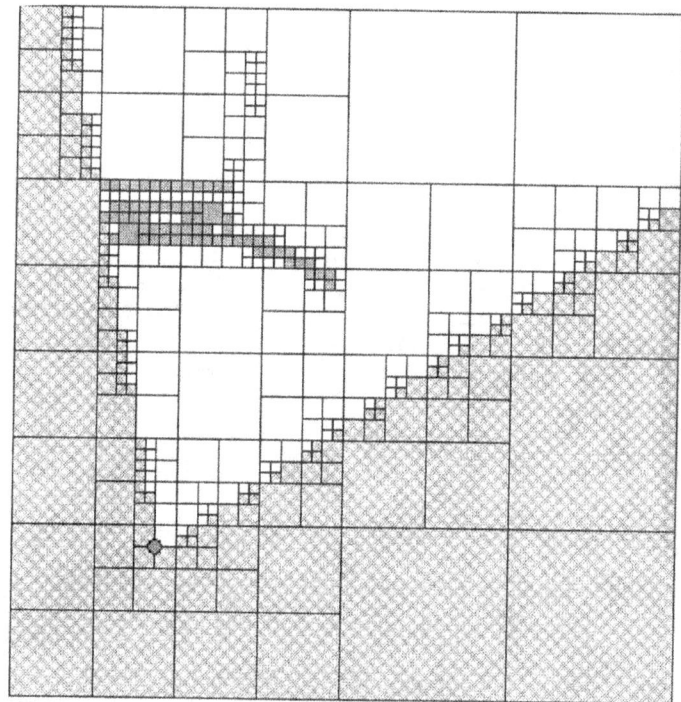

Figure 218: Scan 4

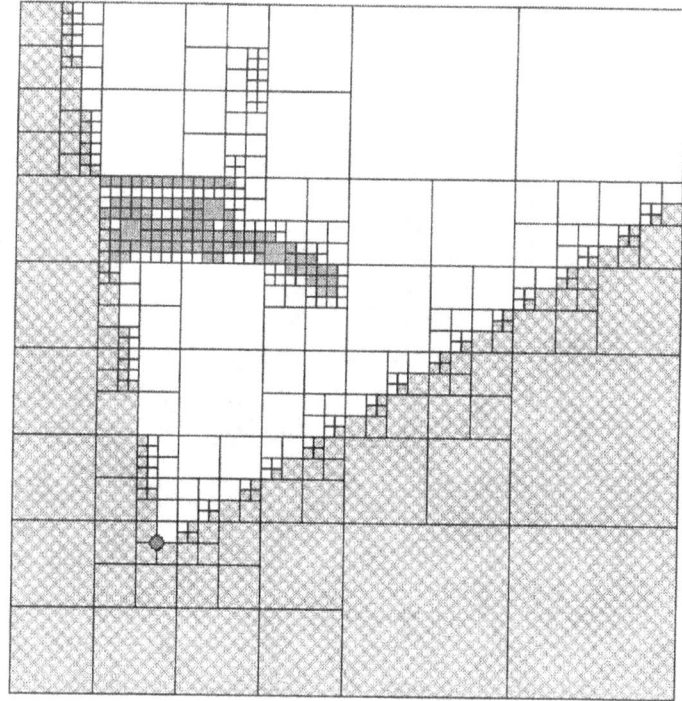

Figure 219: Scan 5

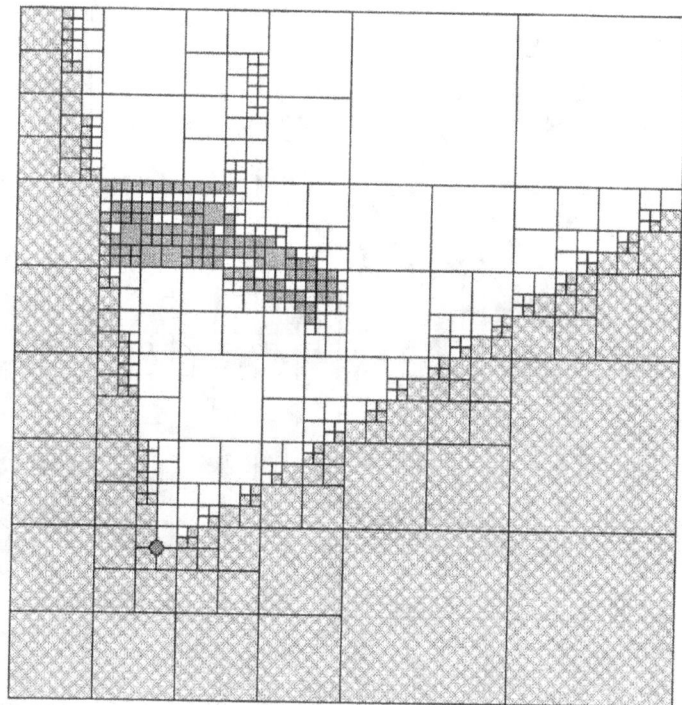

Figure 220: Scan 6

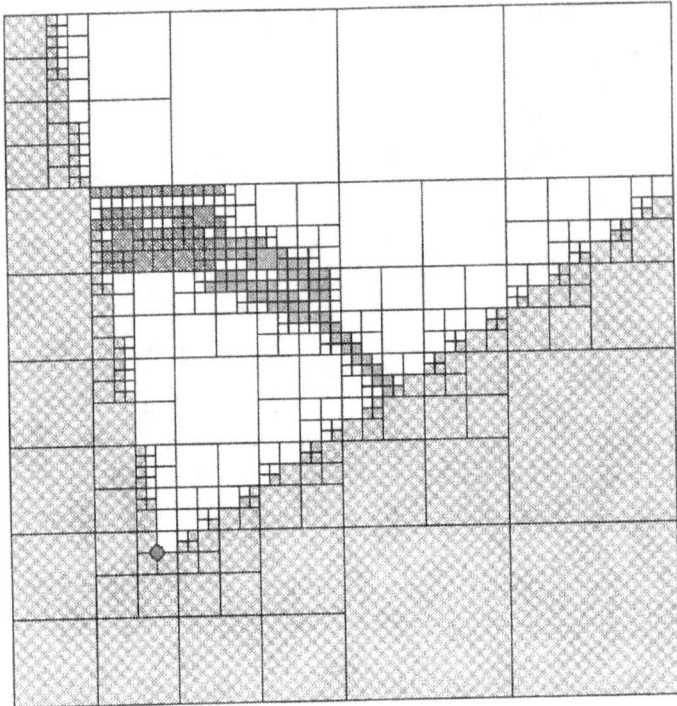

Figure 221: Scan 7

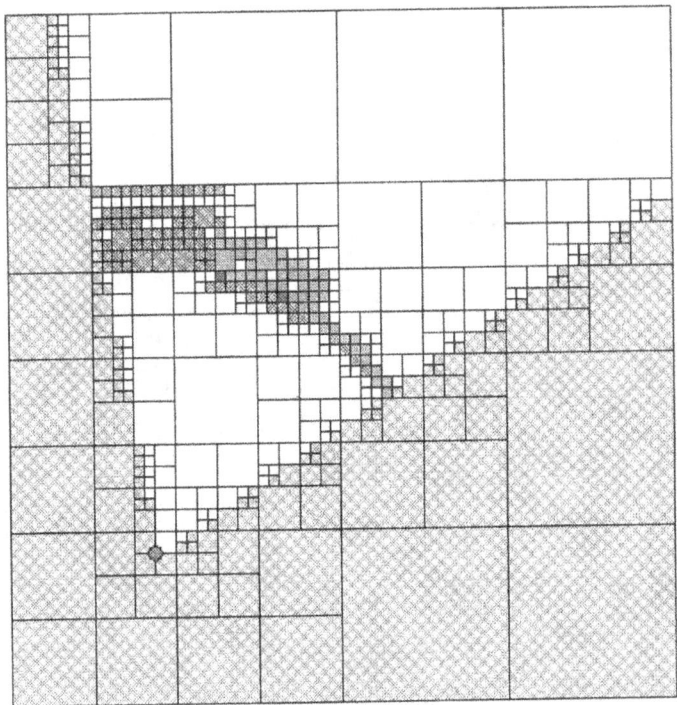

Figure 222: Scan 8

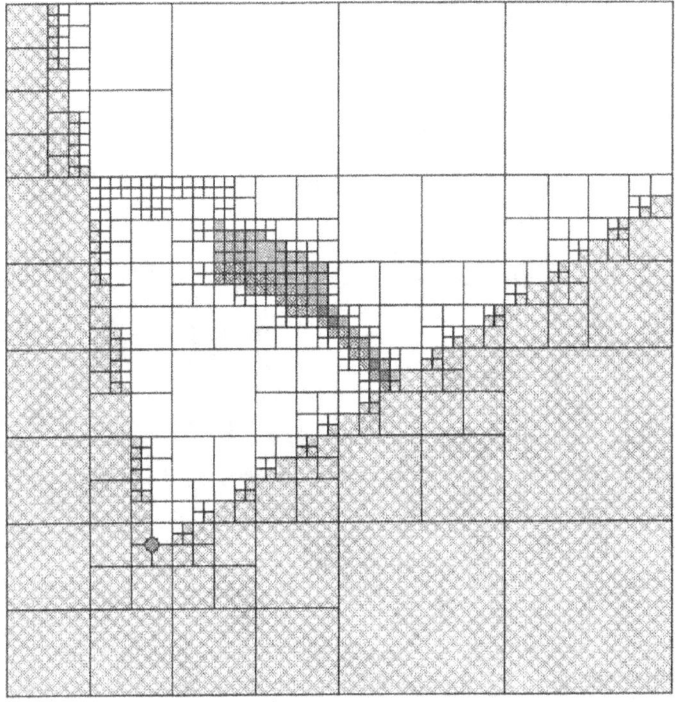

Figure 223: Scan 9

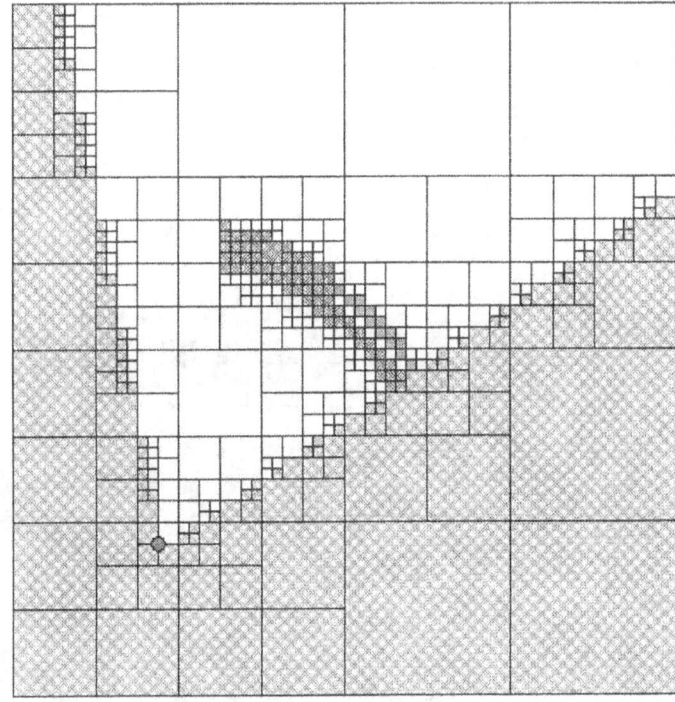

Figure 224: Scan 10

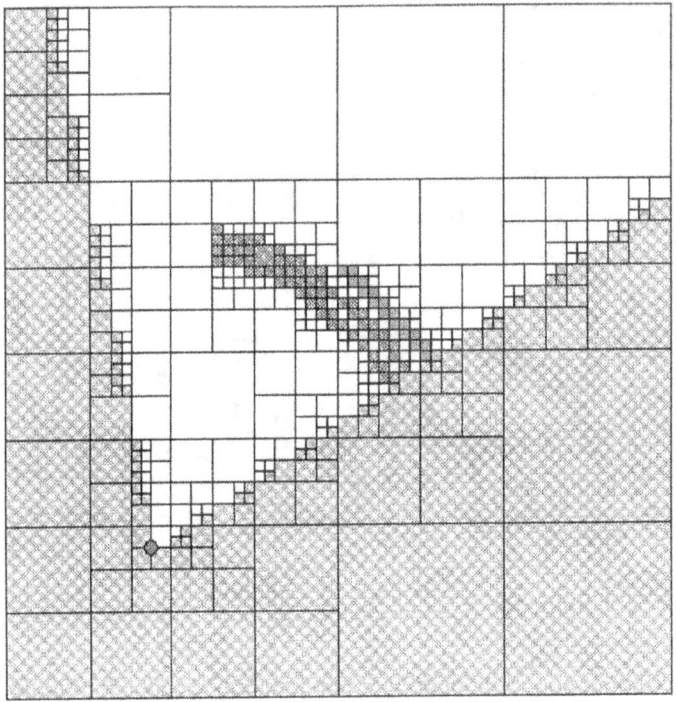

Figure 225: Scan 11

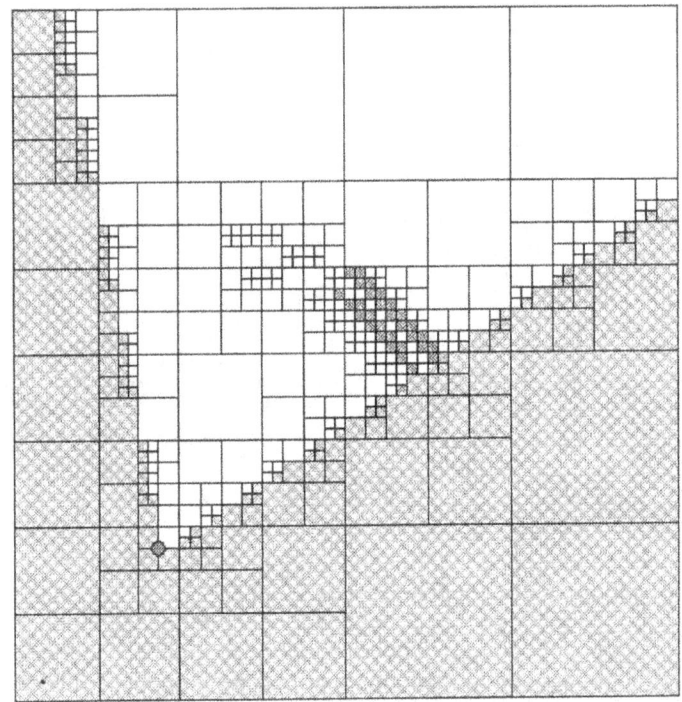

Figure 226: Scan 12

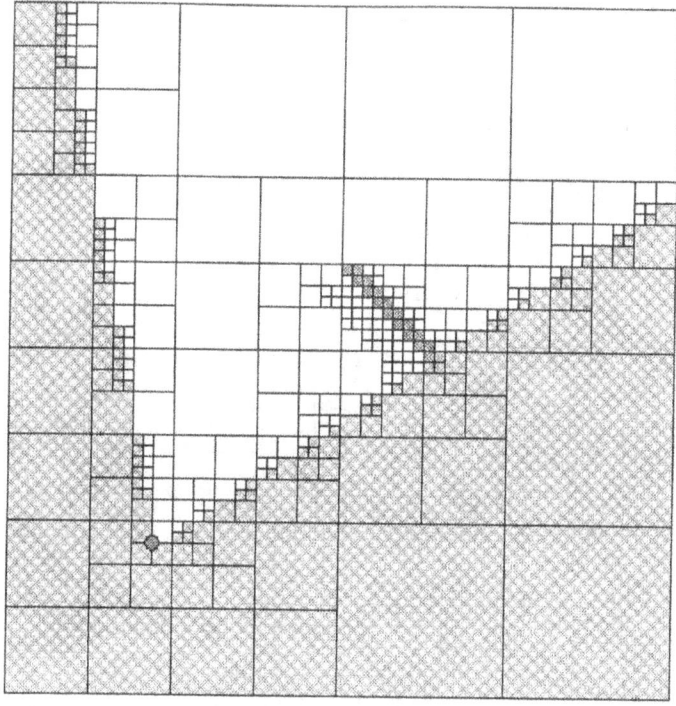

Figure 227: Scan 13

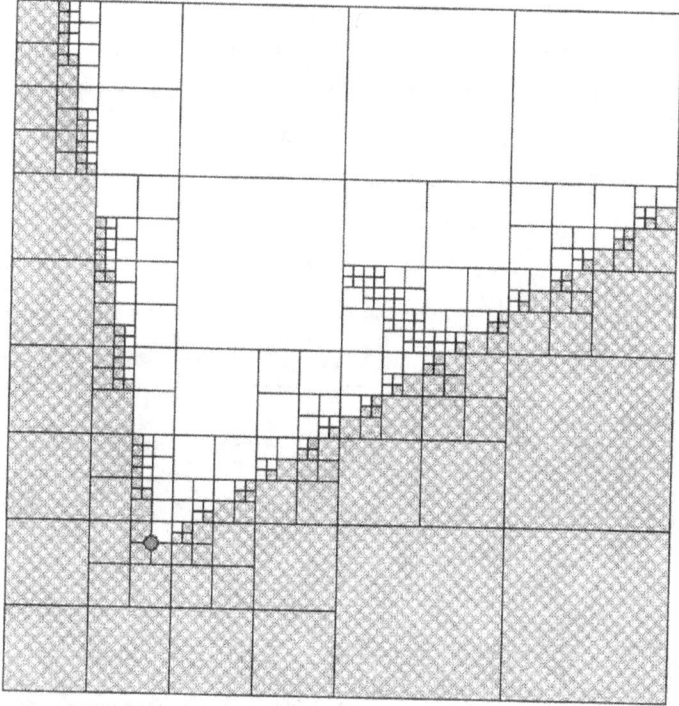

Figure 228: Scan 14

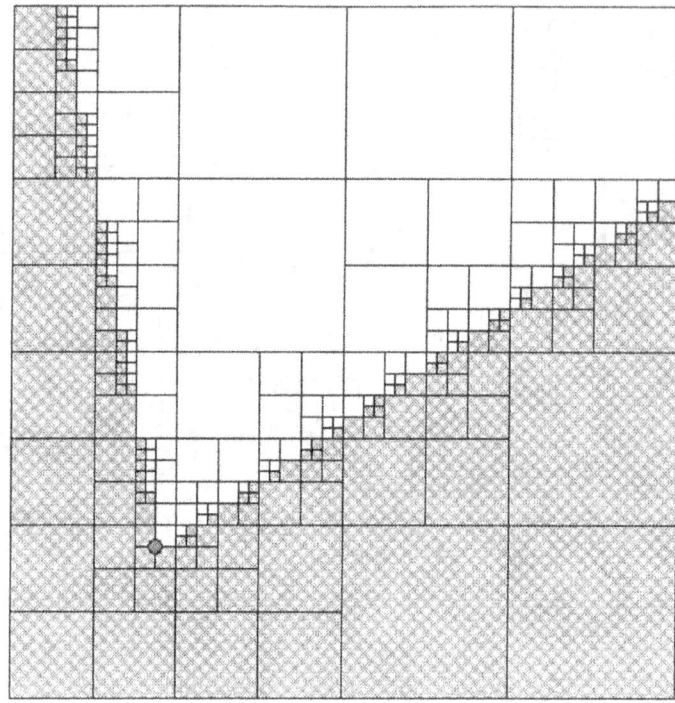

Figure 229: Scan 15

Scan 1 shows the empty map; the area covered by the sensor beams is EMPTY, the rest UNKNOWN. The TIPs in scan 2 show the first position of the obstacle. In scan 3 the obstacle is still in beam 1 but has moved closer to the AMV. In the subsequent scans it can be seen how the obstacle is traced to beam 2 and 3. When it has left a beam the according nodes change to TAILs and finally back to EMPTY. The limited angular resolution of the ultrasonic sensors obviously limits the accuracy of the map. The entire arc is assumed to be occupied, even if only one small obstacle causes the ultrasonic echo to return.

5.3.3.2.2 Moving Obstacle in Corridor

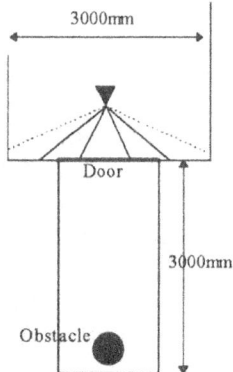

Figure 230: Experimental Environment

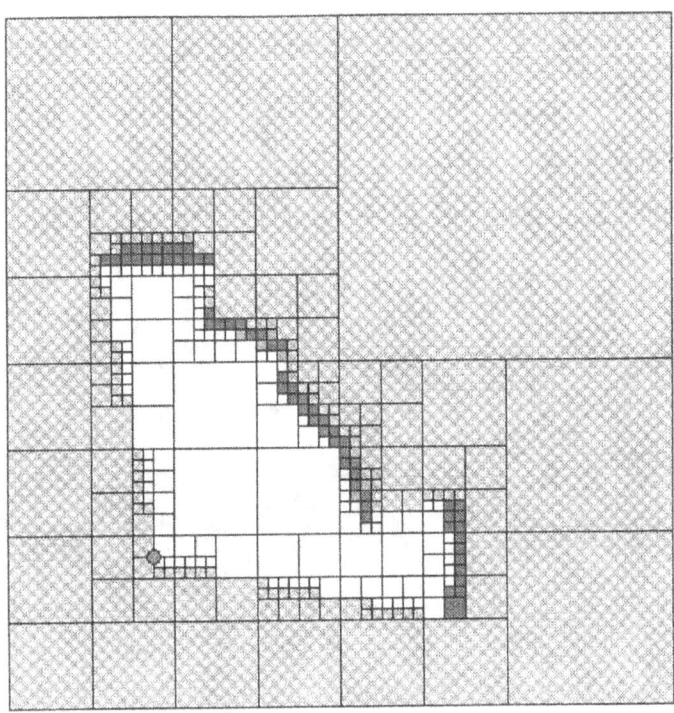

Figure 231: Static Environment

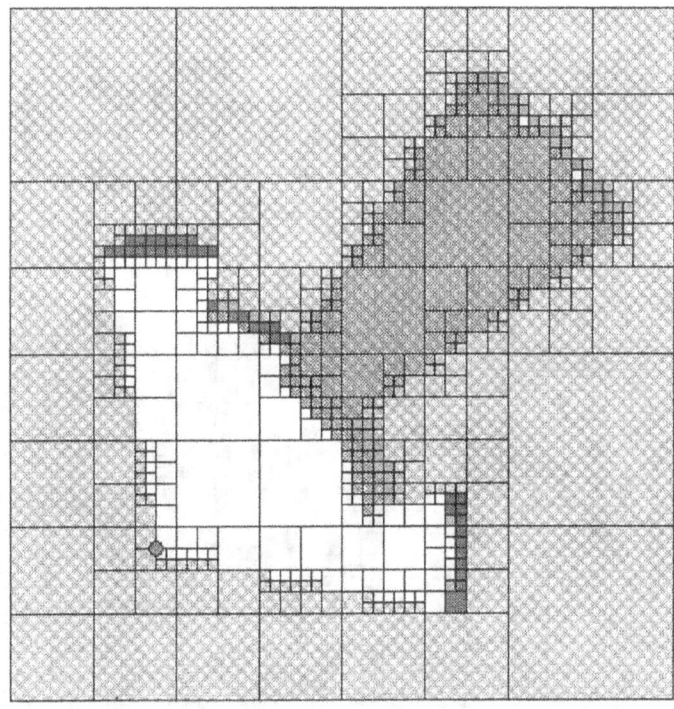

Figure 232: Learning the Open Door and the Corridor

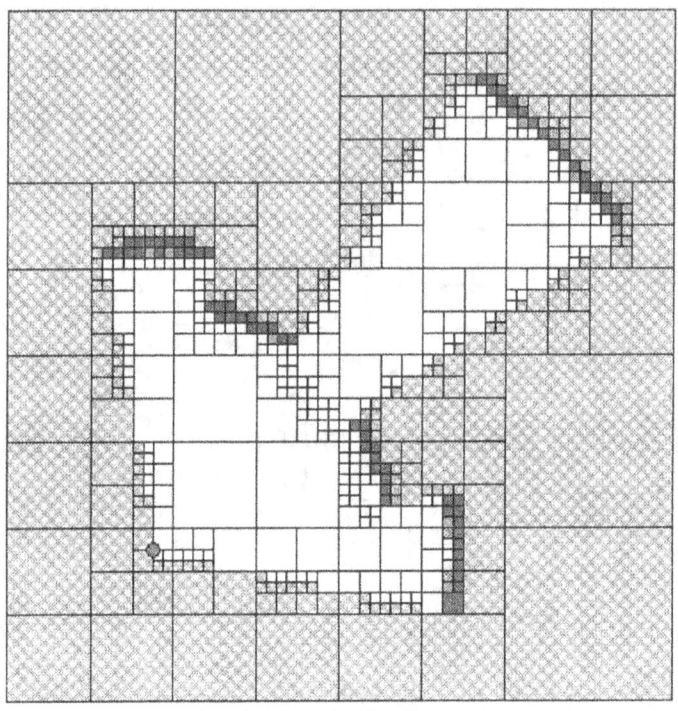

Figure 233: Updated Static Environment

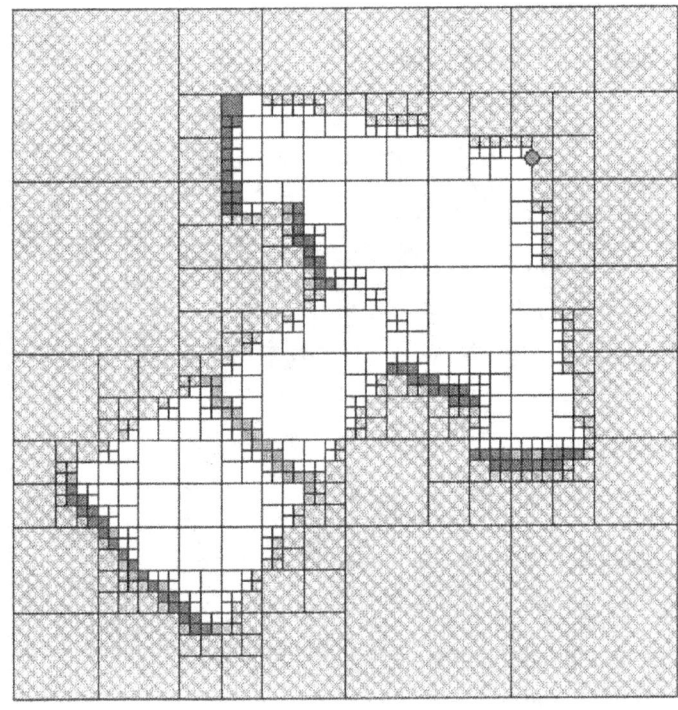

Figure 234: Obstacle is Approaching Sensor

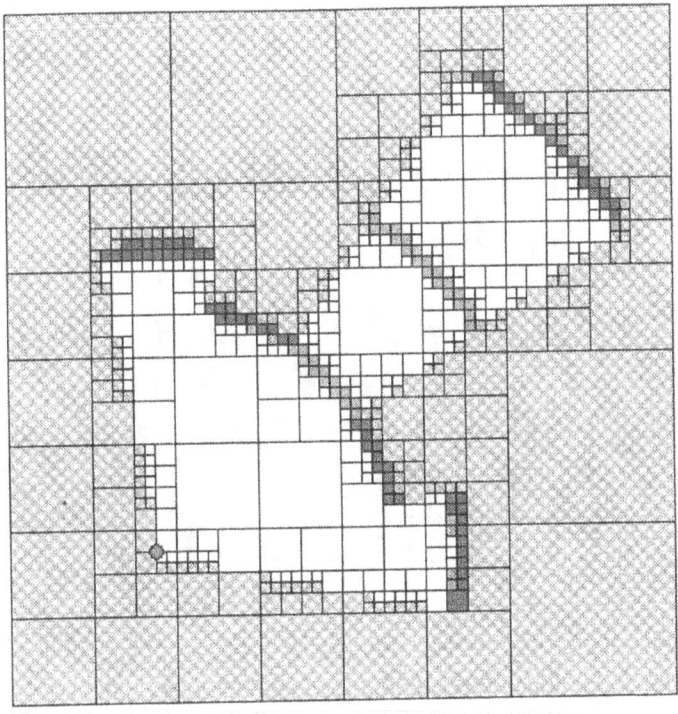

Figure 235: Obstacle is still Approaching Sensor

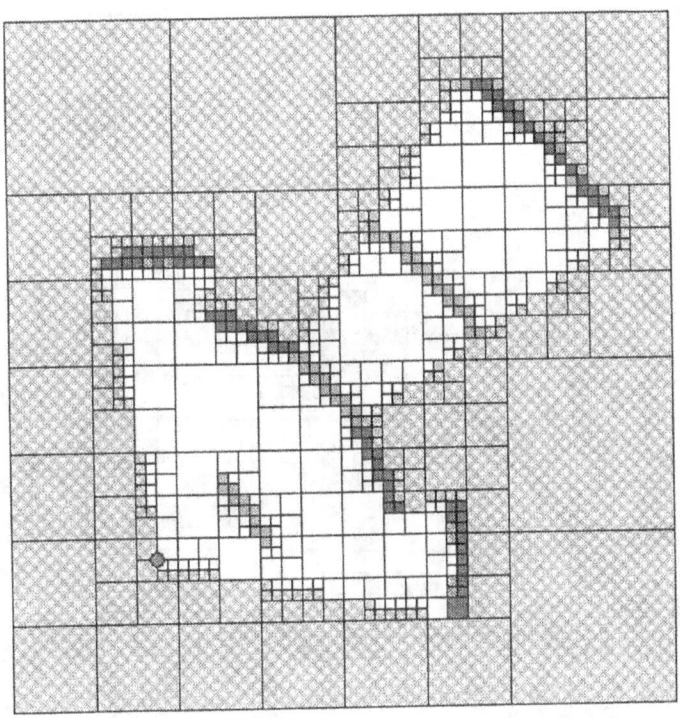

Figure 236: Obstacle is still Approaching Sensor

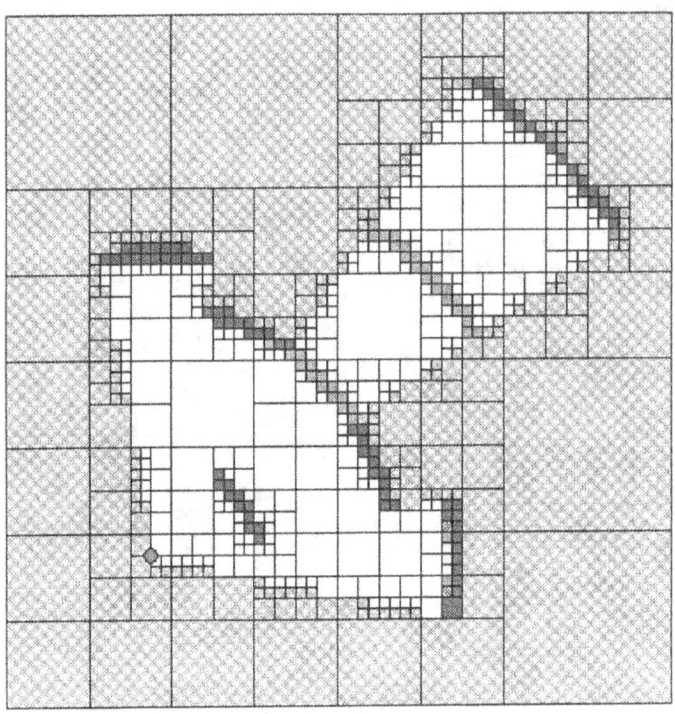

Figure 237: Obstacle has Stopped close to Sensor

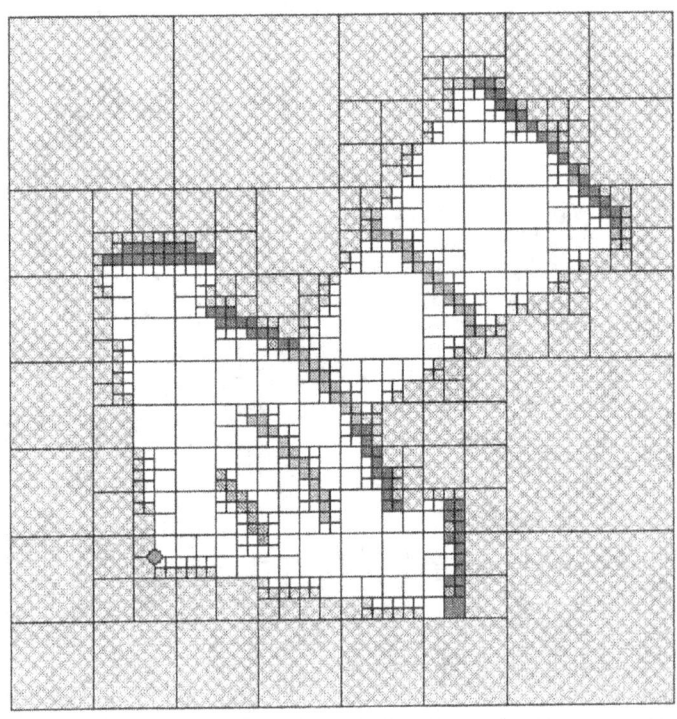

Figure 238: Obstacle Moves Back

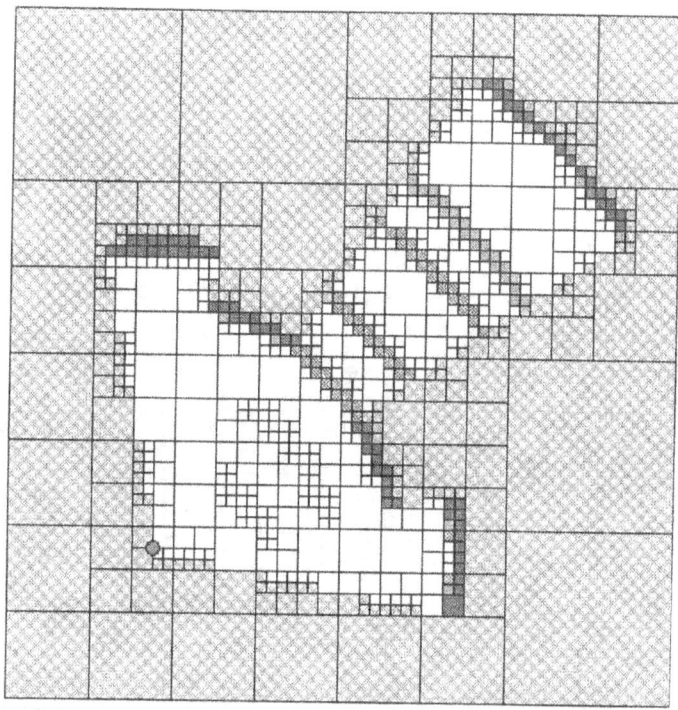

Figure 239: Obstacle Moves still Back

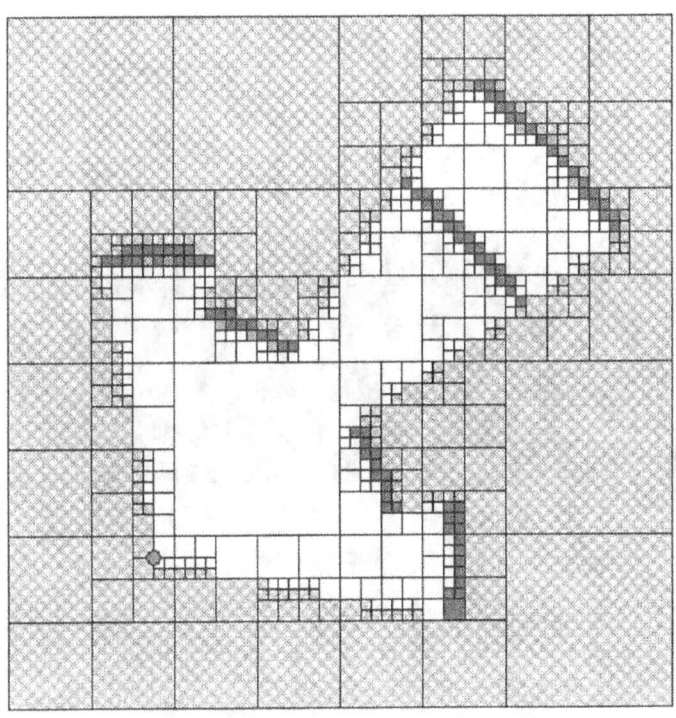

Figure 240: Obstacle has Stopped in the Corridor

The map is initialised as unknown. At first the door remains closed and the map learns its environment (figure 231). In figure 231 the learning process is already completed, and the node states are EMPTY at free space, FULL at walls, or UNKNOWN in areas out of the reach of the sensor beam. As the door is opened, the leaning process is repeated covering the area of the corridor (figure 232 to 233). In figure 234 to 236 the obstacle in the corridor proceeds towards the AMV. At nodes at which the obstacle arrives the node state changes from EMPTY to TIP. The obstacle stops in front of the AMV, such that the map changes to static states (FULL) at this position (figure 237). When moving away from the AMV, it can be seen that the area which is left by the obstacle is covered by TAIL nodes that finally change to EMPTY (figures 238-239).

Figures 241 and 242 show the Probability and Dynamics for this experiment, respectively, in summary.

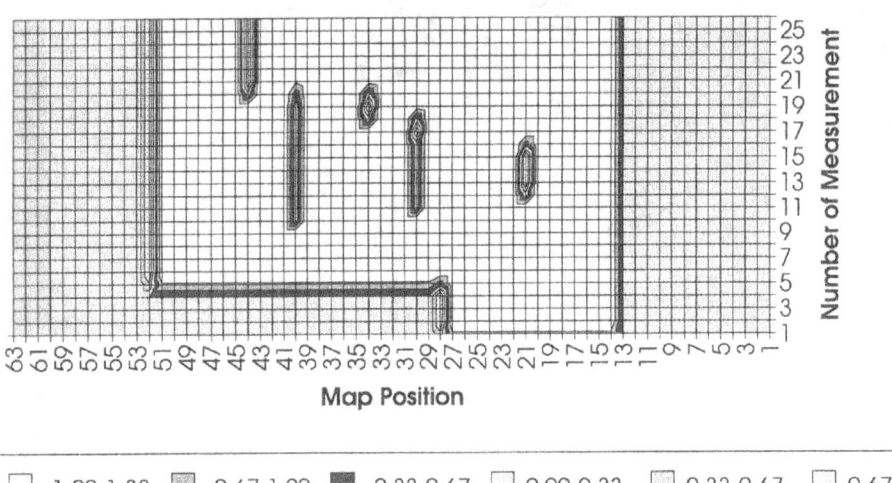

Figure 241: Summary of the Probability

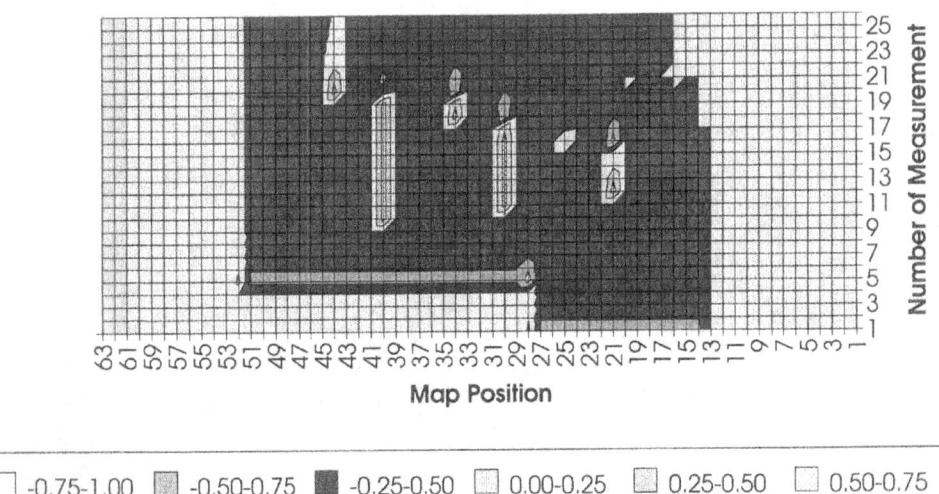

Figure 242: Summary of the Dynamics

6 Conclusions and Suggestions for Further Research

6.1 Conclusions

SUAVE's motion controller has found to be insufficient in accuracy and reactivity due to a high computational effort inherited in the vehicle design: This can only be overcome by using a different vehicle, which is recommended when trying to assess the quality of the Navigation algorithms rather than SUAVE's performance. The dead-reckoning system has proven to be of sufficient accuracy when rotation is excluded from the motion. This should be investigated further combining translational and rotational motion.

The Quadtree Data Structure has found to be appropriate to represent complicated environment structures. The processing speed has been comparable to a regular grid map. However, in maps built from real sensor data the maps still show a significant fragmentation of the information stored: one single sensor reading results in many node-entries. Of course, this is a consequence of the sensor model, too. The node properties Probability P and Dynamics D have enabled the map to reflect static and dynamic properties of the environment very well. Noise in the ultrasonic sensor readings could be filtered well enough using small or medium Kalman Gains. The disturbances through multiple reflections have to be filtered by incorporating the prediction model. The low angular resolution of the ultrasonic sensors has found to be insufficient in order to map small obstacles or details of larger structures.

The Local Navigation Module has proven to find a path to the motion command endpoint whenever a solution path exists. It has also shown its capability to identify impossible missions. The main drawback that became apparent in the simulations is the long path when Local Re-planning is necessary even in static environments. In the simulations this was the case since no Global Navigation was performed and therefore no Global Pre-planning of the path was given. Combing Global and Local Navigation should improve the navigation module in this point.

The potential field navigation was successful to create a collision free, goal approaching and in most cases smooth path. The oscillations observed in the simulations when passing a corner in a narrow corridor are unsatisfying since they endanger the vehicle and slow it down unnecessarily.

6.2 Suggestions for Further Research

The work presented here is the basis for future research and improvements. Many suggestions can be made: Experiments with a Local Map in a regular grid of constant resolution should be performed in order to compare the QDS and the grid for this application. The failures of the MSE found in the navigation simulation should be removed, e.g. the oscillating path when passing by corners. It seems also worthwhile to investigate the possibility of guiding the vehicle with an on-line velocity vector rather than a position setpoint. The communication efforts would be drastically reduced, since the exact provision of the position setpoint would not be necessary anymore. The sensor model needs improvement in order to account for the low angular resolution. One possibility is to detect corners, edges and planes using the technique of Barshan et al. [64]. Another way to solve this problem is to employ a sensor type with higher angular resolution, e.g. a laser scanner. It has to be investigated if the maps obtained with the suggested structure and sensor model is useful for the navigation techniques used in CA^{2}MOV. The memory system has to be completed, the Global Map, the EXTRACTOR, and the UPDATER have to be implemented and improved. Furthermore the connection between Map Building and Navigation has to be established. Maps built with real sensor data have to be used for Navigation purposes. Many adjustment in both, Map building and Navigation algorithms might be necessary in order to create an effective cooperation between both modules.

If the map's task is only to provide the necessary environment information for the navigation module, different map structures should be investigated. The "way" from the raw sensor data to the path planning algorithm should be as "short" as possible. "Short" in this sense means to perform only as many transformation of the data as absolutely necessary. The map should only store information directly deducted form the sensor readings. In the case of ultra-sonic sensors this could be a free distance information in the direction of the sensor beams.

Potential field modelling should be investigated based on a decomposition of the repulsive force into a component parallel and perpendicular to the moving direction of the AMV to overcome the problem of sudden deviations of the path at discontinuities of the field that lead to oscillations when passing a corner in an angle to the walls.

References

[1]   S.M Killough,. F.G Pin,. "Design of an omnidirectional and holonomic wheeled platform prototype", *Proceedings of the 1992 IEEE International Conference on Robotics and Auto mation*, Nice, France, May 1992, Vol. 1, pp. 84-90

[2]   A. Ryden, "Autonomous Vehicle", *Undergraduate Thesis* 1993, The Department of Mechanical and Mechatronic Engineering, The University of Sydney, Australia

[3]   J. Evnas et al., "HelpMate: a service robot for health care", *The Industrial Robot*, June 1989, pp. 87-89

[4]   A. Meystel, "Autonomous Mobile Robots", *World Scientific Singapore*, 1991

[5]   B. Wilcox, "Robotic Vehicle for planetary exploration", *Proceedings of the 1992 IEEE International Conference on Robotics and Automation*, Nice, France, May 1992, Vol. 1, pp. 84-104

[6]   N.J. Nilsson, "Shakey the Robot", *Technical Report 323, SRI International*, April 1984

[8]   E.W. Dijkstra, "A note on two problems in connection with graphs", *Numerische Mathematik*, Vol. 1, pp. 269-271, 1959

[9]   P.E. Hart, N.J. Nielsson, B. Raphael, "A formal basis for the heuristic determination of minimum cost paths", *IEEE Transactions of Systems Science and Cybernetics*, SSC-4 No. 2, pp. 100-107, July 1968

[10]   R. Tarjan, "Fast algorithms for solving path problems", *Journal of ACM*, Vol. 28, No. 3, July 1981

[11]   D.M. Keirsey, E. Koch, J. McKisson et al., "An algorithm of navigation for a mobile robot", *Proceedings of the 1984 IEEE International Conference on Robotics*, May 1984, pp. 574-583

[12]   T. Lozano-Perez, M.A. Wesley, "An algorithm for planning collision free paths among polyhedral obstacles", *Communications of the ACM*, Vol. 22, No. 10, pp. 560-570, October 1979

[13]   T. Lozano-Perez, "Spatial planning: a configuration space approach", *IEEE Transactions on Computers*, C-32, No. 2, pp. 108-120, February 1983

[14]   H.P Moravec, "Obstacle avoidance and navigation in the real world by a seeing rover", *PhD dissertation*, Stanford University, September 1980

[15]   A.M. Thomson, "The navigation system of the JPL robot", *Proceedings. of the 5th International Joint Conference on Artificial Intelligence*, August 1977, pp. 749-757

[16]   R. Chatila, "Path planning and environment learning", *European Conference on Artificial Intelligence*, July 1982, pp. 211-215

[17]   J. L. Crowley, "Navigation for an intelligent mobile robot", *IEEE Journal of Robotics and Automation*, Vol. RA-1, No. 1, pp. 31-41, March 1985

[18]   R. A. Brooks, "Solving the find-path problem by a good representation of free space", *IEEE Transactions on Systems, Man and Cybernetics*, SMC-13, No. 3, pp. 190-197, March 1983

[19]   D. T. Kuan J.C. Zamiska, R. A. Brooks, "Natural decomposition of free space for path planning", *Proceedings. of the 1985 IEEE International Conference on Robotics and Automation*, pp. 168-183, March 1985

[20]   R. A. Jarvis, J. C. Byrne, "Robot navigation: touching, seeing and knowing", *Proceedings of the 1st Australian Conference on Artificial Intelligence*, November 1986

[21]   C. E. Thorpe, "FIDO: Vision and navigation for a robot rover", *PhD dissertation*, Carnegie-Mellon University, Department of Computer Science, December 1984

[21a]   A. Zelinsky, "Environment exploration and path planning algorithms for mobile robot navigation using sonar", *PhD dissertation*, The University of Wollongong, Department of Computer Science, 1991

[22]   A. Zelinsky, A mobile robot map exploration algorithm", *IEEE Transactions of Robotics and Automation*, December 1991

[23]   M. D. Adams, H. Hu, P. J. Robert, "Towards a real-time architecture for obstacle avoidance and path planning in mobile robots", *Proceedings of the 1990 IEEE International Conference on Robotics and Automation*, May 1990, pp. 584-589

[24]   R. C. Arkin, "Motor-Schema based mobile robot navigation", *International Journal of Robotics Research*, Vol. 8, No. 4, pp. 92-112, 1989

[25]   O. Khatib, "Real-time obstacle avoidance for manipulators and mobile robots", *International Journal of Robotics Research*, Vol. 5, No. 1, pp. 90-98, 1986

[26]   B. H. Krogh, "A generalised potential field approach to obstacle avoidance control", *Proceedings of the First World Conference on Robotics Research*, August 1984.

[27]   E. S. H. Hou, D. Zheng, "Mobile robot path planning based on hierarchical hexagon decomposition and artificial potential fields", *Journal of Robotic Systems*, Vol. 11, No. 7, pp. 605-614, 1994

[28]   D.F. Cahn, S. R. Phillips, "ROBNAV: A range based robot navigation and obstacle avoidance algorithm", *IEEE Transaction on Systems, Man and Cybernetics*, SMC-55, pp. 138-145, September 1975

[29]   R. Chattergy, "Some heuristics for the navigation of a robot", *International Journal of Robotics Research*, Vol. 4, No. 1, pp. 59-66, 1985

[30]   R. A. Brooks, "A robust layered Control system for a mobile robot", *IEEE Journal of Robotics and Automation*, Vol. RA-2, No 1, pp. 14-23, March 1986.

[31]   R. C. Arkin, "Motor-Schema based navigation for a mobile robot: an approach to programming by behaviour", *Proceedings of the 1987 IEEE International Conference on Robotics and Automation*, 1987, pp. 264-271,

[32]   R. C. Arkin, "Cooperation without communication; multi-agent schema-based robot navigation", *Journal of Robotic Systems*, Vol. 9, No. 3, pp. 351-364, 1992

[33]   K. Fujimura, H. Samet, "A hierarchical strategy for path planning among moving obstacles, *IEEE Transactions on Robotics and Automation*, Vol. 5, No. 1, February 1989

[34]   J. Canny, "Collision detection for moving polyhedra", *IEEE Transactions on Pattern Analysis, Machine, and Intelligence*, Vol. PAMI-8, pp. 200-209, March 1986

[35]   H. Sammet, M. Tamminen, "Bintrees, CSG trees, and time", *Computer Graphics*, Vol. 20, pp. 121-130, July 1985

[36]   R. Hartley, F. Pipitone, "Experiments with the subsumption architecture", *Proceedings. of the 1991 IEEE International Conference on Robotics and Automation*, April   1991, pp.1652-1658

[37]   M. Watanabe, K. Onoguchi, I. Kweon, Y. Kuno "Architecture of behaviour based mobile robot in a dynamic environment" *Proceedings of the 1992 IEEE International Conference on Robotics and Automation*, 1992, pp. 271-271,

[38] H. J. Warnecke, G. Drunk "Integrierte Sensoraktions-Planung als Neuartige Sensor- und Steuerungsarchitektur für den mobilen autonomen Roboter IPAMAR", *Robotersysteme*, Vol. 3, pp. 209-217, 1987

[39] R. Gusche, F.M. Wahl, "A new navigation concept for mobile vehicles", *Proceedings. of the 1992 IEEE International Conference on Robotics and Automation*, pp. 215-220, May 1992

[40] J. L. Crowley, "Navigation for an intelligent mobile robot", *IEEE Journal of Robotics and Automation*, Vol. RA-1, No. 1, March 1985

[41] R. Bhatt, D. Gaw, A. Meystel, "A real-time guidance system for an autonomous vehicle", *IEEE Journal of Robotics and Automation*, Vol. RA-1, No. 1, March 1985

[42] J. H. Connell "SSS: A. Hybrid Architecture Applied to Robot Navigation" *Proceedings of the 1992 IEEE International Conference on Robotics and Automation*, 1992, pp. 2719-2724

[43] J. Borenstein, Y. Koren, "Task-level tour plan generation for mobile robots", *IEEE Transactions on Systems, Man, and Cybernetics*, Vol. 20, No. 4, pp. 938-943, July 1990

[44] G. Pearson, D. Kuan, "Mission planning system for an autonomous vehicle", *IEEE Transactions on Systems, Man, and Cybernetics*, Vol. 20, No. 4, pp. 834-841, July 1990

[45] J. J. Leonard, H. F. Durrant-Whyte, I. J. Cox, "Dynamic map building for an autonomous mobile robot", *The International of Robotics Research*, Vol. 11, No. 4, August 1992

[47] H. Samet, "An overview of quadtrees, octrees and related hierarchical data structures", *Theoretical foundations of computer graphics*, NATO ASI Series, vol. F40, pp. 51-68, Springer Verlag, Berlin,1988.

[48] H. Samet, "The Quadtree and related hierarchical data structures", *ACM Computing Surveys*, Vol. 16, No. 2, pp. 187-260, June 1984

[49] P. Flajolet, G. Gonnet, C. Puech, J. M. Robson, "Analytic variations on Quadtrees", *Algorithmica*, No. 10, pp. 473-500, 1993

[50] S. Scheding, "Path planning for an autonomous robot vehicle using potential field methods", *Undergraduate Thesis*, The University of Sydney, Department of Mechanical and Mechatronic Engineering, Sydney, November 1994

[51] J. Latombe, "Robot motion planning", Kluwer Academic Publishers, London, 1991

[52]   T. Ikegami, S. Ozono, "A potential field approach to path planning", pp. 23-32, *IEEE Transactions on Robotics and Automation*, Vol. 8, No. 1, February 1992

[53]   A. M. Flynn, "Combining sonar and infrared sensors for mobile robot navigation", *The International Journal of Robotics Research*, Vol. 7, No. 6, pp. 5-14, December 1988

[54]   S. C. A. Thomopoulos, "Sensor integration and data fusion*", Journal of Robotic Systems*, Vol. 7, No. 3, pp. 337-372, 1990

[55]   S. A. Shafer, A. Stentz, C. E. Thorpe, "An architecture for sensor fusion in a mobile robot", *Proceedings of the 1986 IEEE Conference on Robotics and Automation*, 1986, pp. 2002-2011

[56]   M. Beckermann, "A bayes-maximum-entropy method for multi-sensor data fusion", *Proceedings of the 1992 IEEE International Conference on Robotics and Automation*, Nice, May 1992, pp.1668-1674

[57]   D. Marioli et al., "Digital Time-of-Flight measurements for Ultrasonic sensors", *IEEE Transactions on Instrumentation and Measurement*, Vol. 41, No. 1, February 1992

[58]   Anderson, Moore, " Optimal Filtering", Englewood Cliff, NJ, Prentice Hall, 1979

[59]   A. Whiteside, "Map making by an intelligent mobile platform", *Undergraduate Thesis*, The University of Sydney, Department of Mechanical and Mechatronic Engineering, November 1993

[60]   R. Jarvis, „A selective survey of localisation methodology for autonomous mobile robot navigation", *Intelligent Robotics Research Centre*, Monash University, Clayton, Australia

[61]   C. Ming Wang „Localisation estimation and uncertainty analysis for mobile robots", *Proceedings of the 1988 IEEE International Conference on Robotics and Automation* 1988, pp. 1230-1235

[62]   J. J. Leonard, H. F. Durrant-Whyte, „Mobile robot localisation by tracking geometric beacons", *IEEE Transactions on Robotics and Automation*, Vol. 7, No. 3, pp. 376-382, June 1991

[63]   A. A. Holenstein, M. A. Müller, E. Badredin, "Mobile robot localisation in a structured environment cluttered with obstacles", *Proceedings of the 1992 IEEE International Conference on Robotics and Automation*, Nice, France, May 1992, pp. 2576-2581

[64]   B. Barshan, R. Kuc, "Differentiating sonar reflections from corners and planes by employing an intelligent sensor" *IEEE Transactions on Pattern Analysis and Machine Intelligence*, Vol. 12, No. 6, pp. 560-568, June 1990

[65]   E. M. Nebot, G. G. Schenkel, "A hybrid control architecture for autonomous mobile vehicles operating in a dynamic environment" to appear in: *Proc. of the International Conference on Intelligent Autonomous Systems IAS-2*, Karlsruhe, Germany, March 1995